I0109939

Editing Eden

Editing Eden

A Reconsideration of
Identity, Politics, and Place in Amazonia

Edited by Frank Hutchins
and Patrick C. Wilson

University of Nebraska Press
Lincoln and London

© 2010 by the Board of Regents
of the University of Nebraska

All rights reserved
Manufactured in the
United States of America
⊚

Library of Congress
Cataloging-in-Publication Data

Editing Eden : a reconsideration of identity,
politics, and place in Amazonia / edited by Frank
Hutchins and Patrick C. Wilson.
p. cm.
Includes bibliographical references and index.
ISBN 978-0-8032-1612-9 (pbk. : alk. paper)
1. Indians of South America—Amazon River
Region—Ethnic identity. 2. Indians of South
America—Amazon River Region—Public opin-
ion. 3. Indians of South America—Amazon River
Region—Government relations. 4. Culture and
globalization—Amazon River Region. 5. Social
capital—Amazon River Region. 6. Public opin-
ion—Amazon River Region. 7. Amazon River
Region—Social conditions. 8. Amazon River
Region—Economic conditions. 9. Amazon River
Region—Politics and government. I. Hutchins,
Frank, 1959– . II. Wilson, Patrick C., 1970–
F1219.1.A6e35 2010
305.800981'1—dc22
2009039514

Set in Myriad Pro and Quadraat Sans.
Designed by Ray Boeche.

Contents

Illustrations

Figures

Maps

Acknowledgments

This book is the product of considerable hard work by numerous individuals. Without their assistance this project would have been far more difficult and substantially less rewarding. Our first debt goes to the anthropologists who contributed to *Editing Eden*. These accomplished scholars greeted our proposal enthusiastically, and they made this book what it is through the quality of their work and their intellectual commitment. The common themes that emerge in these pages are not a product of chance, but of an engagement among the contributors that began at a panel session at the Latin American Studies Association conference in San Juan, Puerto Rico, in 2006. We are also most appreciative of the editors at the University of Nebraska Press. Matthew Bokovoy, in his role as the acquisitions editor for the press's indigenous studies list, and Elisabeth Chretien, as the associate acquisitions editor, have been supportive of this project from its inception. They skillfully guided us through the different stages of manuscript preparation and were most patient as deadlines were stretched.

Jessica Marcotte and Ashley Haughton, both undergraduate students at the University of Lethbridge, worked tirelessly on proofreading and formatting the text, and this work benefited from their close reading and attention to detail. Andrea Cuéllar, from the Department of Anthropology at the University of Lethbridge, took considerable time away from her research and teaching demands to translate the chapter by Margarita Chaves from Spanish to English.

Finally, each of the authors owes a considerable intellectual debt to the people with whom we do our research. It is only with the collaboration of many friends, colleagues, and acquaintances in the Amazon region that we can feel any confidence in "editing" the representations of this oft-imagined place.

Introduction

Frank Hutchins and Patrick C. Wilson

Editing Eden traditionally has been the job of utopian visionaries, and modesty dictates that we qualify our title at the outset. The Eden around which this book is built, the great basin of Amazonia, certainly has drawn many toward excess—an excess of superlatives, an excess of embellishment, and an excess of drama. Travel writing becomes an exercise in histrionics, ethnography gets tangled in exotica, and would-be saviors of every stripe struggle to salvage the last species, the lost souls, and the pristine places. Thus the Amazon, which is as much as anything a canvas of ever-morphing imagery.

We—editors, authors, anthropologists—are not attempting here to tear apart the canvas or the painters. We are instead reacting ethnographically to new insights and more nuanced ways of thinking about the Amazon and its inhabitants and the complexity of evolving exchanges with others who do not call this place their home. Both the *American Heritage Dictionary* and *Roget's Thesaurus* connect editing with deleting or rewriting, but they also state that "to edit" can mean "to adapt." The tone of the following chapters is closer to the latter concept, where we've drawn on substantive scholarship about

Amazonia to analyze contemporary issues in the region, with special attention to Colombia, Brazil, and Ecuador.

Cultural, linguistic, and archaeological anthropology has produced and disassembled many Amazons. An area theorized to be absent of "civilization" (Meggers 1996) now appears to have been home to a number of complexly organized, and sometimes relatively large, cultural groups (Balée and Erickson 2006; Heckenberger 2004; Roosevelt 1997). Native people whose interests seemed barely distinguishable from the evolutionary path of the natural world that surrounded them are now understood as agents with variable objectives that are not always congruent with those of would-be allies. This book in many ways advances projects that reconsider the images, texts, and discourses on which "the Amazon" has been built. The "natives" written into these accounts are subsequently pluralized, contextualized, and humanized.

Before turning the page on the Amazon of legend, it is worth revisiting moments in history that suggest that "editing" is a fruitful endeavor. The words of Alain Gheerbrant are a good starting point, as he describes the eruption of superlatives that seemed to occur as Europeans experienced the Amazon. "Everything about this land was alien and defied conventional logic," he wrote about these early encounters with Amazonia. "The first Europeans to set foot in Amazonia let their imaginations run away with them and claimed to actually see and hear everything they had hitherto only imagined. . . . Seldom have reality and fantasy complemented each other so well" (1992:47).

The rainforest that Alexander von Humboldt called Hyleia coaxed even men of the cloth to the extremes of imagination. Friar Gaspar de Carvajal, chronicling the Amazon River trip of Francisco de Orellana in 1541–42, wrote of the famous single-breasted Amazon warrior women and a mysterious tribe of white men (Heaton 1934). Padre Cristóbal de Acuña, who accompanied Pedro Texeira on a trip from Quito to Pará in 1639, resorted to a "mixture of fiction and direct observation" (Newton Freitas's introduction to Acuña 1942) in his description of vast riches, hairy fish that nursed their mothers, and elk the size of a year-old mule. Where Orellana and his men "reached a state of privation so great [they] were eating nothing but leather, belts and soles of shoes, cooked with certain herbs" (Heaton 1934:172), Acuña and his crew found an abundance of food so extensive that it could be attributed only to the "Paternal Providence of the Lord, who with just five loaves and a few fish fed 5,000 men" (Acuña 1942:43).

Explorers and scientists who followed similar routes through the Amazon produced stories with equally contrasting accounts of the wonders and nightmares that awaited in the jungle. Charles-Marie La Condamine, an eighteenth-century scientist whom Anthony Smith (1990:163) counts among "a new breed of men . . . forever ready to measure, to sketch, to take note, to examine," arrived in South America as part of French efforts to settle the question of the shape of the earth. After losing much of his party to disease, murder, marriage, and insanity, La Condamine eventually headed home through the Amazon. His reflections on indigenous life in the rainforest describe a simple, lazy, undifferentiated people, who "are all gluttons to the point of voracity" and "pusillanimous poltroons to excess, unless transported by drunkenness" (180).

Alexander von Humboldt followed up La Condamine's work by seeking out the connection between the Orinoco River system and the Amazon basin. Early on, Humboldt and his partner Aimé Bonpland began to document New World wonders that Smith calls "a repository of unending astonishment." Electric fish and the drinkable sap of the milk tree were among the marvels that entertained the explorers until they entered the clouds of swarming, biting insects, leading Humboldt to scribble in his journal, "All hope abandon, ye who enter here" (Smith 1990:236).

Mary Louise Pratt identifies the discourses of Amazonian travel that emerged with the Age of Exploration. La Condamine, she writes, offers two great themes: one is based on hardship and danger, and the second on marvels and curiosities (1992:20). Pratt's analysis in

Imperial Eyes helps us understand how these projects of exploration not only defined colonized lands through a discourse that naturalized conquest and deterritorialized natives, but also defined for Europeans their tasks of rationalizing nature and civilizing culture. Humboldt, she says, who wrote thirty volumes to cover his South American travels, achieved nothing short of the "ideological reinvention of South America" (1992:111).

Cultural geographers and anthropologists reveal how natives have been reterritorialized as myriad interest groups marry identity to place. In the process imaginary geographies are transformed into normative geographies, as documented in many of the following chapters. The creation of normative geographies, and the perception of transgressions within these spaces, can be seen through an examination of how heroes and villains are made in the Amazon. Edenic and "noble savage" discourses have defined for many what the rainforest should look like and the appropriate behavior for those who live there, native or otherwise.

The accounts of Carvajal and Acuña represent experiences from the period Joseph Conrad called "Geography Fabulous," during which travelers based their tales more on speculation than on a pursuit of the truth. La Condamine, Humboldt, and their colleagues in science exemplify the period of "Geography Militant," based on a global search for empirical knowledge. Conrad's final period was "Geography Triumphant," which "marked the irreversible closure of the epoch of open spaces, the end of an era of unashamed heroism" (Driver 2001:4). But in revisiting Conrad's essay, published in *National Geographic* in 1924, Felix Driver contends that the era of Geography Militant is far from over. In tracing the contemporary era of Geography Militant, Driver looks to public culture, or popular geographies, such as tourism, film, the press, and fashion:

Geography Militant has thus not merely survived the processes of modernization and globalization: it has been regenerated in a variety of ever-

proliferating forms, from the pages of fashion magazines to the sale-rooms of auction houses. Rather than simply reactivating forgotten histories of imperial exploration, these enterprises are engaged in the business of producing memories: of making the past meaningful for people in the present. This memory work takes place in many different sites, often far removed from the pedagogy of the classroom or the esoteric knowledge of the library, in objects, images, buildings, places, the flotsam and jetsam of everyday life. (217)

That the Amazon is variously seen as generous or parsimonious, hellish or Edenic, authentic or imagined is evidence of the creative production of its history and meanings. It also reflects the cognitive mapping of a part of the world made extraordinary through travel writing, scientific exploration, economic exploitation, and environmental hyperbole. Complex cultural and natural systems are thus transmuted through the alchemy of the exceptional. Trouble is, people must live with the consequences.

In a chapter in *The Cambridge Companion to Travel Writing*, Neil Whitehead reviews such representational practices from the sixteenth century to the twentieth to expose how Amazonia has long been "an intense object of the imagination." But while this history reveals common threads over the centuries, it also highlights the variety of projects, interests, and renderings that lead Whitehead to conclude that "knowledge of ourselves, not others, is therefore the real discovery that is made through travelers' tales" (2002:137).

These various portrayals of the Amazon, whether originating outside or from within the region, do not represent consistent, continuous narratives. Rather, there are gaps and contradictions in the telling that Candace Slater says reveal different historical perspectives and interpretations of what happens — or should happen — in Amazonia. These indicate differences both within and between outsider and insider stories, although there are also "points of contact" between the story lines, such as recognition by insiders of the various ways they are tied to a larger world (Slater 2002:188). Slater's concern is that a sense of connection from the outside in is less apparent. One consequence of the failure by outsiders to see a larger Amazonian reality, she says, is an environmental and cultural pessimism that sees only a doomed rainforest and vanishing Indians. "The sharp insistence on irreparable loss that is a hallmark of the new pessimism . . . creates a great divide between the past and future, tribal Indian and cultureless beer guzzler, predatory human and threatened nature, the precious 'wild' and the unexciting 'tamed.' In so doing, it conceals a less totalizing, far less clear-cut world in which partial change and surface transformation are at least as common as is outright disappearance" (153).

While these authors suggest that the history of imagining various Amazons is also a history of imagining Euro-American identity by creating its opposite, Whitehead more directly ties these processes to specific projects and periods. What begins in sixteenth-century travel accounts as an effort to textually capture the marvels and package the wonder of geographically and culturally distant lands leads to an "aesthetic of extremes" that sets a tone for later scribes. As a cadre of writers emerges from within the now colonized Americas, their imaginations turn from a general fascination with distance and difference to specificities of people and place. Travel in and of itself is not enough; it must be authenticated by details of cultural and natural features that have fallen under the European gaze. It is at this point that the novelties of native existence beyond the colonial margins are documented alongside a debate about their imminent demise. By the mid-eighteenth century "a sense of nostalgia for the eclipse of a native Amazon . . . really begins to take hold" (Whitehead 2002:130).

As the imagined Amazon moves into the nineteenth century it becomes less a space of wonder and more a place incorporated into the processes of scientific discovery. The rainforest is subjected to empirical practice, not historical speculation, and its native peoples are eulogized, as they "have become irrelevant to the potential of Amazonia for scientific enlightenment" (Whitehead 2002:131). What

Whitehead calls the "Science of Paradise" extends into the twentieth century, revealing the Amazon as naturally pristine but quite unfit for sustained and meaningful human occupation. Ethnographers scramble to salvage what remains of native culture, while the mysteries and wisdom of indigenous knowledge are sopped up and scribbled down for posterity. Modern travel writing, says Whitehead, seeks to take us back one last time for a final check on the exotic and timeless, to reassure us that some remnants still exist. But as travel writers beat the bushes, they shake out only the essentialisms of the past, recast as peculiar anachronisms. "The forest of marvels finally becomes a playground for the absurd as the distance between possible observations and actual experiences invites parody and then plagiarism of the ethnographic form" (136).

The Amazon has frequently and throughout history been conceptualized as a frontier zone: at the edge of the Inka Empire, the untamed fringes of civilization, the margins of state and colonial control, or a vast area of untapped potential for natural resource extraction and development. What these conceptualizations share is the tendency to place the Amazon and its people consistently at the margins of, or make them peripheral players in, grander state, entrepreneurial, or development agendas. Although a specific form of Amazonian orientalism is relevant here, particularly as it relates to modernizing nationalisms in the Andes and Brazil, the "othering" of the Amazon through these representational forms is only one facet of its construction and fails to recognize the complexities and contradictions such representational forms engender. Another dimension of these representations is the Amazon as a region of reaction, responding to external state, colonial, market, or developmentalist forces, those that are thought to be ultimately foreign to, and to have no place in, a traditional Amazonian world. Yet treating Amazonian peoples as simple reactors to these forces and understanding such forces as strictly external ultimately downplays exchanges between Amazonian peoples and state agents, missionaries, capitalist economies, and

NGOS, among others. Much recent scholarship on the Amazon leads us to question simple action-reaction conceptualizations, and more general trends in anthropological theory encourage us to (once again) take seriously local cosmologies in the construction of interpretive worldviews (Sahlins 1988).

One consequence of these narrative constructions of Amazonia is that their tendency to follow specific narrative tropes has guided dominant understandings of the core characteristics of the region and its inhabitants. The schizophrenic metanarratives of noble versus ignoble savages, pristine forests versus dark and dangerous places, and massive development potential versus forested wasteland speak to ways of knowing the Amazon through incoherent yet consistent constructions of space and the capacity to create a mental map irrespective of divergent local historical trajectories. In the present these narratives and the frontier mentalities guiding them make the Amazon an exciting tourist destination, where one can encounter uncorrupted, traditional Indians in their pristine, unadulterated natural spaces while simultaneously making the Amazon and the "uncivilized savages" that inhabit it symbolic of the failure of the modernizing, civilizing missions of European countries. As such, many dominant constructions of the Amazon have hinged on what we would like it to be (or what we fear it is and wish it were not), making the region a vessel for our fantasies and nightmares. This book does not strive to achieve a rewriting of Amazonian narratives, nor does it hope to be comprehensive in its treatment of Amazonia in thematic, regional, or ethnographic scope. It does, however, center on several interrelated themes that bring the contributors together in dialogue.

Indigeneities and Communities

National and transnational indigenous movements have become central subjects of analysis for anthropologists, political scientists, and human geographers, among others. Research on indigenous social movements owes a debt to the Amazon, as some of the most visible early movements found their footing there, primarily oriented around struggles over land and resources. Not only have issues of territorial rights been central to the political agendas of indigenous leaders in the Amazon and elsewhere, but questions of these rights have been intimately tied to indigenous cultural identity more generally, as Alcida Ramos points out in her contribution to this book. In fact, territorial rights often hinge on the ability to make claims as "original inhabitants," making indigeneity part of a political strategy employed to gain official state recognition of these lands made on the basis of ancestral ties to them (Sawyer 2004).

"Primordial" claims to land have been effective political strategies, both by making use of existing legislation for indigenous land claims and by pushing for legal reforms to enhance indigenous rights. In Ecuador, for example, both Amazonian and Andean indigenous movements made use of an antiquated Law of the Commons, put in place in 1937 to promote the organization of agricultural cooperatives as an intermediate step between subsistence farming and commercial farming (Becker 1998). This law protected communal land rights for indigenous peoples, and following the enactment of the Law of Agrarian Reform in 1964 and the Law of Colonization of the Amazon in 1977, both of which contributed to colonization, extractive development, and militarization of the Amazon, indigenous organizations forming at that time utilized the Law of the Commons as a mechanism for obtaining official recognition of community lands in large, contiguous, collectively held units. Two of the earliest of these organizations, the Federation of Shuar Centers and the Federation of Indigenous Organizations of Napo, worked to organize their member communities into associations and cooperatives eligible for collective land title, helping to gain recognition of large territories (Perreault 2003; Salazar 1981).

The global indigenous rights movement in the 1980s and 1990s put international pressure on states to recognize the rights of their indigenous inhabitants. The United Nations International Year of Indigenous

Peoples in 1992 contributed to a countercelebration of the European discovery of the New World, and the United Nations Working Group on Indigenous Peoples and the declaration on indigenous peoples by the International Labour Organization both provide international legal templates for addressing indigenous rights. Indigenous advocacy has led to the adoption of legal reforms In many countries with Amazonian territories, most notably Colombia and Venezuela (see Van Cott 2003), and international pressure has, more generally, been favorable for indigenous political activists who seek to carve out political space for legal reforms and the recognition of rights specific to indigenous peoples.

In fact Amazonian indigenous social movements of the past two decades have not been limited to struggles over territory, but have conceptualized territory within a broader cultural frame. Arguing that cultural expression and history are linked to territory through seeing cultural identity woven into the forest landscape, indigenous leaders have broadened their demands to include the recognition of cultural rights, including bilingual education, the right to practice indigenous medicine, and control of archaeological sites. Linking cultural and territorial rights has uniquely shaped the nature of indigenous social movements as indigenous leaders suggest that it is not land, in a general sense, that is the goal of indigenous struggles, but particular territories linking histories of people to place, or chronotopographies (Uzendoski 2005), and territories are recognized as culturally significant due to how they are made recognizable by specific land-use practices (Sawyer 2004). The success of linking environmental conservation to recuperation or recognition of indigenous land rights has led to some of the most visible of these struggles occurring in contexts in which land use is contested between indigenous peoples claiming ancestral rights and extractive corporations seeking to access forest or mineral resources (Hecht and Cockburn 1990; Turner 1995).

Over time the convergence of interests between those involved in the global environmental movement or interested in sustainable development of the Amazon and indigenous peoples seeking recognition of territorial and cultural rights has led to the growth of shared struggles between these movements. While the internationalization of indigenous movements has been a crucial factor in their ability to press demands against frequently hostile states (Brysk 1996; Perreault 2003; Yashar 1999), this interconnectedness has also had consequences for the ways that states, NGOs, and international observers more generally view indigenous Amazonians. In fact the very strength of the coalition of activists and indigenous leaders, by constructing indigeneities partially with the expectations of the international community in mind, may also be its limitation. If, as international advocates have commonly asserted, Amazonian indigenous peoples represent a key—perhaps the key—to rainforest conservation, and if delimiting indigenous territories is therefore akin to setting aside those territories as parklands, there are demands placed on indigenous peoples that they live according to Western environmental expectations. Anthropologists concerned with the implications of the indigenous-environmental alliance in the form sketched above correctly predicted the backlash by some NGOs when Western expectations were not met (Conklin and Graham 1995; Ramos 1994).

Some of the implications of the webs of interaction by which indigenous identities are constructed both globally and locally are addressed in various chapters in this volume. Contributions by Margarita Chaves and Jean Jackson highlight the complexities of "indigenous" as a category, illustrating both how it eludes easy or coherent definition and how the meanings attached to indigenousness are highly malleable. Chaves examines how state understandings of indigenism have led to the de-Indianization of some groups in Putumayo, while also contributing to the re-Indianization of others. In this context the ongoing violent conflict in the region has contributed to extensive displacement and relocation of people, leading to a disruption of narrow understandings that link indigeneity to ancestral territories. Under the Colombian *resguardo* system indigeneity is recognized when inhabitants can make a historical claim to land, yet in the war-torn Putumayo victims of the conflict have left their rural territories in favor of the relative security of urban neighborhoods, uprooting them not only from territory but, in the eyes of the Colombian state, from their very indigenous nature. These de-Indianized Indians are not granted land title in their new locales in spite of their claims to indigenous identity; instead, colonists in other parts of the Putumayo are having their land claims recognized through the *resguardo* system, ultimately "Indianizing" them in the process.

Jean Jackson provides a detailed and nuanced examination of media representations of indigenous Amazonians over the past fifteen years, identifying themes in the treatment of indigenous peoples in the major Colombian presses. Importantly, she is able to link the predominantly positive representations of indigenous peoples in this time period to the political and social climate in Colombia more generally, as spiraling violence and corruption there have led many to look for alternative models for constructing society. In this context indigenous peoples become moral foils for the malaise of modernity and the ills of Western society (Friedman 1999).

In fact the expectations tied to those occupying the "indigenous slot" become critical in determining who is and is not perceived to be authentically indigenous (Li 2000, 2003), as well as the ethical obligations associated with being a member of that group. Beth Conklin examines the tension associated with indigenous materialism, one taboo for those who are tagged by outsiders with the "indigenous" label. As she illustrates, materialism is not oppositional to the formation of "traditional" affective and kin relationships in Wari' society; instead, materiality forms a critical component of the formation and maintenance of social relationships. When Conklin, in introductions to strangers, is tied by her friends to a litany of material goods she has gifted them, this is not to deny the affective relations she shares with them. Rather, these objects serve as physical evidence that such affective relationships exist. Michael Uzendoski (2004) has made similar observations in the formation of kin ties through shared substances, as has Janet Chernela (2006) for the obligations indigenous leaders have to effectively circulate goods in expressions of generosity. Conklin adds to the discussion the ability of indigenous peoples to make sense of nonnatives through a local system of exchange and incorporate outsiders into meaningful emotional relationships comprehensible through the exchange of material items. Thus the attention that indigenous peoples pay to material objects should not be understood as a result of corruption by consumerism, but as a means of solidifying social relations through exchange.

The complexities associated with defining who is and is not indigenous are widely noted (see, for example, Beteille 1998; Bowen 2000), and the implications of employing indigeneity as a criterion—or the criterion—for the application of special rights have also been debated (Brown 1998; Friedman 1999). Despite academic discussions of the possible pitfalls of utilizing such a nebulous concept in the design and application of legal rights and policy frameworks, politicians, development agents, and those seeking recognition (or seeking to avoid recognition) as indigenous freely employ the label, often with conflicting and contradictory results. The contributors to this volume recognize indigeneity as a social fact, even if defining "the indigenous" and determining with any degree of accuracy who belongs in that category remain futile exercises. As such, some of the most promising anthropological work related to indigeneity explores its use in different political projects and what, exactly, the nature of the indigenous-nonindigenous divide may be.

Michael Uzendoski examines this divide, suggesting that it may not be as stark or clear-cut as it would appear in much of the anthropological literature on the Amazon. Exploring Amazonian fractality evident in stories told by both natives and nonnatives, he emphasizes the exchange of ideas, the sharing of space and sociality, and the telling of stories that intertwine people artificially divided into separate categories by external readings of ethnicity. These stories illustrate the social landscapes of the Amazon, in which native inhabitants and colonists occupy adjacent spaces, where there are growing populations of indigenous peoples in urban sectors, and where those who self-identify as *mestizos* share in the telling of stories that contain structural and thematic similarities to stories told by those who self-identify as indigenous. The constant exchanges between these different Amazonian inhabitants has led to the emergence of shared intellectual traditions and social spaces and the formation of kin ties between groups that are often incorrectly treated separately (as indigenous and *mestizo*) in the anthropological literature.

Cosmologies of Capitalism and Development

Research on Amazonia as well as other regions conceptualized as peripheral zones has paid significant attention to the impacts of capitalism on the social organization of their inhabitants. Framing capitalism as a foreign entity, much of this research has inadvertently contributed to representations of the Amazon as timeless and its inhabitants as victims of the forces of modernity. While forces of colonialism and capitalism have certainly had severe consequences for Amazonian inhabitants at different points in history, anthropology's unique contribution lies in its ability to comprehend the multiple meanings attached to how people understand these forces in their lives. Marshall Sahlins (1988, 1999) has dedicated substantial attention to what he calls "cosmologies of capitalism," his premise being that people may construct radically different understandings of colonial or capitalist forces presumably emanating from Western metropoles, and that they may in fact transform not only the meanings attached to those forces locally but also their very expression in these different contexts. An important contribution of this work lies in Sahlins's ability to demonstrate that frameworks of domination and resistance are limiting our capacity to detect and comprehend the meanings people in different settings attach to so-called global forces in their daily lives. A failure to recognize this runs the risk of artificially privileging Western perspectives at the expense of an adequate exploration of how people in the Amazon, and elsewhere, may attach different significance to how they experience and interact with the supposedly Western forces of capitalism. In fact we should question the validity of assertions that capitalism is a Western phenomenon when at work in different sociocultural contexts; it seems apparent that capitalism itself is transformed in its appropriation and use in diverse cultural settings, as Uzendoski suggests in his chapter (see Bashkow 2000 for an illustrative case from Papua New Guinea).

This suggests that these economic, social, and informational exchanges are occurring in distinct cosmological universes, leading to quite different meanings attached to concepts or ideas that seem, at first glance, to be shared within a "global village." This is an important insight, particularly for those who would wish to support alternative frameworks for understanding the world outside of dominant Western capitalisms. This insight guides the contributions of several of the chapters in this volume. It also represents a departure from most of the research focused on political ecology and extractive and sustainable development in Amazonia.

For example, research from a political ecology perspective has focused attention on access to and control of natural resources, as well as the implications of extractive development on rainforest ecologies and the livelihoods of those who rely on the natural resources of the Amazon for their subsistence (Bunker 1988; Hecht and Cockburn 1990; Roper 2003). This research agenda gained prominence in the 1980s concomitant with growing global concern about the impact of oil and other mining industries, logging, and cattle ranching and agricultural plantation economies on Amazonian ecosystems, and it has made a substantial contribution to our understanding of the relationship among these forces, ideologies of national development, and attempts by an array of national and international organizations and movements, including peasant and indigenous organizations and environmental and human rights NGOs, to avert extractive practices (Fisher 1994; Schwartzman 1999; Schwartzman and Zimmerman 2005). It illustrates the capacity of international alliances to advance conservation agendas and the capacity of many Amazonian groups to link their objectives to those of national and international conservation and human rights organizations. But it also tends to obscure the complexities and contradictions in the relationships between these organizations and their Amazonian interlocutors. Patrick Wilson examines some of these complexities in Amazonian Ecuador through an analysis of the multiple meanings attached to development projects by NGOs, indigenous federation leaders, and base communities of the federation and the conflicts they potentially produce for indigenous representative organizations.

María Clemencia Ramírez examines the role of alternative development projects in contributing to a "taming" of the Colombian Amazon, making coca eradication and alternative development tied to Plan Colombia quite consistent with prior concerns with the Amazon as an uncontrolled frontier zone. The NGOs responsible for alternative development suggest that their role is to transform a "perverse" into a productive social capital, thereby creating viable citizens and enhancing governance in the region. Ramírez, however, illustrates how the rationale and organization behind these development projects fail to take seriously the experiences of local inhabitants, instead criminalizing peasants by implicating them in Colombia's drug problem. Rather than working closely with peasant organizations in the elaboration of development alternatives, the NGOs financed through Plan Colombia have tended to be wary of these organizations because of their suspected ties to the illicit drug trade or violent activity, contributing to the quick demise of the development projects while failing to support local actors potentially inclined to such alternatives.

A related field of research has examined the role of sustainable development in rainforest conservation efforts and in empowering local peoples in the development process. Sustainable development has been heralded as a pathway to environmentally and culturally sensitive economic and political empowerment for historically mar-ginalized peoples. These forms of development have been predicated on specific conceptualizations of the relationship between Amazonian peoples and the natural environment, leading to a plethora of proj-ects promoting ecotourism, agroforestry, and artisan craft production utilizing renewable forest resources. Although substantial attention has been paid to the liberating potential of these projects in economic and cultural terms, only sparse attention has been directed to what these projects might signify for local peoples or what the political implications of these projects may be for indigenous organizations. Several contributions to this volume address these issues.

Frank Hutchins, for example, examines the role of indigenous-operated ecotourism in the production and consumption of culture through the paid encounter between foreign tourists and local peo-ples. Culture here is commodified to the extent that it is the "good" that is being marketed and sold to tourists: tourists pay to see the real Indians. Yet this very process of commodification creates ten-sions within the communities related to how, exactly, culture should be presented to tourists and the mundane but critical question of distribution of resources generated from ecotourism. The tourists themselves sometimes feel uncomfortable as well, suggesting that the cultural presentations are contrived or that the participants are only half-hearted in their dancing, leading the tourists to question the authenticity of the performances. This could lead one to draw the conclusion that the marketing of culture through ecotourism contrib-utes to an eradication of cultural difference and multiple historicities, ultimately resulting in a loss of power through the commodification of culture. Yet, as Hutchins demonstrates, this process is only partial, and those involved in indigenous ecotourism construct their understand-ing of ecotourism from multiple frames and historicities that inform the capitalist production of culture through ecotourism, illustrating how capitalism becomes pluralized in the process.

Beth Conklin and Patrick Wilson similarly focus their attention on economic exchanges. As discussed earlier, Conklin examines the materiality and sociality of gift giving among the Wari', reconciling the discomfort many anthropologists and others feel when affective relationships with friends in the field are discussed in terms of a list of consumer goods they have given them. Her argument relates to two sides of the debate on sowing the seeds of capitalism in Amazonian and other contexts. One side is the role that capitalism has been thought to play in "modernizing" and "improving" culturally and economically impoverished Indians, which has been part of the modernizing agenda of many Latin American states, and missionaries before them (Muratorio 1991; Stutzman 1981). The other side of this debate relates to those who have greeted the incorporation of indigenous peoples into capitalism with despair, treating it as a corruption of a prior idyllic state and resulting in the loss of cultural traditions. Conklin illustrates that both of these are outsider concerns with indigenous Amazonians and tell us very little about how Amazonian peoples conceptualize their socioeconomic relationships. By taking seriously Amazonian cosmologies of capitalism, she is able to demonstrate how attention to the exchange of material goods has locally inscribed meaning that defies explanation through Western capitalist understandings of exchange.

Patrick Wilson focuses on the implications of sustainable development projects sponsored by NGOs for the exercise of leadership in an indigenous federation. Exploring notions of corruption and collaboration from the vantage points of the Napo Kichwa of Ecuador's Amazon and the sustainable development NGOs working in the region, he suggests that divergent understandings of the appropriate and inappropriate use of project resources contribute to an inadvertent undermining of leadership authority. Unlike NGO staff, who are concerned with fiscal responsibility, effective indigenous leadership is contingent on leaders' ability to mobilize and circulate desired goods in conspicuous displays of generosity. As indigenous leaders have been increasingly removed from the development process in favor of working through intermediary NGOs, these leaders have been unable to control the flow of the projects, thereby leading to a decline in the legitimacy of the leaders and the indigenous organizations they represent.

Editing Eden had its genesis in a panel discussion at the Latin American Studies Association meeting in San Juan, Puerto Rico, in March 2006. Since then, contributors have deepened and polished their work, and two respected anthropologists, Alcida Ramos and Neil Whitehead, have added commentaries. This volume includes insights from well-established scholars and budding ideas from junior scholars. These academics come from both North and South America. The lives of indigenous people and colonizers alike are analyzed, along with the merchants, tourists, environmentalists, missionaries, and anthropologists who move in and out of their worlds. Research and reflections in the following chapters span history and historicities. The common thread through all chapters is, obviously, the Amazon. It is the hope of the editors that, while we continue to acknowledge the contributions of scholars who helped us see the ways the Amazon is produced and represented by outsiders, we also begin to decipher the voices and actions of people going about the business of living in this part of the world.

References

Acuña, P. Cristobal de. 1942. *Nuevo descubrimiento del Gran Rio de las Amazonas.* Buenos Aires: Emece Editores.

Balée, William, and Clark Erickson. 2006. *Time and complexity in historical ecology: Studies in the neotropical lowlands.* New York: Columbia University Press.

Bashkow, Ira. 2000. "Whiteman" are good to think with: How Orokaiva morality is reflected on whiteman's skin. *Identities* 7 (3): 281–332.

Becker, Marc. 1998. Una revolución communista indígena: Rural protest movements in Cayambe, Ecuador. *Rethinking Marxism* 10 (4): 34–51.

Beteille, Andre. 1998. The idea of indigenous people. *Current Anthropology* 39 (2): 187–91.

Bowen, John R. 2000. Should we have a universal concept of "indigenous peoples" rights? Ethnicity and essentialism in the twenty-first century. *Anthropology Today* 16 (4): 12–16.

Brown, Michael F. 1998. Can culture be copyrighted? *Current Anthropology* 39 (2): 193–222.

Brysk, Alison. 1996. Turning weakness into strength: The internationalization of Indian rights. *Latin American Perspectives* 23 (2): 38–57.

Bunker, Stephen G. 1988. *Underdeveloping the Amazon: Extraction, unequal exchange, and the failure of the modern state.* Chicago: University of Chicago Press.

Chernela, Janet M. 2006. *Lex talionis*: Recent advances and retreats in indigenous rights in Brazil. *Journal of Latin American Anthropology* 11 (1): 138–53.

Conklin, Beth A., and Laura R. Graham. 1995. The shifting middle ground: Amazonian Indians and eco-politics. *American Anthropologist* 97 (4): 695–710.

Driver, Felix. 2001. *Geography militant: Cultures of exploration and empire.* Malden MA: Blackwell.

Fisher, William H. 1994. Megadevelopment, environmentalism, and resistance: The institutional context of Kayapó indigenous politics in central Brazil. *Human Organization* 53 (3): 220–32.

Friedman, Jonathan. 1999. Indigenous struggles and the discreet charm of the bourgeoisie. *Australian Journal of Anthropology* 10 (1): 1–14.

Gheerbrant, Alain. 1992. *The Amazon: Past, present, and future.* Translated by I. M. Paris. New York: Harry N. Abrams.

Heaton, H. C., ed. 1934. *The discovery of the Amazon, according to the account of Friar Gaspar de Carvajal and other documents.* New York: American Geographical Society.

Heckenberger, Michael J. 2004. *The ecology of power: Culture, place and personhood in the southern Amazon, AD 1000–2000.* London: Routledge.

Hecht, Susana, and Alexander Cockburn. 1990. *The fate of the forest: Developers, destroyers and defenders of the Amazon.* New York: HarperCollins.

Li, Tanya Murray. 2000. Articulating indigenous identity in Indonesia: Resource politics and the tribal slot. *Comparative Studies in Society and History* 42 (1): 149–79.

———. 2003. *Masyarakat adat*, difference, and the limits of recognition in Indonesia's forest zone. In *Race, nature, and the politics of difference,* ed. Donald S. Moore, Anand Pandian, and Jake Kosek, 380–406. Durham NC: Duke University Press.

Meggers, Betty. 1996. *Amazonia: Man and culture in a counterfeit paradise.* Washington DC: Smithsonian Institution Press.

Muratorio, Blanca. 1991. *The life and times of Grandfather Alonso: Culture and history in the Upper Amazon.* New Brunswick NJ: Rutgers University Press.

Perreault, Thomas. 2003. Making space: Community organization, agrarian change, and the politics of scale in the Ecuadorian Amazon. *Latin American Perspectives* 30 (1): 96–121.

Pratt, Mary Louise. 1992. *Imperial eyes: Travel writing and transculturation.* New York: Routledge.

Ramos, Alcida Rita. 1994. The hyperreal Indian. *Critique of Anthropology* 14 (2): 153–71.

Roosevelt, Anna, ed. 1997. *Amazonian Indians from prehistory to the present: Anthropological perspectives.* Tucson: University of Arizona Press.

Roper, J. Montgomery. 2003. Bolivian legal reforms and local indigenous organizations: Opportunities and obstacles in a lowland municipality. *Latin American Perspectives* 30 (1): 139–61.

Sahlins, Marshall. 1988. Cosmologies of capitalism: The trans-Pacific sector of the "world system." *Proceedings of the British Academy* 74:1–51.

———. 1999. What is anthropological enlightenment? Some lessons of the twentieth century. *Annual Review of Anthropology* 28:1–23.

Salazar, Ernesto. 1981. The Federación Shuar and the colonization frontier. In *Cultural transformations and ethnicity in modern Ecuador,* ed. Norman E. Whitten, 589–613. Urbana: University of Illinois Press.

Sawyer, Suzana. 2004. *Crude chronicles: Indigenous politics, multinational oil, and neoliberalism in Ecuador.* Durham NC: Duke University Press.

Schwartzman, Stephen. 1999. Reigniting the rainforest: Fires, development and deforestation. *Native Americas* 16 (3/4): 60–63.

Schwartzman, Stephen, and Barbara Zimmerman. 2005. Conservation alliances with indigenous peoples of the Amazon. *Conservation Biology* 19 (3): 721–27.

Slater, Candace. 2002. *Entangled Edens: Visions of the Amazon.* Berkeley: University of California Press.

Smith, Anthony. 1990. *Explorers of the Amazon.* London: Viking.

Stutzman, Ronald. 1981. El mestizaje: An inclusive ideology of exclusion. In *Cultural transformations and ethnicity in modern Ecuador,* ed. Norman E. Whitten, 45–94. Urbana: University of Illinois Press.

Turner, Terence. 1995. An indigenous people's struggle for socially equitable and ecologically sustainable production: The Kayapo revolt against extractivism. *Journal of Latin American Anthropology* 1 (1): 98–121.

Uzendoski, Michael A. 2004. Manioc beer and meat: Value, reproduction and cosmic substance among the Napo Runa of the Ecuadorian Amazon. *Journal of the Royal Anthropology Institute* 10:883–902.

———. 2005. Making Amazonia: Shape-shifters, giants, and alternative modernities. *Latin American Research Review* 40 (1): 223–36.

Van Cott, Donna Lee. 2003. Andean indigenous movements and constitutional transformation: Venezuela in comparative perspective. *Latin American Perspectives* 30 (1): 49–69.

Whitehead, Neil. 2002. South America/Amazonia: The forest of marvels. In *The Cambridge companion to travel writing,* ed. P. Hulme and T. Youngs, 122–38. Cambridge: Cambridge University Press.

Yashar, Deborah J. 1999. Democracy, indigenous movements, and the postliberal challenge in Latin America. *World Politics* 52 (1): 76–104.

Part 1

Myth, Meaning, Modernity, and Representation

1. Indigenous Capitalisms

Ecotourism, Cultural Reproduction, and the
Logic of Capital in Ecuador's Upper Amazon

Frank Hutchins

The finger points at me, indicating that I'm now expected to sling a drum over my shoulder, beat out a rhythm, scoot around the wooden floor, and initiate a courtship dance with a Kichwa woman on the other side of the room. It's all part of a cultural presentation on the last night of a student trip to Capirona, an indigenous community involved in ecotourism in Ecuador's Upper Amazon. I've watched or participated in this scene a dozen times, most often as a researcher, but this time I am the leader of a student group. At the end of each visit to Capirona, community members first perform traditional music and dance and then ask visitors to join in both the performance of Kichwa culture and in a production of the visitors' own culture.

Student evaluations after the program included comments such as "The 'dance' on the last night seemed contrived and packaged for tourists . . . it seemed the locals felt obligated to dance" and "I felt like they were there trying to serve us like a hotel — I didn't feel it was a good cultural experience." Similar comments were generated by visitors to other Kichwa projects in the area (Schaller 1996) and were frequently associated with a sense that the performances lacked authenticity or genuine interest on the part of the dancers.

The public display of culture, questions of land use (cut and sell the trees, or show them to tourists?), and the division of labor and profits all contribute to contentious and ongoing dialogues that reflect the "indigeneities" discussed in the introduction to this volume. Negotiations over how to manage economic capital and cultural or social capital bring together concepts and resources from places that may be geographically and culturally distant. Finding a middle ground where compromises between the local and the extralocal might be worked out can be a conflictive process, as Wilson (this volume) points out in his discussion of contrasting leadership styles between generations of Kichwa in Ecuador's Amazon as they respond to development initiatives.

Ecotourism offers an interesting window through which to observe these negotiations, as it involves economic, cultural, spatial, and environmental issues. Capirona and eight other lowland Kichwa communities in Ecuador's Napo region make up a network organized to develop community-based ecotourism. They are part of a growing trend in which communities, principally indigenous, search for alternative development models that ostensibly protect natural resources and sustain local cultures. The process draws participants more directly into the global tourism market and a capitalist system of exchange and commodity production. It also creates a unique type of reflexivity, wherein "culture" must be identified, packaged, priced, and produced for tourist consumption. This "thingified" culture is often clumsy for performers and audiences alike, appearing as fallout from a market invasion. But indigenous communities aren't sucked naïvely into globalization, nor are they hurled back out as residue. They unquestionably lose some ground and gain some ground. What's most interesting, however, is the ground they are regularly negotiating. Sahlins, reflecting on the agency of indigenous cultures, argues that "even the subjects of Western domination and dependency-relations act in the world as social-historical beings, so their experience of capitalism is mediated by the habitus of an indigenous form of life. In the upshot, the capitalist forces are played out in the schemata of a different cultural universe" (1999:xvi).

In this chapter I consider production and consumption of culture through ecotourism, one of many global-scale "projects" (Tsing 2000) that influence meanings important to Kichwa life in the Upper Amazon. Specifically, I analyze whether the production of culture as a tourism commodity is simply the settling of capitalistic processes that lead to the abstraction of labor (Marx's concept) and alienation (and crude objectification) of indigenous societies. If so, then the end product is the destruction by capital of heterogeneous histories (and historicities), a concomitant loss of power through identity politics, and a general withering away of diverse possibilities for belonging in the world.

I investigate this via research materials gathered in Napo Province, Ecuador, since 1997. The materials (interviews, observations, government documents, NGO documents, industry pamphlets and reports) come from traveling with tourists, staying in host communities of Kichwa people, visiting travel agencies, and attending travel exhibitions and conferences. This happened during a fifteen-month period in 1997–98 and during summer field trips each year between 2003 and 2008. My position is that, although cultural commodification is certainly part of tourism among the Kichwa, their labor—and hence cultural reproduction—is not totally absorbed by capital. Local practices, beliefs, and historicities (Whitehead 2003) still anchor Kichwa people in a variety of ways, even as the ground that holds the anchor shifts with regularity. This is a position not unlike that advocated by Mascia-Lees and Himpele writing on globalization in *Anthropology News*, where they urge conceptualizing the global and local not as geographical binaries, but as inseparable processes of meaning making. Anthropological subjects and objects, they maintain, should be theorized as "existing simultaneously in multiple frames of meaning,

5

in differing magnitudes of practice, and multiple domains of materiality" (2006:11).

Before I can elaborate on this simultaneity I need to explain the ways that Upper Amazonian Kichwa, and indeed many indigenous people turning to ecotourism, are integrated into contemporary market processes. While the area under investigation (generally around the provincial capital of Tena) has long been a contact zone of economic and cultural exchange, ecotourism offers a more intense market incursion into participating communities, as well as possibilities for reconfiguring that market by integrating indigenous perspectives and interests. I begin by looking at how indigenous culture has become a "thing" available for use by governments, organizations, and tourism entrepreneurs (both indigenous and nonindigenous). Reification makes possible the transplantation of cultural items into legal documents, development plans, political positions, and market strategies. This appears to be part of the logic of capital being worked out via the global practice of tourism. I then look more specifically at how tourism operators, governmental and nongovernmental organizations, and indigenous groups have manipulated these cultural items to design, promote, and carry out activities categorized as ecotourism. This also looks like the unfolding of a capitalist process within which product differences (namely, cultural elements) are minimized so that the particular commodity can more easily enter the flows of global exchange.

This version of globalization, however, is too linear. There are histories outside the history of capitalist forms that continue to influence subjectivities and frame responses to the demands of the state and the blandishments of the market. Acknowledging these influences helps us understand how, according to Sahlins, "the world is also being re-diversified by indigenous adaptations to the global juggernaut" (1999:ix). In the final section I use reflections on Marx's writings by Dipesh Chakrabarty to examine ways Kichwa people pluralize capitalism by continuing to practice traditional forms of communal work, by pressing for legal reforms that recognize collective tourism projects (as opposed to purely private enterprises), and by creatively distributing profits. These responses are tied to ways of living not prefigured by market forces, ways captured by Chakrabarty in his discussion of "History 2" (detailed in the closing section). "The idea of History 2," he writes, "allows us to make room, in Marx's own analytic of capital, for the politics of human belonging and diversity. It gives us a ground on which to situate our thoughts about multiple ways of being human and their relationship to the global logic of capital" (2002:102).

In describing the larger, structural picture that includes global-scale tourism, I use Hannerz's (1992) model of four frameworks (form of life, market, state, and movement) that organize cultural flow. This allows me to track the reification of culture and the commodification of identities through tourism (particularly through the state and market frameworks), while also considering points of resistance and alternative models (most visible in the form of life and movement frameworks). This process is locally grounded and analyzed with the help of Whitehead, Whitten, and Scott, whose works add the critical dimensions of agency and creative response that involves both resistance and selective accommodation. In the end I hope to have delivered a story of socioeconomic hybridization, characteristic of places where something called a "global force" arrives via complex circuitry, is refitted by particular histories and perspectives to be more locally palatable, and is then allowed to continue a course through places big and small. Like Chakrabarty, I seek to "produce a reading in which 'capital'—the very category itself—becomes a site where both the universal history of capital and the politics of human belonging are allowed to interrupt each other's narrative" (2002:106).

This "interruption of narrative" is exemplified in Uzendoski's contribution to this volume, where he muddles the local/global dichotomies by suggesting that Kichwa people see themselves as part of a much more fluid world. This context for living is governed neither by linear

7

historical processes nor by rigid geographical categories, but is shaped by the ongoing relationships among people, places and nature.

Uzendoskl's work points to interesting ways that Amazonian cultures represent a challenge to the simplistic reading of historical change and the dangers in clumsy conflations of globalization, capitalism, and modernity. The Amazon as a uniquely imagined place both geographically and culturally, and as a real space located physically, politically, and economically at the margin of many margins, is a rich site for exploring contemporary contractions, compressions, corrections, and conversions that are all shot through with the foreign and the familiar.

The often bloody rendering of rainforest resources, from canopy to subsoil, is part of a history played out in the shadows of the global marketplace. Roger Casement (in Taussig 1984) threw light into this shadow world in the early twentieth century when he described the dark side of imperialism and resource extraction in Africa and the Amazon. More recently Carolyn Nordstrom (2007) has done the same in her investigation of illegal trade and illicit markets across the globe. In the Amazon these processes have helped create a particular political economy that affects, and is consequently acted upon, by various groups filtering the changes through their respective norms and worldviews that the authors of this volume reveal to be quite diverse. I consider such diversity as it relates to tourism and how plural lifeways and histories fare as this industry expands across Amazonia.

Reifying Culture

Tourism, Ecuador's third leading industry and a key interface between that country and much of the rest of the world, is directly involved in the creation of an "imaginary geography." Attempts to order knowledge and engage in "imaginative seduction" have historically implicated travel and travel writing in the production of imaginary geographies and "imaginary topographies" (Chard 1999:10). Tourism is a magnifying glass, albeit with a distorted lens, through which outsiders see countries such as Ecuador. Within these countries tourism acts more like a carnival mirror, warping images but nevertheless offering some semblance of reality. Ultimately tourism plays an important role in the "visual and discursive imaginings of space and place" that are "crucial in Ecuador as a postcolonial state" (Radcliffe 1996:25).

Tourism, projected at the start of this millennium to be the world's largest industry, generates its own complex networks of relationships and interdependencies that reach into almost every corner of the planet. In Ecuador, with 953,196 foreign visitors in 2007 (Ecuadorian Ministry of Tourism, Department of Statistics 2008, www.turismo.gov. ec), the industry is touted by the government, private agencies, indigenous organizations, and NGOs as a primary source of development and foreign exchange. In an editorial in Quito's major newspaper, *El Comercio* (September 1, 2000), Kurt Freund Ruf echoed industry and government sentiment when he referred to tourism as "a potential gold mine" and a "key element of sustainable development for Ecuador."

The history of tourism in the Upper Amazon, and its relationship to indigenous peoples, must be considered within the larger political economy of Ecuador. Throughout much of the republic's history, the Ecuadorian government has ceded control of its Amazon region to other entities, mainly those relating to religion and commerce. The Oriente, as it is often called, was "off the discursive 'mental map' of metropolitan decision-makers" until the late nineteenth century, when it was first mentioned in 1861 in the Constitution as a province and gradually recognized for its potential resources (Radcliffe and Westwood 1996:110). This reflects not only a political distancing of the area, but a cultural and cognitive distancing as well. As Taylor points out, many coastal and Andean peoples have mixed feelings about the Amazon in terms of national identity: "In their view the Amazon region and its inhabitants are a different world, historically and sociologically as well as geographically; at best a promising though rowdy frontier, at worst a dumping ground for vague utopian ideas, rebels, and down-and-outs" (1999:196).

The attraction of the Amazon as a tourist destination is related to its biological diversity, its international image as a major environmental resource, and its reputation as home to some of the remaining "primitive" peoples left on the planet. For the Ecuadorian government and the tourism market, these attractions provide opportunities to diversify tourism offerings that have traditionally focused on the Galapagos Islands and some highland regions (especially Quito, Cuenca, and Otavalo), while also holding out an acceptably green development option for the rainforest.

For indigenous communities and some NGOs, exploitation of these natural and cultural resources offers a development alternative and, theoretically, a way to sustain environments and cultures. At least rhetorically these organizations push for a form of tourism development rooted in indigenous history, values, and worldviews. In a May 22, 2008, press release by the Ministry of Tourism, Galo Villamil Gualinga, president of the Federación Plurinacional de Turismo Comunitario del Ecuador (FEPTCE), described community tourism as an alternative for "living well." He said *bien vivir* is what "indigenous people practice through their ancestral knowledge of foods, natural medicine, customs, traditions, care for natural riches; this is in essence what we want to share with the rest of the world" (my translation). This concept (referred to this time as *buen vivir*) emerged during the drafting of Ecuador's new Constitution during the summer of 2008. Carlos Pilamunga, a Constitutional Assembly member from the indigenous Pachakutik Party, explained in a newspaper interview that the elements of *buen vivir* inform all indigenous positions related to the new Constitution: "Western-style development takes into account only the political and the economic. We insert the cultural, pluri-nationality, and the environment. . . . It's not just capitalistic economic growth, but also a valorization of our labor, so that we won't be exploited by those who control political and economic power" (*El Comercio*, June 29, 2008).

From an anthropological standpoint, analyzing the evolution and impacts of ecotourism requires a discussion of culture and nature as "things" that are packaged, marketed, and sold. Hannerz sees culture as integrated networks of meaning that are externalized in overt forms. Meanings are managed and interpreted on a variety of scales, all of which are interconnected through a wide range of ever-changing contacts. In his analysis of these interconnections, Hannerz is looking for a corrective to a problem identified by Sally Falk Moore (1987) as a "zone of ignorance" between the micro and macro. This is accomplished, he says, by paying less attention to the parts of this global system "than to the interfaces, the affinities, the confrontations, the interpenetrations, and the flow-through, between clusters of meaning and ways of managing meaning" (Hannerz 1992:22). To more effectively monitor and interpret this flow-through, Hannerz conceptualizes four frameworks: the form of life (the cultural process in small-scale societies), the market (through which cultural commodities are moved), the state (through its attempts to manage meaning), and various movements (collective efforts to raise consciousness and transform meanings). The fact that there are asymmetries of power in virtually any set of relationships means the flow of meanings is variable at any given time.

Hannerz's frameworks allow us to see culture as both produced by and a means of responding to tourism. The state, for example, is the predominant regulatory force that defines the structure of the industry. Tourism operators and agencies are expected to abide by laws that govern health and transportation standards, the licensing of guides, treatment of the environment, and taxation. The state, primarily through the Ministry of Tourism (and earlier through the Corporación Ecuatoriana de Turismo, or CETUR), is also directly involved in promoting the country as a tourist destination. It publishes materials, takes out advertisements, and has a presence at tourism conferences and exhibitions. At this point the market becomes more directly involved, as operators and agents peddle their various products nationally and internationally. State entities and industry interests also push to extend tourism activities into new areas, incorporating more and more of the country into a commercial network. Indigenous culture is an important part of the package of attractions, as reflected in a promotional campaign organized by the Ministry of Tourism for World Cup 2006 in Germany. During this campaign, titled "Shaman on Tour," a bus filled with representatives of different indigenous groups visited various German cities. A shaman was included, and at each city on the tour he performed cleansing ceremonies on local authorities. The minister also suggested that the shaman visit stadiums where the Ecuadorian soccer team would play its World Cup games, to scare away bad spirits and negative energy.

In a more general sense the state and market systems are directly involved in authorizing and legitimizing activities that transform place. As neoliberal economic policies erode the role of the state and encourage decentralization and the privatization of once-public industries, state and market activities tend to run into one another. There continue to be "centering relationships" between producers and consumers, between the governors and the governed, that involve particular points (retail shops, markets, public offices and institutions, etc.) where meanings are produced and disseminated. But in Latin America and other developing regions these points often combine both market and state activities, so that the commercial and the political, the public and the private are more difficult to distinguish. The tourism industry in Ecuador, for example, is undergoing a "modernization process" designed to make it more competitive with other Latin American countries. A private-public initiative seeks to reduce financial and legal barriers for foreign investors in the tourism sector, create a unified image for promoting Ecuador, and develop a "culture of service, security and quality through internal consciousness-raising" (*El Comercio*, July 10, 2000).

This process involves various representational practices that may or may not align with the indigeneities and historicities referred to in the introduction. Hannerz, with his concept of a "cultural apparatus," points to how this apparatus "connects one person or a relative few (creators, personified symbols, performers, players) with a greater many who are more passive (clients, spectators, audiences), in relationships the core of which is a provision of meaning" (1992:82). The relationships generated through this process are asymmetrical, suggests Hannerz, due to scale (the ideas of the few are widely distributed to the many) and input quantity (some contribute more to the pool of meanings than others). The cultural apparatus is thus composed of those people and institutions that are in the business of "affecting minds" and whose purpose is to "meddle with our consciousness" (83).

In a world in which words and ideas flow ever more freely between people, the media play an especially important role in processing and distributing meanings. Technological capabilities and the power to control media distribution networks can lead to significant asymmetries, says Hannerz, especially in the management of symbol systems and the production of messages. As Jackson explains in this volume, the media can play an important role in circulating images of indigenous peoples nationally and internationally. These practices of representation often pry cultural elements away from context, which results in a boiling down of identity, or the creation of a narrow litmus test of "authenticity," that can have significant repercussions for affected peoples (see Chaves, this volume).

The notion of culture as something that can be revitalized and distributed reflects the philosophy of the Programa Nacional Nuevo Rumbo Cultural, a cultural recovery project directed by Ecuador's Ministry of Education and Culture. In the Amazonian city of Tena the office of Nuevo Rumbo assembled for its Project of Rescue, Diffusion, and Continuation of Culture in Napo several booklets on medicinal plants and archaeological sites in the region. Culture was promoted through video projects, cultural training centers, research endeavors, and training manuals for teachers. Culture also has legal protection in the 1984 Law of Culture. That law guides activities of the National

13

Council of Culture, which is charged with "affirming national identity through the impetus of programs of cultural preservation, formation, and diffusion" (Consejo Nacional de Cultura, www.cncultura .gov.ec).

The rhetoric of indigenous cultural protection and respect marks a significant discursive departure from that of *mestizo* making in the nation-building projects of earlier decades (Stutzman 1981). In a multiethnic society such as Ecuador's, with distinct cultural groups in the coastal, highland, and Amazonian regions, it is no small endeavor to harmonize interests and create social, political, and economic space for diverse groups. But, as Laura Rival points out in her study of bilingual education among the Huaorani in Ecuador's Amazon, "cultural continuity depends more on understanding in practice than on the internalization of collective representations" (1997:137). Rival reported her observations of Huaorani schoolchildren assembled at the end of the year for a cultural presentation organized by teachers. They were dressed in outfits with little relation to Huaorani traditions and performed a dance that was "to a large extent made-up" (142). Her point is that bilingual education and cultural revalorization efforts often ignore everyday practice and the complexity of social worlds through which social life is reproduced. The school, in the paradoxical position of making modern Ecuadorian citizens while trying to preserve indigenous lifeways, "folklorizes cultural traditions by decontextualizing them and teaching them as if they were narratives from the past" (142). This exposes the dark side of folkloric production, where the ostensible support of cultural diversity obscures deep-rooted injustice. As José Almeida Vinueza puts it, "Governmental claims to recognize the value of cultural diversity through a mere discourse of cultural equality tend to effectively erase or avoid issues of political domination and social inequality" (2005:95).

With Ecuador's decentralization project many of the tasks of organizing, promoting, and regulating tourism are falling to municipal governments. The government of Tena, in its Strategic Development

Plan, determined that strategic north for the plan is ecotourism, which, through its carefully managed growth, is also supposed to improve health, education, and production (Tena Municipal Government 2000). The plan reflects many of the goals of sustainability woven into development and environmental discourse over the past three decades. It calls for curricular changes in local schools, where students learn the importance of ecotourism, cultural pride, and environmental preservation. One section of the plan is titled "Objectives, Strategies, Goals and Projects for the Subprogram of Amazonian Identity" and outlines ways the municipal government will meld a wide variety of subjectivities into an essentialized Amazon subject. The features of this singular subject emerge from the "Objectives" for this part of the plan, which include "socializ[ing] in the population the elements of cultural identification of the Amazon region in general, and the Canton in particular," and "rescu[ing] the millenarian traditions and customs of indigenous peoples in the proposals for creating pedagogic materials."

In their analysis of similar processes among the Ese Eja along the Peruvian-Bolivian border, Peluso and Alexiades track the stages through which indigenous pasts and traditions are reinterpreted to provide both state and market actors, along with some NGOs, a degree of ecological and moral legitimacy in their development and conservation plans. Through international tourism and environmentalism hunting and other subsistence activities are rescripted as more nature-friendly practices and then re-presented to indigenous people as pure cultural elements. As a result, note Peluso and Alexiades, "Ese Eja notions of subsistence, hunting, the past, and 'culture' are subverted and conditioned by the complicity of state and market and transformed into commodities that are consumed according to late capitalism's theory of value" (2005:8).

Analyzing the cultural flow, the externalized meanings, and the "interfaces, the affinities, the confrontations" identified by Hannerz helps fill in the gaps between the macro and the micro. Another framework

15

for analysis is the tourism market, which even more effectively reifies culture and packages it as commodity. The tourist town of Baños, at the foot of Tungurahua Volcano and in the doorway of the Ecuadorian Amazon, peddles Indian culture on almost every street. More than a dozen travel agencies sell rainforest tours, most offering visits to or stays in indigenous communities. The commodification of culture and the primitivism used to sell tour packages are intensified as operators vie for the business of European, Asian, and North American travelers eager to experience the Amazon. Visits to the center of Baños in 1998, and later in 2004 and 2006, revealed the town as a key node in the tourism network. "I sell Huaoranis," said a man behind the desk at Sebastian Moya Travel Agency. The representative at Auca Tours (*auca* or *awka* is the Kichwa term for "savage" and is often used to refer to the Huaorani) promised that the Indians on his tour are the "most primitive in South America." You could also visit the Shuar, but "now they are almost civilized. There isn't much to see." As with tendencies in anthropological representation, the tourism market sees in indigenous people a "historyless character." This "despondency theory," according to Sahlins, is more about Western longings for a pristine other than it is about any local realities. The result is a temptation to use "other societies as an alibi for redressing what has been troubling us lately" (Sahlins 1999:v).

The marketing of indigenous culture through selective representation reveals how tourism plays out in Ecuador within the state and market frameworks. A consideration of Hannerz's two other frameworks, movements and form of life, takes us closer to local experiences and provides a sense of how tourism is accommodated, resisted, and reworked in particular places.

Community-Based Ecotourism

On March 21, 2001, Antonio Vargas, president of the Confederation of Indigenous Nationalities of Ecuador, issued the following statement about the takeover by Cañari Indians of the country's most important Incan ruins:

Exercising our constitutional rights as people of Cañar, we have regained custody of the Temple of the Sun of Ingapirca, in the presence of 22 communities and the backing of all indigenous organizations and institutions of the province as of this day 12 of March, to demand of the national government an executive decree that officially restructures the current Directorate of Administration, Development and Maintenance of the Fortress of Ingapirca and other archaeological sites existing within the Cañari Nation. . . . We want to say to the tourists who have visited the Temple of the Sun that from the 12 of March, you should feel comfortable with the security, respect and solidarity of the communities present. In this manner, we push the development of a new style of touristic development, leaving behind the mistreatment and profanation that others have given to the Cañari Nation, as if we were pieces of the past in a museum, in order to present ourselves as a culture with history and dignity that actively participates in its own projects of self-development. (www.llacta .org/organiz/coms/com28.htm, my translation)

The takeover of the Incan ruins of Ingapirca in Ecuador's Cañar Province was a dramatic move at a symbolically important site. The fortress, constructed during the reign of the Inca ruler Huayna Capac (1493–1525), sits amid the lands of the Cañari people, who have long resisted domination by outsiders (Rojas 1988). Vargas's statement on the takeover revealed important details about ambitions within the indigenous movement and issued a call for alternative paths toward development, representation, and tourism. While challenging the power of state and local authorities to manage indigenous history and representations, Vargas nevertheless located the protest within the legal and political language of the sovereign state. And though he indicated that indigenous control of the site signaled the birth of a new form of management over cultural materials and meanings, he took care to reassure tourists that they are still welcome. Both the protest and the statement point to changes in consciousness and communication (the statement was issued over the Internet) that Brysk

(2000) says represent a new form of politics emerging from indigenous movements. In Ecuador this means an overt challenge to long-held meanings and long-standing social relations, but not to the extent of challenging the state as a legitimate model for governance.

States and markets have historically had predominant influence over nation-building and economic development projects. But these projects, and the meanings and social relations that guide them, have never been—and certainly are not today—without challenge from other social sectors. These challenges may arise from grassroots mobilizations, but increasingly they combine base movements with more extensive networks of national and transnational actors. Examining contemporary indigenous movements in Latin America, Brysk sees clear evidence that pluralistic forms of participation are on the rise as Indians and their allies confront and reconfigure historical meanings: "Like David battling Goliath, tribal villages unexpectedly challenge the states, markets, and missions that seek to crush them. Even more unexpectedly, their scattered triumphs come from Goliath's own arsenal: from the United Nations to the World Wide Web. Indigenous movements derive much of their impact from an unlikely combination of identity politics and internationalization. In the spaces between power and hegemony, the tribal village builds relationships with the global village" (2000:2).

Tourism, especially the ethno and eco varieties, is intimately connected to development and cultural identity issues in a country such as Ecuador. It is fertile ground for investigating Hannerz's frameworks of movements and form of life, which take us to more anthropologically interesting territory and into those "spaces between" mentioned by Brysk. It is in these spaces where resistance and accommodation produce hybrid forms that mix identity politics with economic development. In this section of the chapter I focus on movements and form of life as reflected in an organization (Federación Plurinacional de Turismo Comunitario del Ecuador, or FEPTCE) and a Kichwa ecotourism network (Red Indígena de Comunidades del Alto Napo para

Convivencia Intercultural y Ecoturismo, or RICANCIE, best translated as the Indigenous Network of Upper Napo Communities for Ecotourism and Intercultural Living) that represent hybrid forms of tourism development. In various ways these organizations commodify cultural products, ply tourism markets, and seek profits. But this is done, albeit in a sometimes conflictive way, by retooling the market machinery of tourism to better serve the particularities of local indigenous political and social life. By reviewing documents (reports, evaluations, meeting minutes) in the RICANCIE office, traveling to communities with tourists, attending conferences and exhibitions in Quito, and interviewing tourists, tour operators, and community members, I was able to trace the evolution of this hybrid system.

The emergence of community-based ecotourism in Ecuador is historically rooted in the larger indigenous movement, which gained significant momentum throughout the 1990s as groups pressed for self-determination. During this period and on into the present indigenous groups directly challenged the status quo in Ecuador and other parts of Latin America. The indigenous movement's most emphatic statements were made with uprisings in 1990 and 1992. Whitten refers to the earlier protest (Levantamiento Indígena) as "the greatest mobilization of people in Ecuadorian history" (Whitten, Scott Whitten, and Chango 2003). Luis Macas and other indigenous leaders have stated publicly that the movement seeks, not a geopolitical separation from Ecuador, but a reconfiguration of the nation-state as plurinational and pluricultural (Macas, Belote, and Belote 2003:221).

In addition to bilingual education and legal recognition of indigenous medicine and legal systems, the movement aims to increase control by indigenous communities over resources and development. Ecotourism, emerging out of the environmental and sustainable development movements, is central to many community development plans. Although much of the rhetoric surrounding indigenous tourism projects highlights the preservation of nature and culture, these are also commodified as ecotourism is carried out through a global-scale market system. At a meeting to discuss possibilities for ecotourism as a development alternative for indigenous communities, the following comments were made by various participants in reference to marketing culture and nature (my translations):

Indigenous people can't continue giving out their knowledge for free. Culture is worth something because it is different and you can convert it into money that, at the same time, can serve to maintain values and customs. (Salmón, Schulze, and Gaviria 1998:18)

The day that we realize that by conserving our language, conserving the ceramics in which we serve our lunch, maintaining our typical dress, our cooking recipes, our dances, and that they will pay us and that this is the principal source of attraction, we're going to understand that tourism, far from killing our culture, reinforces it. (28)

It's necessary to train the communities and indigenous people in subjects that are new to them, such as those that involve their growing relationship with the market economy. (9)

These comments were made at a conference hosted by the community of Capirona, which was the first member of the RICANCIE project. The project, described below, was developed and is operated by a group of Kichwa communities and the indigenous federation that represented them. The *runa*, as they refer to themselves in their own language, differ by region throughout the Amazonian provinces; the designation Canelos Kichwa generally refers to those in Pastaza Province, and Quijos or Napo Kichwa refers to those along the Napo River and up toward Baeza in the Andean foothills. The cultural area discussed in this chapter encompasses Kichwa groups in the upper part of the Napo, especially in the Tena-Archidona area.

The RICANCIE project is a pioneer in indigenous, community-based ecotourism. The network was born in the early 1990s with the guidance and support of the Federación de Organizaciónes Indígenas del Napo (now the Federación de Organizaciónes de Nacionalidad Kichwa del Napo), but it has gradually gained a degree of autonomy. As of July 2007 RICANCIE included nine Kichwa communities, ranging in size from eighteen families in Cuya Loma to fifty-six families in Huasila Talag. Tourist numbers have grown from a few hundred to over a thousand in good years. A central office in Tena, with a manager, a treasurer, and community liaisons, promotes attractions, communicates with potential tourists and travel agencies, and provides logistical support for each trip. The all-inclusive tours, averaging around forty dollars per day, offer the visitor hikes through the forest, displays of traditional practices (shooting blowguns, making baskets and traps, dances, healing ceremonies), and recreation on local rivers and lakes. A RICANCIE report in 2002 said the organization benefited two hundred families, or two thousand Kichwa people. The central office takes a 25 percent cut of tourism income to cover administrative, marketing, training, and infrastructure costs, while the remaining 75 percent goes to the communities to divide or invest as they see fit.

As RICANCIE developed, administrators and supportive NGOs worked to teach and strengthen business and technical skills. The RICANCIE plan of operations for 1997, for example, included the strategy of turning the ecotourism project into "an alternative for insertion into the market," which requires the "urgent strengthening of skills and technical accompaniment of people directly involved in the service and administration of the program, maintaining the principles of community business." Activities such as these are part of a basic philosophy of encouraging self-sufficiency by building perspectives at the local level.

The efforts to make the RICANCIE project a hybrid experiment, mixing market objectives with traditional communal interests, are reflected in a variety of letters, reports, and meeting records accumulated in the central office. An undated RICANCIE report that appears to have been written in the early years of the organization refers to its ambitions to "successfully demonstrate that ecotourism is an economic alternative and that the communities, with force and will, are capable of starting up businesses unfamiliar to indigenous people." These ambitions for enterprise are qualified with the "communal" tag, making RICANCIE a pioneer in alternative tourism development. Several documents refer to the objective of positioning RICANCIE communities in the tourism market with "a different and unique image." This includes both cultural elements such as language, myths, foods, music, and dance and a creative way of making dark historical moments such as "the conquest and Spanish colonization, missionaries, masters, and rubber barons, the hacienda system, and petroleum exploitation" part of the tourist experience. The reputation of RICANCIE has spread within and far beyond Ecuador and has helped it develop and maintain a transnational network of allies and interests.

The incipient experience of RICANCIE with community-based eco-tourism generated debate within indigenous organizations about the role ecotourism could play in community development. Part of that debate focused on questions of legality and the insertion of communal projects into the formal politico-economic system of the tourism industry. This, I would argue, signaled the development of certain perspectives that eventually formed a view from above with regard to ecotourism's role in preserving indigenous identity. A number of documents from the Federación de Organizaciónes Indígenas del Napo, the Confederación de Nacionalidades Indígenas de la Amazonia Ecuatoriana, the Confederación de Nacionalidades Indígenas del Ecuador, and the Coordinadora de las Organizaciónes Indígenas de la Cuenca Amazonica reveal the emergence of a dialogue at various levels concerning the importance of recognizing commu-nally operated projects as central to indigenous identity. In building support for their arguments these organizations appealed for help to NGOS, sympathetic legislators, and educational institutions at home and abroad. For example, in a 1995 proposal the Coordinadora de las Organizaciónes Indígenas de la Cuenca Amazonica reached around the state and sought financial aid from a Danish NGO to hire legal help in "changing the Tourism Law in favor of indigenous organizations." Support for the proposal was also sought from the United Nations representative in Ecuador, the president of Ecuador's Congress, legislators from the indigenous party Pachakutik, and the minister of tourism. Each letter asked that community-managed ecotourism be recognized as a legitimate activity, protected and supported by Ecuadorian tourism law. The organizations expressed a desire to be "owners of their development" through a process of "democratizing the economy."

These efforts to challenge both the laws that govern tourism operations within Ecuador and the rules that govern the market economy are part of a battle fought through much of the life of RICANCIE. Ecuadorian laws that prevented communities from incorporating as tourism operators led to the project's being shut down several times in the 1990s by the government Corporación Ecuatoriana de Turismo for operating illegally. The response by RICANCIE to CETUR officials was to meet with them as required and then secretly keep the project running. All the while RICANCIE officials were working with other indigenous groups to change Ecuadorian tourism law to allow for community-run projects. The pressure to rewrite tourism law in Ecuador, applied initially by RICANCIE but ratcheted up by other organizations, eventually led to changes. Articles 3 and 12 of the 2002 Tourism Law legitimize and, at least in legal terminology, support community tourism operations.

The same year that the tourism law was rewritten the Federación Plurinacional de Turismo Comunitario del Ecuador was created to "promote and strengthen community tourism initiatives in order to improve the quality of life of our peoples and nationalities." A FEPTCE report written for the Ministry of Tourism in June 2006 begins with a description of the oppression suffered by indigenous people since the conquest. The report moves on to discuss tourism as directly tied to the political and economic system of exploitation, which through the closing decades of the twentieth century resulted in a situation in which "the only relation with tourism was through the flashes of the cameras. Private enterprise grew from earnings made from the sale of tours into our territories and from the sale of our cultures, and we became visited things: 'wild nature' and 'exotic cultures,' postcards for tourism promotion, even though tourism didn't leave us any benefits" (FEPTCE 2006:2, my translation).

The FEPTCE report lays out problems and potentials within the tourism industry using a language that is at times explanatory, at times suggestive of development strategies, and at times confrontational. In stating that indigenous people are as qualified as any among the white or *mestizo* population to manage tourism enterprises but simply lack opportunities and resources, the document states (apparently to Ministry officials), "You should know that it is not a lack of capabilities, but rather of opportunities for preparation and training. Do you actually believe that there are human beings predestined to know a science or discipline for no other reason than genetic inheritance?" (FEPTCE 2006:4, my translation). The document calls on the government to develop strategies to support and promote community tourism. The "Principles of Community Tourism" are divided into environmental, cultural, social, economic, and political principles. These encompass a variety of objectives much broader than a mere profit motive. The protection of the environment, the promotion of cultural identity, the strengthening of self-esteem and autonomy, the diversification of the communal economy, and the right to "be heard as a group, and not as individual people" are included in the principles. An appendix compiles objectives and actions for realizing FEPTCE goals.

The concept of community is applied broadly, and often vaguely, by FEPTCE and other governmental and nongovernmental organizations, suggesting a taken-for-granted characteristic of all indigenous social and political arrangements. But as Ramírez discusses in this volume, definitions of community are sometimes constructed by outside organizations, such as those promoting development programs, using borrowed concepts such as "civil society" and "social capital" that may not accurately reflect local realities. Indigenous organizations also use the language of "community" and "authenticity" as a strategy for gaining desirable resources. Killick describes how the Ashéninka of Peru, who traditionally have lived in scattered households with the nuclear family as the primary social unit, "found themselves having to conform to the state's idea of how people should live, and then having to deal with the new social structures that this created" (2008:37).

Wilson, in this volume and elsewhere (Wilson 2003, 2008), has written about the influence of NGOs and other organizations in Ecuador's Upper Amazon, revealing the tendencies and resulting consequences of essentializing concepts such as "community" and "indigenous" in the construction of development projects. This is indeed part of the meaning-making process that occurs within and between the frameworks outlined by Hannerz. "Community" has currency and, in the case of ecotourism, has evolved to fill a particular niche in the market. But applied broadly and unreflexively it masks the diversity of organization and opinion that can be significant in any human collective.

Just as "eco" has become a popular tag that enhances the marketability of things, places, and activities, so has the term "community." The network of NGOs, lobbying groups, and tour operators that support community tourism has grown significantly in recent years. Among indigenous groups, however, this is not simply a marketing gimmick. The efforts of RICANCIE and FEPTCE, while connected in many ways to the indigenous movement, are best analyzed through Scott's concept of infrapolitics. Protests and *levantamientos* represent open resistance, but less visible struggles to rewrite legal standards or adjust inequitable structures can also create space within which hybrid forms incubate. The realm of open resistance to domination, says Scott, "is shadowed by an infrapolitical twin sister who aims at the same strategic goals but whose low profile is better adapted to resisting an opponent who could probably win any open confrontation" (1990:184).

The "opponent" can be an elusive target, as late capitalism has a way of obfuscating processes and institutions that perpetuate social and economic inequality. But Whitten helps us identify a "globalizing ideology" associated with modernity that is generative of particular structures of power and stratification. This ideology includes profit seeking; science for economic gain; phenotypic color coding of labor; concepts of humans as vestiges or relics of an antipodal past; the growth of wealth; fetishism of commodities; commodification of land, labor, and humans; ethnic cleansing; the hypostasis of racial fixity; and the power of print languages (Whitten 2003:28). Within this exhaustive list one can locate many elements that make up the contemporary global tourism industry, especially with regard to the processes of commodification and folklorization of peoples seen as tourist attractions. Whitten goes on to underscore the critical message of his edited volume that reveals myriad voices and actions that challenge the globalizing ideology of modernity in Ecuador: "Millenarianism in its multiple manifestations confronts these forces of modern globalizing ideology as people endeavour to restore human dignity to its inevitable diversity and to forge interculturality on the anvil of this very human difference" (28).

This is what organizations such as RICANCIE and FEPTCE aim to do. By mostly "infrapolitical" means they push not to fully replace the extant political economy, but to emplace indigenous concepts and interests within the system as vehicles for change that are connected fundamentally to social and economic justice. Some of this happens offstage, in the form of hidden transcripts (RICANCIE's ignoring orders to close its "illegal" operations or turning to shamans to bring powerful spirit allies into the battle); other efforts have become part of the public transcript (active lobbying in Quito to change laws). Many of the changes that are pushed quietly, or more vocally, destabilize the management of meaning that emanates from the state and market powers. This is often (though not always) connected to broader social movements that aim to transform meanings. These arise, Hannerz reminds us, out of local forms of life, but also increasingly come to absorb global and cross-cultural interests. Thus RICANCIE and FEPTCE have supporters across the globe, often from the environmental, sustainable development, and indigenous rights movements. These have the *potential* to transform a global-scale activity such as ecotourism into a set of activities that challenge the globalizing ideology described by Whitten. Largest among the challenges, perhaps, is the job of recognizing and reacting to efforts by private and government sectors to appropriate and commercialize those elements that give ecotourism the best opportunity to function as a true alternative to mass tourism. In the final section of this chapter I use ideas from Dipesh Chakrabarty, supplemented with the concept of historicities as described by Neil Whitehead, to think through ways that this challenge might cohere.

History 2

Writing in an edited volume titled *Cosmopolitanism*, Chakrabarty reflects on Marx's idea that capital, through the exchange of commodities, renders insignificant the differences between products. As Chakrabarty puts it, "The commodity form does not as such negate difference but holds it in suspension so that we can exchange things as different from one another as beds and houses" (2002:84). Even though products may be materially different, the common substance that mediates difference in the productive process is human labor, an "abstract labor" that is in contrast to the specific labor of the independent artisan or worker. For Marx abstract labor becomes "a homogeneous and common unit for measuring human activity," says Chakrabarty (83). It is made so by the disciplinary practices of factory and governmental regulation.

I see this debate as relevant to my discussion of conventional tourism and potential alternative, hybrid forms of tourism because both (to different degrees) involve the commodification of culture and nature. Although the capitalist mode of production with regard to factory work differs in important ways from that associated with a service industry such as tourism, there are still significant disciplinary and regulatory forces in the service industry that tend to abstract labor and erode the harder edges of difference. When these productive processes involve cultural and historical materials the potential implications are weighty. This suggests that, despite efforts and ambitions to the contrary, community tourism in the end offers social and economic "alternatives" in name only. More important, it points to ways that globalization (in the form of tourism), and the logic of capital that it currently operates under, subjugates cultural particularities as units exchangeable in the world market are produced.

Chakrabarty raises another possibility, however. His argument that precapitalist pasts are part of most cultures and can influence the terms under which they participate in a global economy is built around differences he associates with "History 1" and "History 2." The logical presuppositions of capital—the historical conditions that had to fall into place (divorcing labor from land to create the wage worker, for example)—are not understood as history until the capitalist system has fully come into being. In other words, we couldn't understand the preconditions of capitalism without first understanding how capitalism worked out in practice. The history of "capitalism-as-becoming" is thus a retrospective history, written and understood by those who can reflect on and make meaning of its past. Marx called this capital's antecedent "posited by itself." "This is the universal and necessary history we associate with capital. It forms the backbone of the usual narratives of transition to the capitalist mode of production. Let us call this history—a past posited by capital itself as its precondition—History 1" (Chakrabarty 2002:98).

Marx contrasts History 1 to a second kind of history, History 2, which Chakrabarty elaborates on. This second history also has antecedents to capital, but they are not established by capital itself (that is, they do not contribute to the self-reproduction of capital). Chakrabarty writes, "I therefore understand Marx to be saying that antecedents to capital are not only the relationships that constitute History 1 but also other relationships that do not lend themselves to the reproduction of the logic of capital. Only History 1 is the past 'established' by capital because History 1 lends itself to the reproduction of capitalist relationships" (2002:98). Chakrabarty points out that, although Marx says History 1 is forever trying to subjugate the "multiple possibilities that belong to History 2," there is no certainty that this has been, or will be, a completed process. History 2, then, might be thought of as a "category charged with the negative function of constantly interrupting the totalizing thrusts of History 1" (101).

The commodification of culture in the tourist industry has all the hallmarks of a chapter in History 1. As a product this culture is selectively defined, represented, promoted, and consumed in a way that makes it palatable to visitors from many points beyond the destination site. Labor is often abstracted in the process, as shamans, storytellers, dancers, potters, and healers are interchangeable actors, emerging sometimes overnight to fill the slots created by tourist expectations. The bearer of labor, it would seem, is daily aligned more closely with the logic of capital as reproduced through agencies, operators, guides, and travel writers. But, as I hinted at in my discussion of RICANCIE and FEPTCE, there are disruptions in the narrative of History 1.

As the editor of *Histories and Historicities in Amazonia*, Whitehead (2003) says there are myriad stories in the Amazon, stories that aren't written overtly into conventional histories. The selective, Eurocentric histories are defended as such because it has been generally assumed that indigenous experiences are "uninteresting or unknowable." This absence of history is replaced by an "eternal present" tied to narratives of first contact and exotic marvels, which are frequently echoed in tourism literature. But there are indigenous perspectives on life's events old and new, and these can be categorized as "historicities." These versions of the past are embedded in shared experiences of the landscape, in oral traditions, and even in indigenous narratives captured within more conventional histories.

These historicities are not localized, inward-focused perspectives on the circumscribed world of the native. Rather, they are more fluid, dynamic accounts "designed to mediate the disjunctural" and manage an "engagement with that which is understood as external" (Whitehead 2003:xvi). Here we seem to have much of History 2, a heterogeneous cacophony of voices that may at times harmonize with those creating History 1 through markets and states, but that also articulate the particular experiences and ambitions of specific groups.

In relation to the cultural flow described by Hannerz, these voices shout most audibly from the form of life and movements frameworks. There are historicities guiding the work of indigenous federations, just as there are historicities that influence responses to tourism problems and opportunities. They are indeed forever threatened, and sometimes overcome, by "the totalizing thrusts of History 1." But they are also where we might look for true hybrid forms. In such a search, however, one should not expect to encounter seamless cultural compounds. Instead there are more likely to be stress fractures, ragged edges, and various anxieties as scales change, values are challenged, and worldviews are filtered through new cultural kaleidoscopes.

Discussing capitalism and commodification as "negotiated" processes in Kichwa communities glosses over the potential contentiousness involved. Gossip, shamanistic attacks, and verbal and physical fighting are part of the experience of working through the arrival of new resources and new resource allocation systems. Sahlins's advice, to consider the "structural position money is accorded in the cultural totality," is a useful insight (1999:xvi–xvii). The infusion of resources into a Kichwa community is filtered through a set of social relations influenced by the concept of limited goods and the envy (*envidia*) that boils up as those resources become unevenly divided. Money, then, takes a structural position among a web of relations frequently frayed by jealousies and rewoven according to *ayllu* (kindred) practices. These are the contextual nuances often missing from references to "community" in the generic form.

In his rich account of the Canelos Kichwa in Pastaza Province, Ecuador, Whitten details how the envy of one *runa* toward another can lead to the mobilization of spirit helpers who cause harm in the form of invisible darts: "In the very simplest form of this procedure a man merely places his hand over his mouth in the same way as he covers the blowgun when he blows a dart, takes aim at the person he wishes to harm, and blows. A spirit helper leaves his throat and speeds toward the victim" (1976:145). Shamans can catch and return such darts, setting off a cycle of attacks and counterattacks that may draw in innocent victims. Illness and death are often attributed to these attacks, with repercussions rippling throughout a community.

Tod Swanson locates particular resource concentrations for the Napo Kichwa in mountains (*urcu*) and in the deep pools (*cocha*) of rivers (personal communication). These finite resources circulate locally, with competition among various *ayllus*. When one family or community receives more of a good than another, less is available from the total amount of resources, and the result is *envidia*. In the competition for ecotourists and their money, says Swanson, this can translate into the belief that when one community takes tourists into the forest, another might use its spirit allies to lock up the animals so that the tour is unsuccessful.

To write of *runa* social relations as driven only by access to resources is simplistic and misleading. Uzendoski writes at length about Kichwa notions of value and reciprocity. The former, he says, are not measured concretely in weights, quantities, and currencies, but within the larger social context of giving and receiving. These "social forms of value" are more accurately thought of as gifts rather than commodities. "Commodities are alienable; they are produced and circulated as if they exist independent of people. . . . By contrast, the defining feature of gifts is that they are not alienable and function, metaphorically and pragmatically, as conceptual extensions of people. Gifts assume and follow the social forms of persons. They are morally charged entities that create relations" (2005:3).

Building on the concept of conviviality as it relates to native Amazonian societies (Overing and Passes 2000), Uzendoski discusses exchange as the everyday expression of one's needs and desires and the response to those of others. This give-and-receive process early on became part of his fieldwork experience. "Mutual desires structure value, and it was always better to meet someone else's need than to address one's own. To meet the desires of the others with whom one shares life is to live convivially, to realize intersubjectivity as a socially meaningful being. This complex of ideas and practices constitutes the cultural forms of the value process" (Uzendoski 2005:113).

Although the interpretations outlined by Swanson and Uzendoski appear on the surface to be contradictory statements about Kichwa sociality, they need to be connected to the shape-shifting nature of Kichwa kinship. Uzendoski describes the concept of *ayllu* as dynamic, reflecting a system of relations much more flexible than blood kinship. "The notion of kinship carries with it the idea that people share not only a common substance but also a common destiny that requires sharing things and the experiences of life. At the same time, just as those who become close and share life become kin, those who lose their connections can become lost to one *ayllu*" (2005:65). In such a case people could join another *ayllu*, or even several over a lifetime. Kin groups thus flow into one another rather than existing within rigid boundaries. As circumstances change, rivalries and alliances also change.

I have several ethnographic examples of just such rending and mending. The community of Unión Venecia was one of the early members of the RICANCIE network and regularly received tourists to its cabins along the Napo River on the road to Misahuallí. But in a dispute over money and labor contributions one faction burned the cabins and heaved the cooking stove into a pool in the Napo. The community remained divided, and the tourism project in ashes, in 2008.

Another enduring conflict has pitted a shaman, Augustín Grefa, against his home community of Río Blanco. This Kichwa community, about a two-hour hike from the Napo River just before it reaches Ahuano, is also a founding member of RICANCIE. There are different versions of the dispute, but all revolve around the division of profits from the ecotourism project. One generally agreed-upon issue is that the project cabins were built on the shaman's land, and his attempt to get rent angered some community members. There was also a belief, which surfaced during my fieldwork in 1998, that he gained more than others from ecotourism because of visitor interest in his knowledge of medicinal plants and traditional healing techniques. Gossip about this arrangement eventually turned to violence, and he was expelled from the community and briefly jailed under charges of using witchcraft to kill several villagers. A RICANCIE evaluation document from 2005 referred to falling tourist numbers because of "accusations of sickness and death from members of the community by witchcraft caused by member leaders from the same community" (RICANCIE 2005:53).

Discussing these events in the summer of 2006 from his home in Tena, Augustín referred to *envidia* as a significant problem caused by money. He said that short-term profits earned by cutting the forest to plant crops, or calling oneself a shaman in order to guide and earn money from tourists, are damaging both to Kichwa culture and to the sacred places in the forest. The forest spirits, or *supay*, leave their sacred homes and take up residence in humans. They have the power to do both evil and good, and in humans they can lead to drinking, fighting, robbery, and spousal abuse.

These social and supernatural dramas can be seen as the beginning of the end of indigenous culture, or as the messy interface of cultural systems that produce frictions before their differences are resolved. Sahlins opts for the latter, which can lead to an "indigenization of modernity" (1999:x). The RICANCIE project has survived for seventeen years. There has been turnover in leadership and in community membership. There are ongoing concerns about impacts on cultural life and the ability to maintain enthusiasm for projects that rise and fall with the vagaries of international tourism, national political conditions, and all things local (from climate to health conditions to ever-changing development options). But as I spoke with RICANCIE's first director, Tarquino Tapuy (now with FEPTCE), in July 2008 he was preparing to enter the community of Capirona to help resolve conflicts and rejuvenate the network's flagship project.

Cultural Dissolution, Cultural Preservation, or Transculturation?

Capirona manages its tourism profits through communal decisions. Kichwa-speaking teachers are hired to replace unreliable teachers sent by the government, low-interest loans are made to members for emergencies and development projects, and money is allocated for health care needs. I watched one morning as a group of German tourists was fed and sent off in canoes, and then I stayed around to witness the construction of a new canoe by a *minga*, or communal work party. Workers with their tools came from all paths leading to the community center, where a large tree trunk had been hollowed out. They worked the wood together, built a fire to scorch it for protection from insects, and tarred the edges to seal it. They smeared charcoal and clay on each other's faces, equalizing all who participated. Meanwhile women prepared a communal meal, the shaman treated a girl with chest congestion, and stories, jokes, pranks, and shots of cane liquor animated the scene. Much of the group had arrived for tourism-related work, and the canoe would be used to transport future tourists. But the form of life bubbled up from local meanings about how to work, how to laugh, and how to heal—essentially, how to practice conviviality.

Uzendoski challenges the notion that the Kichwa are a people in transition from being "authentic indigenous" to "acculturated mestizo"; he says that what is really happening is a process of "transculturation." This means there are fluid boundaries "across which identities are exchanged or transformed" (2005:15). Although he is writing about intermarriage between Kichwa and other cultural groups, the description applies as well to the intermarriage between Kichwa ways of living in the world and those of others. There is unquestionably accommodation resulting from this—some acquiescence to the logic of capital that so forcefully unfolds in places big and small. But indigenous people in Ecuador and elsewhere are inserting their histories into legal structures, into market formulas, and into considerations of how to develop socially, economically, and politically.

References

Brysk, Alison. 2000. *From tribal village to global village: Indian rights and international relations in Latin America.* Stanford: Stanford University Press.

Chakrabarty, Dipesh. 2002. Universalism and belonging in the logic of capital. In *Cosmopolitanism,* ed. Carol A. Breckenridge, Sheldon Pollock, Homi K. Bhabha, and Dipesh Chakrabarty. Durham NC: Duke University Press.

Chard, Chole. 1999. *Pleasure and guilt on the grand tour: Travel writing and imaginative geography 1600–1830.* Manchester UK: Manchester University Press.

Federación Plurinacional de Turismo Comunitario del Ecuador. 2006. *Turismo comunitario, una alternativa para la mejora de la calidad de vida y la defenza de los territorios de las nacionalidades y pueblos del Ecuador.* Quito: Federación Plurinacional de Turismo Comunitario del Ecuador.

Hannerz, Ulf. 1992. *Cultural complexity: Studies in the social organization of meaning.* New York: Columbia University Press.

Killick, Evan. 2008. Creating community: Land titling, education, and settlement formation among the Ashéninka of Peruvian Amazonia. *Journal of Latin American and Caribbean Anthropology* 13 (1): 22–47.

Macas, Luis, Linda Belote, and Jim Belote. 2003. Indigenous destiny in indigenous hands. In *Millennial Ecuador: Critical essays on cultural transformations and social dynamics,* ed. Norman E. Whitten. Iowa City: University of Iowa Press.

Mascia-Lees, Fran, and Jeff Himpele. 2006. Reimagining globality: Toward an anthropological physics. *Anthropology News* 47 (5): 9–11.

Moore, Sally F. 1987. Explaining the present: Theoretical dilemmas in processual ethnography. *American Ethnologist* 14:727–36.

Nordstrom, Carolyn. 2007. *Global outlaws: Crime, money, and power in the contemporary world.* Berkeley: University of California Press.

Overing, Joanna, and Alan Passes, eds. 2000. *The anthropology of love and anger.* London: Routledge.

Peluso, Daniela M., and Miguel N. Alexiades. 2005. Urban ethnogenesis begins at home: The making of self and place amidst Amazonia's environmental economy. *Traditional Dwellings and Settlements Review* 16 (2): 1–10.

Radcliffe, Sarah A. 1996. Imaginative geographies, postcolonialism, and national identities: Contemporary discourses of the nation in Ecuador. *Ecumene* 3 (1): 23–42.

Radcliffe, Sarah, and Sallie Westwood. 1996. *Remaking the nation: Place, identity and politics in Latin America*. London: Routledge.

RICANCIE. 2005. Ejecución de talleres de identificación, evaluación de productos turísticos y elaboración del plan estratégico 2005. Ten, Ecuador: RICANCIE.

Rival, Laura. 1997. Modernity and the politics of identity in an Amazonian society. *Bulletin of Latin American Research* 16 (2): 137–51.

Rojas, J. Heriberto. 1988. *Miscelanea de arqueologia Canari*. Azogues, Ecuador: Editorial Fondo de Cultura Ecuatoriano.

Sahlins, Marshall. 1999. What is anthropological enlightenment? Some lessons of the twentieth century. *Annual Review of Anthropology* 28 (1): i–xxiii.

Salmón, Jaime Iturri, Juan Carlos Schulze, and Luz Beatriz Gaviria, eds. 1998. *Entre retos y rutas*. Quito: Programa Regional de Apoyo a los Pueblos Indígenas de la Cuenca del Amazonas.

Schaller, David T. 1996. Indigenous ecotourism and sustainable development: The case of Río Blanco, Ecuador. Master's thesis, University of Minnesota.

Scott, James C. 1990. *Domination and the arts of resistance: Hidden transcripts*. New Haven: Yale University Press.

Stutzman, Ronald. 1981. El mestizaje: An all-inclusive ideology of exclusion. In *Cultural transformations and ethnicity in modern Ecuador*, ed. Norman E. Whitten Jr. Urbana: University of Illinois Press.

Taussig, Michael. 1984. Culture of terror—space of death: Roger Casement's Putumayo report and the explanation of terror. *Comparative Studies in Society and History* 26 (3): 467–97.

Taylor, Anne Christine. 1999. The western margins of Amazonia from the early sixteenth to the early nineteenth century. In *The Cambridge history of the native peoples of the Americas*, vol. 3, part 2, ed. F. Salomon and S. B. Schwartz. Cambridge: Cambridge University Press.

Tena Municipal Government. 2000. *Plan estrategico de desarrollo*. Tena, Ecuador.

Tsing, Anna. 2000. The global situation. *Cultural Anthropology* 15 (3): 327–60.

Uzendoski, Michael. 2005. *The Napo Runa of Amazonian Ecuador*. Urbana: University of Illinois Press.

Vinueza, José Almeida. 2005. The Ecuadorian indigenous movement and the Gutiérrez regime: The traps of multiculturalism. *PoLAR: Political and Legal Anthropology Review* 28 (1): 93–111.

Whitehead, Neil L., ed. 2003. *Histories and historicities in Amazonia*. Lincoln: University of Nebraska Press.

Whitten, Norman E., Jr. 1976. *Sacha Runa: Ethnicity and adaptation of Ecuadorian jungle Quichua*. Urbana: University of Illinois Press.

———. 2003. Introduction to *Millennial Ecuador: Critical essays on cultural transfor-*

mations and social dynamics, ed. Norman E. Whitten Jr. Iowa City: University of Iowa Press.

Whitten, Norman E., Jr., Dorothea Scott Whitten, and Alfonso Chango. 2003. Return of the Yumbo: The *Caminata* from Amazonia to Andean Quito. In *Millennial Ecuador: Critical essays on cultural transformations and social dynamics*, ed. Norman E. Whitten Jr. Iowa City: University of Iowa Press.

Wilson, Patrick. 2003. Market articulation and poverty eradication? Critical reflection on tourist-oriented craft production in Amazonian Ecuador. In *Here to help: NGOs combating poverty in Latin America*, ed. Robyn Eversole. Armonk NY: M. E. Sharpe.

———. 2008. Neoliberalism, indigeneity, and social engineering in Ecuador's Amazon. *Critique of Anthropology* 28 (2): 127–44.

2. Fractal Subjectivities

An Amazonian-Inspired Critique of Globalization Theory

Michael A. Uzendoski

En los patios de las casas los delfines tocan sus guitarras
y enamoran a las muchachas.

Juan Carlos Galeano, "Leticia," in *Amazonia*

In the mind's eye, a fractal is a way of seeing infinity.

James Gleick, *Chaos: Making a New Science*

Anna Tsing (2004), like many other current theorists, has been writing innovative things about globalization. Her recent book problematizes "scale" in a way that questions the local/global dichotomy through the trope of "friction." Her work joins that of many others complicating anthropology's traditional focus on the local by shifting more focus to processes of globalization. Globalization study owes much to the work of Arjun Appadurai, who has emphasized how global "flows" make local reproduction "fragile," contradictory, displaced, and destabilized (1996:198). The stories considered here, however, defy reduction to the local, but they also make little sense when viewed from Appadurai's idea of "scapes" or Tsing's metaphor of "friction." What about people who view the local as global and vice versa, a perspective described by Mascia-Lees and Himpele, in which "ethnographic collocation . . . [can] occupy two (or more) places simultaneously" (2006:9)? As I will show, contemporary Amazonian storytellers conceptualize themselves as fully modern subjects, but they define their subjectivity through fractal relationships with animals, spirits, and nature—relationships that I argue define Amazonian sociality in the first and last instance (Kelley 2005). These relationships do not oppose locality and globality; they show that people are defined simultaneously by the local and the global, part and whole, and the one and the many.

Indeed Amazonian realities complement and undermine capitalism's presumed homogenizing of things and thing-like relations, as well as contradict the supposed monopoly capitalism has on global processes. As Hutchins, Whitehead, and Chaves demonstrate in their chapters in this volume, Amazonian historicities wreak havoc on modernity's universalizing projects and "interrupt" the "totalizing thrusts" of capital (Chakrabarty 2002:101, cited in Hutchins, this volume). The fractal forms of Amazonia, as I hope to show, articulate the body as defined by alternative subjectivities that can engender alternative modernities, social movements that question capital (Chakrabarty 2002; Parameshwar Gaonkar 2001; Uzendoski 2005a; Whitten and Whitten 2008).

I first look at a story told in 1997 by a *mestizo* person about a dolphin that impregnates her sister-in-law.[1] This story is from the Leticia area of Colombia, and it was taped by the Amazonian poet Juan Carlos Galeano, who wishes that it be used here. I next consider another *mestizo* story from Iquitos, Peru, that was told to me during a fishing trip in the spring of 2006. This story involves an encounter with the *boa negra* (black boa snake) and a near-death experience. I next consider a native story told to me in Kichwa during 2006 in the Upper Napo region of Ecuador.[2] This story is about the disappearance of a boy who becomes a governor in the spirit world. I also look at emergent genres of storytelling in Amazonia, specifically the poetry and folktales created by Juan Carlos Galeano (2000, 2005, in press) and "electronic" Kichwa music, called Runa Paju, from Amazonian Ecuador. These materials allow me to address how fractal relations of the body cross social and cultural boundaries, including my own relationship with Juan Carlos and the storytellers discussed here.

I have chosen these three stories and materials because they are compelling accounts that reveal how fractal principles can be used to conceptualize an emergent subjectivity that has not been much discussed in relationship to globalization. Despite the diversity of materials I consider, the relations show an underlying conceptualization of subjectivity as embedded in the larger flows and material exchanges with animals, spirits, and nature—relationships that move through and transform the sociality and social logics of capitalism itself.

Chaos Theory and Fractality in
Social Anthropology and Amazonian Anthropology

By "fractal" I refer to relations in which the whole and its parts are made similar, creating a relational world based on self-similarity (Jackson 2004:1l; Mosko and Damon 2005). Ruth Richards describes fractals as "forms . . . born from infinity; by definition, they can look similar on infinitely receding or expanding scales" (2001:72). Fractals are found not only in nature, but also in culture and in the patterns of globalization. Recently, for example, Appadurai has suggested that newer approaches to culture should draw on fractality explicitly:

What I would like to propose is that we begin to think of the configuration of cultural forms in today's world as fundamentally fractal, that is, as possessing no Euclidean boundaries, structures, or regularities. Second, I would suggest that these cultural forms, which we should strive to represent as fully fractal, are also overlapping in ways that have been discussed only in pure mathematics (in set theory, for example) and in biology (in the language of polythetic classifications). Thus we need to combine a fractal metaphor for the shape of cultures (in the plural) with a polythetic account of their overlaps and resemblances. (1996:46)

Appadurai's use of fractality allows one to see modernity's universalizing thrusts as creating similar kinds of relationships throughout time and space and across boundaries. However, Appadurai focuses on what Hutchins (this volume) refers to as "History 1."[3] History 1 is "the universal and necessary history we associate with capital. It forms the backbone of the usual narratives of transition to the capitalist mode of production" (Chakrabarty 2002:668). While Appadurai's (1986, 1996) schemes may help one to see the processes of modernity at large through the various scapes and commodity flows his work brings into view, these are not the stuff of History 2, which does not naturalize commodity relations.[4]

In History 2 the past is created in the fractal forms of culture that generate alternative modernities and alternative conceptualizations of the world. History 2, unlike History 1, does not belong to the reproduction of capital. This notion of History 2 is similar to Whitehead's (2003) paradigm of "historicity." As Whitehead asserts, historicities are "the cultural schema and subjective attitudes that make the past meaningful," ways of knowing the world that undermine the usual narratives of History 1, globalization, and modernity (xi). Historicities, being fractally configured, usually posit the past as a recurring set of relations that extend into the future.

Theorists have been writing about the dynamics of something like History 2 in Amazonia as complexes of self-scaling relations, although these relations have not been described in explicit terms of fractality. Here one might speak of "Amazonia at large," a kind of fractal world-system defined by social and cultural principles distinct from those of the reproduction of capital. In these schemes one finds that the future and past are interconnected nonlinearly.

Evidence for such relations permeates Amazonian ethnographies. Consider Lévi-Strauss's mythological permutations in *The Raw and the*

Cooked (1969), where myths from multiple cultures and geographic regions appear like transmutations of the relations of one myth. Pierre Clastres's notion of a "society against the state" spins out recurring dynamics that are inverted between the Amazonian region and the state societies of the Americas, a fractal set of relations and transformations that address nonlinear dynamics. In a memorable example of fractal thinking, Clastres writes, "'Things in their totality are one.' A startling utterance, of a kind to send Western thought reeling back to its beginnings. Yes this is indeed what Guarani thinkers say, what they are continually proclaiming—and they pursue its strictest consequences, its most unsettling implications" (1989:171).

In Ecuador Canelos Kichwa potters juxtapose chthonic imagery of the anaconda and other animals with oil bosses, church figures, and other images of state authority. This "duality of power patterning" (Whitten 1985) occurs throughout stories, mythology, art, music, and fiesta rituals. These patterns reveal the Canelos Kichwa strategy of subordinating modernity to Amazonian historicity by collapsing the future with the origins of the world, a process of "ending everything" (see Whitten and Whitten 2008:154).

The Bororo of central Brazil define themselves through two major principles of the world, *aroe* and *bope*, which are dynamic but opposing processes that define all living things. Although these terms are hard to define, the *aroe* might be glossed as "soul" or the principle of timeless identity, and the *bope* something like "life processes" that are responsible for all change, including life and death itself, and also such processes as rain, natural disasters, sex, and production and consumption (Crocker 1977, 1986). *Aroe* is linked to enduring "spirit," naming, and social structure; *bope* is linked to processes of *raka*, or blood.

These dynamic forces define and move through all living organisms, transcending the boundaries of species, individual, and time and space. In the Bororo world one finds the *aroe* and *bope* forms fractally configured; they define conceptions of the body, speech

events, rituals, practices, village structure, shamanism, and food production, consumption, and circulation.

The *aroe* and *bope* recur in everything. They define how people are
born, mature, and die, but they also define the world in a particular
Bororo way; they are the pattern of Bororo historicity and are principles at the root of why the Bororo are so "vigorous" and "obstinate"
in their rejection of Brazilian modernity (Crocker 1977:130). One might
argue that the Canelos Kichwa incorporate History 1 and transform
it, whereas the Bororo treat History 1 with disdain. Both strategies,
however, involve using fractal relations to denature History 1 by as-
serting indigenous historicity. There are many other examples, and
Heckenberger has noted similar patterns in the literature: "Amazonian
ethnotheories of the body, the person, and the world, are critical examples of this pattern of cascading (self-scaling), series of sameness/
otherness, alterity and mimesis, for theoretical and ethnographic reasons" (2005:261). A broader, regional approach to Amazonian History
2 might help anthropologists theorize nonlocal complexity in ways
that could transform understanding of historicities, global processes,
borders and boundaries, alternative modernities, subjectivity, and
fractal cosmologies, topics currently at the center of anthropology
and related disciplines.

Story 1

This story was told by Inia Geoffrensis in Ligia Villar (Leticia), Colombia,
in the summer of 1997. The narrator is a Spanish-speaking *mestizo*
whose ancestors were native, but the specific group or groups are
unknown. The story is an eyewitness account. The main character
is the narrator's sister-in-law. I am working from a tape recording,
originally in Spanish, of the story.[5]

*This story is about my sister-in-law and it is a true story. My sister-in-law
spent much time alone at home because her husband was in a business
that caused him to travel a lot. She stayed home and minded a small
store that sold sugar, moonshine, and other small items.*

43

Every night my sister-in-law would hear strange noises in her house of someone walking with very wet rubber boots. She saw a figure move through the light but she only saw a shadow. She said, "Who is there?" But no one responded.

That night she dreamed and dreamed of a very elegant white man.

One night she went to bed, and when she turned off the light she felt something cold in the bed. She tried to see what it was but it was only shadows. She asked, "What is this? Who is there? Is it a demon?"

And the next day she woke up with a tremendous headache and felt nauseous. She felt different. And when she went down to the shore to wash her clothes, a huge dolphin jumped and turned over and over right in front of her. It was like the dolphin was watching her. And she wondered why this dolphin was pursuing her.

She got a feeling. The ancient grandparents used to say that dolphins could turn into men, and right there she got this feeling. "Ay, my God, this dolphin is a man," she said. "He is pursuing me."

That night again she was alone, she couldn't sleep. She was afraid. Then another night, a very rainy night, she got another feeling while asleep. She felt someone touching her. When she woke up she knew that she had been impregnated. She began to experience symptoms of pregnancy.

Then her husband came home finally and noticed that his wife was pregnant. He got angry and jealous and could not understand why she had disrespected him. She begged his understanding and cried and cried and cried. After four months her husband left her because of her indiscretion, but the truth was that it was not her fault.

She began to get pains, normal ones for five or six months. And one day she woke up sick. She called out to her husband's mother and she came. The woman feared that she was going to have a miscarriage. But the truth was that she gave birth to two dolphins.

My mom was the midwife and delivered those two dolphins. She said, "My God, these are not babies. They are dolphins." She almost fainted on the spot. So we decided to wrap them in a towel and let them go in the *river. As soon as they touched the water they swam off. That night she had strong dreams. She dreamed of the dolphin. He said to her, "Thank you. Thank you for giving me my two babies."*

Analysis

The key relations in the dolphin story can be conceptualized through the fractality of humans and nature, land and water, masculine and feminine, Amazonianness and whiteness. The story's basic relation is that of masculine to feminine, represented in the woman's relationship to her husband.

The woman's husband must leave her quite often for his business transactions. The externality of modernity's commodity structure imposes itself on the core family relationship of the household. In the man's absence, however, a new "man" arrives. He is not only attractive but also white, and thus represents, at least on the exterior, modernity in the flesh (see Slater 1994). The man in reality is a dolphin who has shape-shifted.[6] He sleeps with the woman and impregnates her. The woman notes that he feels cold, perhaps because he is of the river domain and gives off little bodily heat. The dolphin-man also makes the woman dream, and she realizes she is pregnant through her dream. When the woman's husband returns, he thinks his wife was unfaithful and leaves her at the four-month mark of pregnancy. The power of the dolphin is its ability to change its body. Not only does he transform into a human, but he also combines his corporeal substance with the woman's to make his own young, and the woman becomes a mother of dolphins.

The cosmic body here is the mutual feeding and shared flow of substance between masculine and feminine, dolphins and humans, and the river and forest domains. The dolphins benefit from the reproductive powers of humans, and humans take advantage of the river for their own food. People do not eat dolphins, but dolphins are thought to help them obtain fish and other aquatic nourishment. The woman's ordeal is one of many exchange moments in a larger and more complex circulatory system, where people, souls,

45

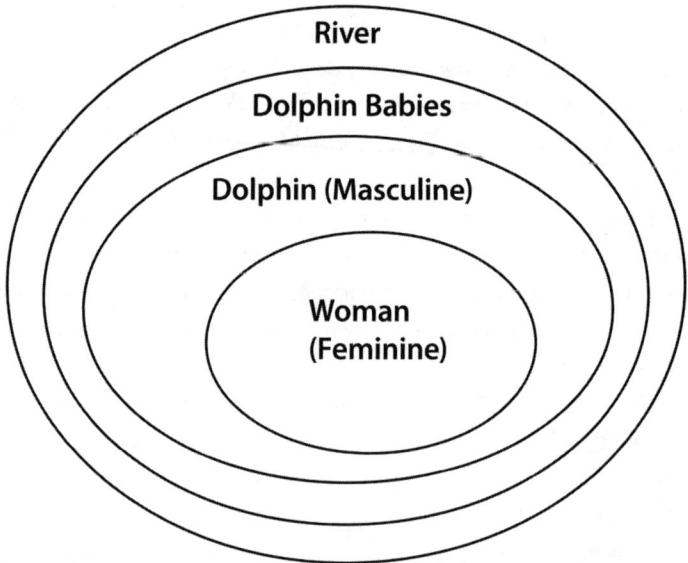

Fig. 1. The cosmic body in story 1.

substances, food, and social relations flow between the human and aquatic domains.

The story also brings modernity into the cosmic body by incorporating historical nuances and family history into the relations. The opposition of whiteness to Amazonianness in Peruvian society is conveyed by the image the woman sees of the dolphin, who appears to her as a "very elegant white man." Like white people, dolphins are exotic, powerful others, but the relationship is not purely structural, nor does it reflect something about white hegemony. The dolphin, a shape-shifter, presents himself clothed in the key symbols of the modern world, the very thing the woman's husband is chasing in his business dealings. Unlike a lot of humans, dolphins understand that modernity is all about corporeal appearances.

Story 2

This story was narrated by Walter, who lives on a floating house near the city of Iquitos, Peru. Walter is a descendent of Cocama people. He claims not to speak Cocama fluently, but says, "I know enough words to get my *masato* [manioc beer] when I need it." Walter considers himself an Amazonian and easily moves between native and nonnative aspects of life. He works for the military and resides in a floating urban neighborhood.

Walter recounts this story as a personal experience. An interesting aspect of his life is that when he was a young man he appeared as a debt-peon in Werner Herzog's famous film *Fitzcarraldo* (1982). The story was told to me when I was on a research trip with Juan Carlos Galeano in April 2006. Walter told the story during a fishing trip and again in his house a few days later. I recount the story here from memory and the tape recording we made.

One day I was walking back from my chagra *[field] when I was younger, and along the trail I saw something* surcando *[jumping] with shiny skin. It was a beautiful black* víbora *[viper snake], and I dispatched its head with a machete blow. I flicked the head aside with my machete and then immediately became drawn to the beauty of the snake's skin. It glistened in the light and so I peeled it off and put it in my bag.*

When I returned home I hung the skin up to dry and decided that it would make a very nice belt. My old belt was broken, so I used the viper's skin to make a new one.

Once the belt was ready I put it in my pants and began wearing it. Soon after I began wearing the belt I became violently ill. I had a fever, diarrhea, aches and pains, and felt very weak. The fever lasted for days and would not subside, so my mother took me to see the doctor at the health clinic. The doctor gave me medicines, but they did not work. I had fever, fever, fever for days and was not getting better. I was sure I was going to die.

My mom then decided to take me to the shaman to see if he could find out what was wrong with me. He examined me and then asked me to tell him if I had done or seen anything strange around the time when I had gotten ill. I told him no, but that several days before I had fallen ill I killed a simple black víbora. *I then told him that I made a belt out of its skin and that I had been wearing the belt.*

The shaman became animated and said, "That was no víbora! That was a boa negra *[black boa snake]! I knew it!" Before I had come to see the shaman he had dreamed of the* boa negra, *and so this explained his dreams. The shaman said, "Quickly, bring me the belt!" My brother ran home quickly and fetched the belt. The shaman scolded me, "This is the* boa negra. *This is the* boa negra, the boa negra, *not some ordinary snake. This is the source of your problems. He has made you ill."*

The shaman then undertook a program necessary to heal me. He dispatched the belt very carefully, burying it far away, and took precautions that the illness would not also pass to him. He cleansed me several times and took ayahauasca *[a hallucinogenic drink made from a rainforest vine, used by shamans to see into the spirit world] to fight off the* boa negra's *powers, although it was a difficult struggle, because the* boa negra *is very strong. If it wasn't for that shaman I would have died. That is the story of my experience with the* boa negra *and how I barely escaped with my life.*

Analysis

The main fractal relationship in this story is the potency of the *boa negra,* which represents the human interconnectedness with the forest domain through predatory flows. The *boa negra,* like the dolphin, is a shape-shifter. He transmits his shamanic power through his skin, even after he is physically dead. His body makes Walter ill in a way modern medicine cannot cure. Similarly the *boa negra* makes the shaman dream and conveys to the shaman his predatory potency from the perspective of the cosmic body.

The story features the motif of human-animal predator-prey relationships. In the beginning of the story Walter's role as predator becomes reversed through the snake's shamanic potency, which transforms Walter from predator to prey as his body becomes open to the cosmic forces at play. That the boa is prey is only an appearance, since he is a cosmic being. Like dolphins, boas never seem to be what they really are.

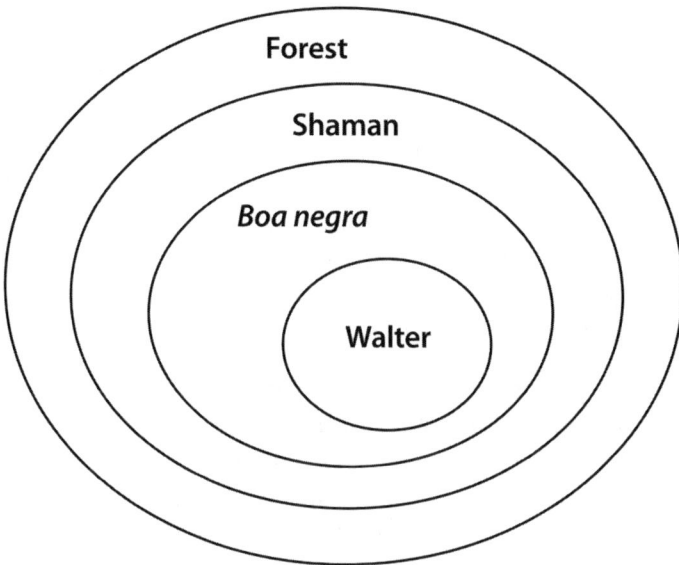
Fig. 2. The cosmic body in story 2.

The story also fractally engages modernity from the perspective of cosmic realities and what Marx described as commodity fetishism. Walter, thinking that he has hunted a nice skin, attempts to turn the living boa into a "thing" with use-value. Walter uses the skin to make a belt, a potential commodity. Mosko (2005:27) has noted that commodities are fractally configured if one follows Marx's analysis of modernity, since the relations that define things also define the relations among people. The *boa negra*, however, has a cosmic body and thus cannot be transformed into a mere thing. For Walter the belt is more like poison. The *boa negra* teaches us that his predatory capabilities allow him to fetishize commodity fetishism.

The cosmic body in this story is the connection of Walter to the *boa negra* (through his encounter and making the belt), the shaman, and the forest. His body rejects the Western theory of biogenetic healing because of its embeddedness in larger cosmic flows of predation with forest beings. The shaman, because he is an expert in the cosmic fractality of bodies, finally heals Walter when modern medicine cannot.

Story 3

This story was told to me by Bandiro, a Napo Runa person from the community of Pano, Ecuador. This narrative involves the history of the name of the river Achiyacu and is an important tale in the history of the community of Sapo Rumi. This story is regarded as family history. The events described happened several generations back. The story was told to me in the Kichwa language (Upper Napo dialect) in July 2006, and I recount it from memory.

This is a story that the older generation told me. When I was little I always wondered where the name Achiyacu came from, as it was the name of our river. As I got older I began to inquire into the name of this river. I bothered my uncles and grandparents until they finally began telling me stories about the past. Most people today do not know this history because the events happened a long time ago. They know the name Achiyacu but do not know what the name means or where it comes from.

The story begins with a boy, who was around thirteen or fourteen years old. The boy lived over there, near that bank, where there used to be a house [points to a place near the bank where there is nothing but weeds]. One day the boy disappeared. He just vanished. His parents were very worried, so they consulted a shaman, who took ayahauasca to find out what had happened.

During the ritual the shaman saw that the spirits under that very large stone [points to the very large stone] had taken him down to the under-world because they had desired him to be one of the governors of their city. The shaman tried to free the boy, but the spirits had a hold of him by all his arms and legs. He could not free him. They decided that more help was needed, so they enlisted the help of more shamans.

During the next session the powerful shamans all took ayahauasca together in an attempt to free the boy. When they traveled to the un-derworld they saw that the boy had become old. He had grown a white beard and looked wise. They used all of their might to free him, but the spirits held on as tight as can be, holding him by his arms and legs. The shamans decided that they needed even more help.

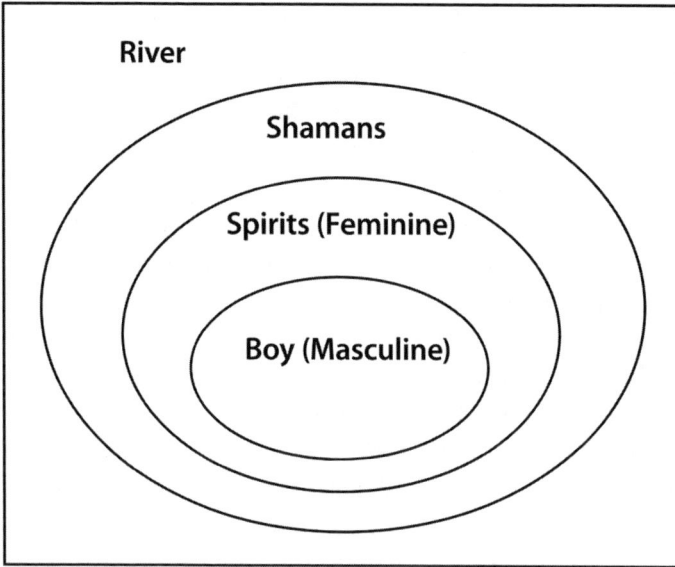

Fig. 3. The cosmic body in story 3.

The shamans enlisted the help of several more powerful shamans and they all took ayahauasca again. This time they again saw the boy, but the spirits were prepared and wrapped around him so tightly that the shamans finally gave up. They saw that the spirits had named him Achi, which means "old" and "wise" in this dialect of the Kichwa language. They also saw that the young boy now had a wife and several children and was a governor of a city. The shamans then declared that this river was "Achi's domain" and thus named the river Achiyacu, which means "old river."

Analysis

This story again features aquatic potency, but the main characters are spirits (*supai*), who represent animal subjectivities in the context of their own world(s). Like the first story about dolphins, this one is framed in terms of the cosmic body that involves circulatory relationships of people, souls, energies, and food among the aquatic and human domains. The story focuses on questions of human-animal-spirit reproduction, but involves "marriage by capture," whereby a human boy becomes a son-in-law to a family of powerful spirits. The story is another version of the very common Amazonian motifs of human-animal intersexuality and affinity.

The landscape reflects the potency of the animal spirits. A very large stone marks the entrance to their world, and the river, the key source of sustenance for the community, is stocked by them. The taking of a young human boy to serve as a governor in their city reflects the motif of animal spirits being masters of modernity. They are reported to have airplanes, trains, and cars in their cities, and they often take people to visit their cities when they dream.

The naming of the river after the boy becomes a spirit governor is an interesting fractal relationship of naming. As in the modern world, the river is named after an old person with government authority whose new name conveys that idea in a word. In the Tena dialect of Amazonian Kichwa, *achi* refers to an elder person of authority. It implies kinship. Naming the river Achiyacu conveys a kinship connection to the spirits who live in the city underneath the large rock.

Unlike white people, however, the spirits do not try to develop or modernize the human world at the expense of the forests and rivers. The spirits have mastered and perfected their version of modernity, so much so that there is no pollution, no poverty, no alienation, and no market forces. It is a generous and giving modernity that provides for human needs in the rivers and forests. Such is Achi's legacy, a relative who sends fish for his human descendants to eat. One day he may call on them again to help govern the place.

Fractal Principles in All Three Stories

As Gleick has noted, fractality is about "a particular, well-defined, easily repeated set of rules" (1987:98). These three stories from diverse regions in Amazonia share a set of similarities. The rules seems to be quite simple, but they permit infinite complexities of possible relations:

1. Humans and animals are not qualitatively different beings.

Animals have souls, intelligence, and subjectivity and can marry with and have children with humans.

2. The major question of the human-nature relationship is one of corporeal flow between humans and nonhuman nature. Animals and humans are intersexual beings.

3. Animals, when they use their cosmic bodies, become masters of mimicry and shape-shifting.

4. Animals often give humans what they want and desire, including allowing their children to become prey so that humans will live well.

5. Animals often deceive humans to get what they want and desire, including making humans prey so that they themselves can live well.

6. Because humans do not really know what animals and spirits want or when they may strike, animals and spirits are unpredictable and dangerous. We often do not even know what hits us, especially when they want our blood.

7. The animals use the human fascination with modernity to deceive us. This makes them even more dangerous.

These rules can be further simplified if one eliminates the implicit assumptions of Amazonian cosmology, animism (see Descola 1992, 1996), perspectivism (Viveiros de Castro 1998), and dark shamanism (Fausto 2000, 2004; Whitehead 2002; Whitehead and Wright 2004). The most basic rules are 3, 4, and 5, which can be glossed as mimesis (Taussig 1987, 1993; Uzendoski, Hertica, and Calapucha 2005; Uzendoski 2005a), and predation or sorcery, since rules 4 and 5 are both predatory principles that involve perspective switching between human and animal subjectivities. Rules 1, 2, 6, and 7 are groundwork or implications (modernity) of the more basic rules. In the materials presented here, the core relations that the storytellers have emphasized are cosmic embodiment, predator-prey exchanges and circulatory relations, and the fulfillment of mutual desires and attractions. That these

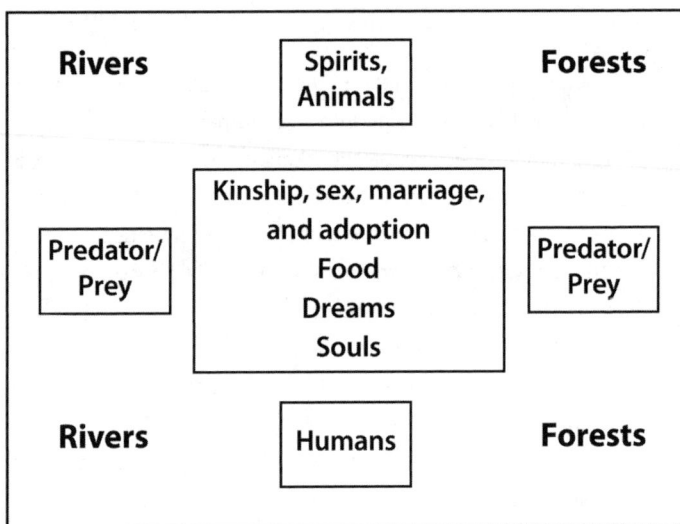

Fig. 4. The general form of the cosmic body.

desires are fully articulated with the tropes of modernity is perhaps a new twist. These relationships can be represented in a diagram of the more general scheme of the cosmic body.

I am arguing that the cosmic body represents the most encompassing of the relations in the stories. Like Dumont's notion of hierarchy, the cosmic body encompasses the individual body, gender, and sociality. It is often in the background of daily life, but in specific instances, such as the ones I have discussed here, corporeal connectedness to animal and spirit predation surges to the forefront. As I have demonstrated in analyzing the stories, exchange relationships between the animal and spirit world and the human domain encompass the daily lives of individuals. The encompassing power of animals and spirits, as both providers and predators, represents the mystery and daily presence of the cosmic body.

Natives and Nonnatives

There is an artificial divide separating anthropologists interested in the native cultures of Amazonia and others, such as literary scholars and environmentalists, who tend to focus on nonnative populations.

It is as if these different populations do not share territory or exchange ideas, things, or artistic works. Much of cultural anthropology deals with Amazonia as if it were populated only by natives. Similarly scholars who work with nonnative peoples write about Amazonia as if it were devoid of the indigenous peoples or cultural features of indigenous derivation.

The reality of the place is much more complex. Native and nonnative peoples often share space, intermarry, and tell stories to one another. In Napo, Ecuador, as in many other places, *colonos* (colonists) have carved out spaces along rivers and along the edges of indigenous settlements. While urban areas are usually dominated by nonnative peoples, rural areas are much more heterogeneous. In the Iquitos region there are populations of *ribereños* (river people) with an indigenous cultural lineage but who no longer possess an overt "native" identity or speak a native language. These peoples are distinct from the *colonos* in that they have a deep knowledge of Amazonian ecology and cultural patterns. Throughout Amazonia one can find a continuum of native-nonnative relationships that are rich and complex.

Natives and *ribereños* share a common intellectual tradition, whereas most *colonos* are newcomers to these ideas. *Colonos* often resist these ideas, whereas *ribereños* like Walter embrace them. A defining feature of the cultural patterns of natives, *ribereños*, and even some *colonos* is the notion of cosmic corporeal fractality with nonhuman nature. The prevalence of *mestizo* urban shamans in Iquitos, the largest city in the Peruvian Amazon, speaks to the adaptation of nonnatives to native concepts of fractality with nature. The work of Candace Slater (2000) reveals that a similar intellectual tradition has emerged in the Brazilian Amazon among nonnatives there. The cosmic body appears to be an intellectual tradition of considerable complexity and influence.

Today Amazonian notions of fractality increasingly appear in new forms of expression, but the cosmic body remains a central theme. Also, alphabetic writing, poetry, video, and emergent styles of music are becoming common. Despite these changes the fractality of human-nature relations remains a defining characteristic of how people conceptualize and define their subjectivity. Let us now explore some contemporary, nonnative Amazonian artistic expressions in more detail.

Fractality and Friendship

I begin this section with my friendship with Juan Carlos Galeano, whom I met in 2001 at Florida State University while he was in the middle of his first project dealing with Amazonian oral traditions. Galeano, a poet and translator, grew up in the area of the Caquetá River of the Colombian Amazon. However, like many of us he made his life far away from his natal home and did not think of his home as a place of much interest. He was interested in other endeavors. After some years of living abroad he came to see Amazonia in a different light and as a source of poetic inspiration. Later in his career he decided to embark on a project to record and study the folktales from places throughout Peru, Colombia, Ecuador, Venezuela, Bolivia, Brazil, and British Guyana. Juan Carlos was about to embark on a trip to Ecuador and asked me if he could take something there for me. We hardly knew each other, but the opportunity to send gifts to Ecuador was one I could not pass up.

I sent with him some gifts for my Napo Runa host family who had adopted me as a son (churi) during my stay in 1994 (see Uzendoski 2005a). I made up a package of clothing for Fermin Shiguango, my yaya (father) and principal mentor of the Kichwa language and culture. I drew a map on the back of an envelope for Juan Carlos to get to Fermin's house, which was some distance (a forty-five-minute hike) from the road. An experienced traveler, Juan Carlos arrived with little problem and was greeted as if he were a member of the family himself. He spent some days there.

Fermin is a storyteller and a shaman, and my relationship with Juan Carlos began through him. Fermin told Juan Carlos who I was to him in the Amazonian context. He emphasized that I was his son and pointed out the things I did while I was there. In these descriptions he exaggerated, but the stories were meant to show my cosmic connection to Fermin's family and to the forest and rivers of their home. For example, Fermin pointed to a place in the forest where I had killed a peccary, even though I had never killed such an animal while living with him. He pointed to the places where I spent time and the spaces I considered my favorites, especially by a large stone near the river. Juan Carlos was taken aback by the love they had for me, since he assumed that I was like many others intellectually interested in the rainforest but who seemed to lack a deeper cosmic connection to the place. (See Beth Conklin's chapter in this volume, which describes similar kin-making processes.)

Fermin then gave Juan Carlos the gift of some healing experiences, and Juan Carlos taped a story titled "Puma yuyu" (The Jaguar Plant) from Fermin in Spanish, which Juan Carlos later rewrote according to his own poetic sensibilities (see Galeano 2005, in press). I had learned about *puma yuyu* years before from Fermin and had published my own anthropological analysis of its mythology and ritual uses (Uzendoski 1999). Although our work on *puma yuyu* is in different genres, both publications capture the religious thinking behind the plant and its role in the cosmic body, not just in the abstract, but as it came to define certain events in Fermin's life. My essay emphasizes Fermin's lineage and connection to the mythical and transformative substance of primordial jaguars; it is an anthropological analysis of native mythology and ritual, with an emphasis on Kichwa language and culture. Juan Carlos's rendition is not at all faithful to the original, nor is it framed in assumptions of native versus nonnative. His is a Spanish story completely rewritten to fit a poetic sensibility.

Juan Carlos's version (in press) emphasizes how Fermin's family viewed the death of Fermin's mother (still living when I wrote my piece) through the *puma yuyu* complex. Juan Carlos's story preserves the essential fractal relationships of the cosmic body, despite his poetic

innovations and social omissions of Kichwa-ness. I quote from the
English translation:

*Eventually death came from heaven and the old lady died peacefully. They
gave her a Christian burial and later, relatives would bring flowers to her
grave every week. This went on until one day one of the granddaughters
went to visit and found that something had dug a hole in her grave. "It
was as if an animal had dug in to eat her remains, or as if someone had
tried to rob her bones to do witchcraft" said the priest and some others.*

*But they were wrong, and her relatives were not worried, because,
according to the sorcerer, the pumayuyu turned her into a jaguar after
death and she was still in this world. Her relatives had a very happy party,
because their grandmother now was walking freely and eating the best
bush meat.*

When Juan Carlos returned from Ecuador we immediately became
close friends, mainly because we now had the context of a shared
intellectual tradition. He had immediately grasped the significance
of *puma yuyu* as part of the general form of the cosmic body. I saw
that he had a deep commitment to Fermin's intellectual tradition,
to his cosmic view of the world. He saw me as someone who could
understand his poetry. Juan Carlos published his version of the *puma
yuyu* story, along with forty-one other stories, mostly told by *mestizo*
storytellers from other Amazonian countries, in *Cuentos Amazónicos*
(2005, appearing in English translation in 2009). Fermin's story fits
in seamlessly with the others, which are so diverse that their linear
connections (where they are from, whether native or nonnative, their
cultural traditions) are in chaos. But the order appears at the level of
the underlying relations.

Later Juan Carlos and I decided that we would collaborate on projects. In April 2006 I made a trip to Iquitos to spend some time research-
ing stories with him; he was working on a documentary film focusing
on the storytellers and shamans behind his folktale book. As I came
to know and talk with the storytellers he was working with, it became

increasingly clear that there were fractal similarities between these *mestizo* stories and the indigenous ones I knew from Ecuador. I also realized that Juan Carlos's poetry was actually part of a larger tradition of emergent Amazonian art. In Iquitos, for example, there are many urban nonnative artists engaged in painting, music, and storytelling (see Luna and Amaringo 1991). Many of these artists use *ayahauasca* for creative inspiration, but they all draw on the Amazonian intellectual tradition of the cosmic corporeality in expressing their art. They see themselves as continuing a wise tradition (*sabio*) that originated among native groups, but which they are expressing through different mediums. These urban artists communicate and work with native artists who continue in their own traditions of ceramics, weaving, and storytelling. Natives are taking up new forms of expression as well.

A Few Thoughts on Fractal Boundary Crossing

Most of Galeano's stories and poems are told by *mestizo* people in Spanish, but they show a connectedness to the indigenous world. Much recent research has shown that this boundary between *mestizo* and indigenous is more fluid than previously thought, and Galeano's writing reveals this fluidity in a creative way. It shows a common subjectivity that transcends ethnicity but does not obliterate its social presence. Stories travel, but more to the point is the intellectual traditions of religious thought represented in them. Modernity is not simply replacing indigenous realities in a linear fashion with cold, rationalistic truths about the world. Amazonian realities are present and active in defining the subjectivity of the nonindigenous, who now represent the majority of the population in many regions. I have described these relations elsewhere as an "alternative modernity," a concept that can be defined as the cultural transformation, and questioning, of modernity's most basic social and cultural assumptions (see Uzendoski 2004b, 2005a, 2006). Hybridity might be a similar way of describing how such processes occur, but, as I try to show in this chapter, hybridity in

Amazonia is shaped by specific forms of subjectivity, as also discussed by Hutchins in his chapter on indigenous tourism.

In *Folktales of the Amazon* (Galeano in press) the indigenous are the background interlocutors of the stories, but they are also a defining part of the present dynamic by which modernity is transformed and hybridity is given a specific shape. In one of Galeano's stories, "Yara's Gift," an indigenous man takes on the role of shamanic interpreter and explains what happened when a man from Lima has a troubling experience with a fish-woman. The man from Lima possesses a dolphin tooth given to him by an indigenous friend.

Towards dawn he woke up again. This time he heard something like an animal flopping on the ground and a soft guitar and violin music coming from the river. He looked through the crack of the door and saw a lovely fish writhing on the dry dirt of the yard. The fish was a curvinata, and he wanted to catch it, but he grew fearful, and again stayed put. The fish's death agonies continued; then the sounds stopped and the music faded.

When his workers returned, the man told them what had happened. They explained that surely that was the Yara who had come to charm him. "What stopped her was the dolphin tooth you wear on your neck," one of the Indians who worked for him said. "But, sir, now that you have seen the Yara, it will be very hard for you to fall in love with another woman, no matter what city or country you go." (Galeano 2005:28–29)

One can imagine such encounters and interactions throughout Amazonia, where people from the outside are actively taught by natives to interpret experiences from a fractal subjectivity defined by the cosmic embeddedness of the body. As the story points out, the encounter with the fish-woman changes the man forever. His subjectivity is altered; he no longer will be able to find love, for his body and soul have been taken over by desires flowing into the unseen world.

Ira Bashkow's (2004) essay on boundary crossing provides a way of conceptualizing relations among social actors who share space but are not isolated groups. Bashkow develops a neo-Boasian perspective on boundaries using linguistic notions of "isogloss" (a dialect boundary) to provide a sense of boundaries as sites of "differentiation." However, the boundaries do not, by themselves, exclude or contain (450). I think this idea is a good one for thinking about relations between the indigenous and nonindigenous in Amazonia. Although there are real boundaries between the indigenous and the nonindigenous, and within these groups as well, the presence of the boundaries also invites their being crossed. These processes are similar to linguistic overlapping and differentiating that occur among dialects of a language. Bashkow, for example, writes, "Contrary to our naive view of dialects as discrete entities, the isoglosses of distinct features often fail to coincide; instead they form tangled patterns of crisscrosses and loops, making it impossible to establish a definitive line of demarcation between dialects" (451). I think the notion of tangled patterns of crisscrosses and loops goes far in explaining the complex coterminous relations that exist between and within the indigenous and *mestizo* worlds. These patterns, by no coincidence, also emerge in the poetic sensibilities of Galeano's stories.

The fractality in the stories reflects an Amazonian theorization of this problem where boundary crossing and looping are not just major themes but also modes of social action. The storytellers are less concerned with cultural boundaries than with natural boundaries, but all "boundaries are meant to be crossed" in the Amazonian world, to borrow a phrase from Santos-Granero (2002). Such processes of boundary crossing, which involve multitudes of natural and social "others," define and permeate Amazonian cosmologies and practices of social reproduction.

Techno-Kichwa Fractality

Napo Runa popular music, called Runa Paju (Runa magic or power), is another example of crossing over and fractality, but here we have natives borrowing from Hispanic, Andean, and African South American traditions in order to express their own religious sensibilities. Although musicians sing Kichwa lyrics and refer to their underlying cultural realities, they incorporate electronic keyboards, foreign instruments, and new musical elements into this hybrid form of religious practice. Indeed popular Kichwa music, which still expresses many conventional religious principles, has gone techno. The musical group Playeros Kychwa (who choose to spell "Kichwa" in their own way) refer to themselves as *los Yachak de la Tecnokychwa*, which roughly translates into "the shamans of techno-Kichwa."

One Playeros album, volume 3, contains two new styles of "traditional" Amazonian music, "Cumbia del Indio" and "Salsa Kichwa." However, the hybridity in this music is used as a means to further Amazonian religious thought. Rather than impoverish the traditional themes, the singers incorporate foreign elements to transform them. In the song "Salsa Kichwa," for example, the lyrics say that this music, *Runa taki*, is transforming "all of Amazonian Ecuador." A *taki* is not a secular thing; it is a song with shamanic power, designed to do something in the world, such as heal or make someone feel happy (see Uzendoski, Hertica, and Calapucha 2005). Like Galeano's poetic stories, the Playeros are an excellent example of how fractality crisscrosses and loops into new genres.

Consider the popular Playeros Kychwa song "Chini panga" (Stinging Nettle Leaf), whose lyrics have an explicitly fractal structure:

Chini panga shina	Like a nettle leaf
Asi*chini*mi	I make laugh
Chini panga shini	Like a nettle leaf
Waka*chini*mi	I make cry
Ruku ñañawara asi*chini*mi	My older sister, I make laugh
Jipa ñañawara asi*chini*mi	My younger sister, I make laugh

The fractality emerges when one considers the sounds and meanings of the Kichwa words, for the grammatical suffix *chi* (a causative, "to make do") resonates explicitly with the word *chini* as a sound quality. These are in addition to the fractal qualities of the music itself, which

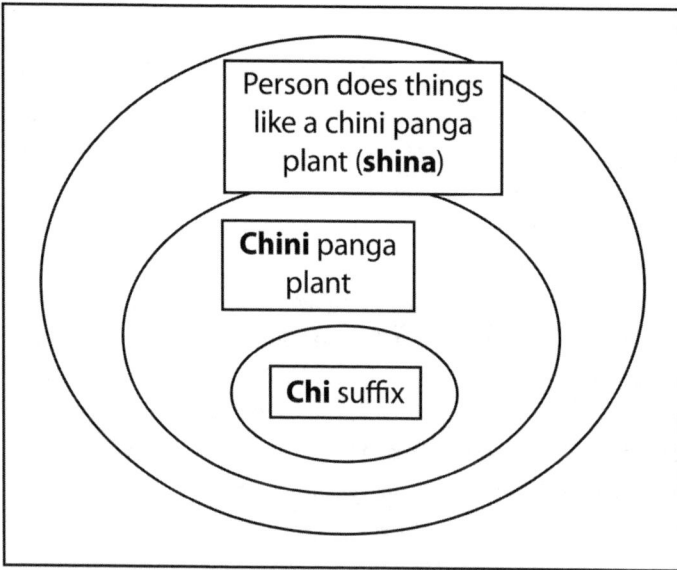

Fig. 5. Fractal relationships in the Playeros Kychwa song "Chini panga."

I do not consider here. The song creates clear self-similar meaning relationships among the *chi* suffix, the *chini panga* plant, and the actions of the subject, who takes on the qualities of the plant in being "sharp" and "strong" (*chini panga shina*, or like a nettle leaf). Although the song is incredibly simple, its use of fractality invokes the notion of the cosmic body, for bodily actions (laughing and crying) are linked to plant qualities (sharpness and strength). The song is a perfect example of Kichwa fractality as employed in emergent aesthetic expressions. (In the figure, the word *shina* means "like.")

Conclusion

In this chapter I have analyzed narrative materials from several locations in Amazonia to show how people use fractal forms to define subjectivity in relation to other people, things, the forest, spirits, and globalization. Despite the diversity of materials considered, the relations show an underlying conceptualization of humans as intersubjectively defined by relationships with larger wholes that are not reducible to globalization theory itself. My analysis of three stories showed how people configure experiences such as pregnancy, illness, and death through the body's cosmic embeddedness in nonhuman nature (the spirit world of animate subjectivities). The stories help people make sense of globalization and are not simply local. They show how real people transform the commodity logics of capitalism using Amazonian notions of fractality. In the first story a dolphin shape-shifts into a modern white man, a predatory outsider. In the second story a nice belt made of snakeskin contains the death-power of a boa, who is the giver and taker of all life. In the third story a contemporary river becomes a place animated by erotic spirits that kidnap the young but also provide the source of all life through fish and water. These stories show that although capitalistic globalization may be present and socially powerful, it remains subordinate to the social flows of the cosmic body, flows that define and determine human subjectivity in the first and last instance.

I also discussed the problem of boundary negotiation in Amazonian thought and practice to show the complexity involved in relations between native and nonnative subjectivities. I analyzed how materials and relations move between languages, cultures, and emergent genres by comparing my own work with that of the poetry of Juan Carlos Galeano. I used the story of my becoming friends with Juan Carlos via our interrelatedness to the cosmic body, an intersubjectivity that spans the boundaries of ethnicity, upbringing, academic disciplines, and the nation-state boundaries of Amazonian regions and the United States. Similarly I looked at the modern electronic music of Amazonian Kichwa speakers (Runa Paju) as a way to show how multiple native and nonnative elements are combined in conveying cosmic corporealness. The song "Chini panga," though short and simple, demonstrates the fractal principles present in contemporary native Amazonian expressive practices.[7]

The flexible subjectivities of shape-shifting discussed in this chapter belie a fractal logic of scale that allows persons—whether human, animal, plant, or spirit—to assume multiple manifestations in local settings. Such shape-shifting occurs commonly today in narratives of experience that deal with globalization and in which spirits assume the appearance of worldly beings (pilots, doctors, businesspeople, even anthropologists) in the midst of remote forests, urban centers, or rural villages. Such stories, as I mentioned earlier, defy analysis in terms of either anthropology's long-standing focus on the local or its more recent efforts to theorize culture in terms of globality.

The materials considered here reflect possible infinite variations of subjectivity as embedded in the larger flows and material exchanges with animals, spirits, and nature. These configurations, which span large geographic distances and myriad social boundaries, reflect an Amazonia at large, a reproductive philosophy that spins out infinities of fractal relations among and within human and nonhuman beings, societies, and civilizations. These recurring relations, as I have argued, belong to a reality of historicities, which in the case of Amazonia implies also the "cosmic body," those fractal processes that interrupt and denature modernity-as-capital.

Notes

I would like to thank the editors of and contributors to this volume for allowing me to participate in this interesting project. I thank Walter and his wife, Bandiro, Juan Carlos Galeano, Edith Calapucha Tapuy, and many other people (too many to name), who have given me insight into and inspiration for the ideas presented here. I also thank Frederick Damon, Roy Wagner, and George Mentore for their passionate teachings on chaos theory, fractality, self-scaling systems, and holography during my training at the University of Virginia. I also thank Neil Whitehead for our communications involving "love" and "desire" and the ambiguity of shamanic and mystical experiences. All shortcomings and mistakes, however, must be attributed to my own deficiencies.

1. I use the term *mestizo* to mean someone who self-identifies as nonnative and does not speak a native language. I realize, however, that the boundaries between "native" and "mestizo" can be and often are ambiguous.

2. All of my work thus far, which spans fourteen years in indigenous communities in Upper Napo, has focused on Amazonian Kichwa speakers (see Uzendoski 1999, 2003, 2004a, 2004b, 2004c, 2005a, 2005b, 2006; Uzendoski, Hertica, and Calapucha 2005). The current research, which represents an effort to branch out, was inspired by a brief research trip to Iquitos, Peru, in the spring of 2006. This trip was partially funded by Florida State University.

3. Hutchins (this volume) interprets Chakrabarty's reading of history: "I . . .

understand Marx to be saying that antecedents to capital are not only the relationships that constitute History 1 but also other relationships that do not lend themselves to the reproduction of the logic of capital. Only History 1 is the past 'established' by capital because History 1 lends itself to the reproduction of capitalist relationships" (Chakrabarty 2002:98). Chakrabarty points out that, although Marx says History 1 is forever trying to subjugate the "multiple possibilities that belong to History 2," there is no certainty that this has been, or will be, a completed process. History 2, then, might be thought of as a "category charged with the negative function of constantly interrupting the totalizing thrusts of History 1" (Chakrabarty 2002:101).

4. Graeber writes, "As so often with grand declarations that the age of totalizing frameworks is over, the actual effect [of Appadurai 1990] is to draw attention away from the current attempt to impose the largest and most totalizing framework in world history—the world market—on just about everything. This leaves skeptics such as me ... wondering whether the ideology of the market (freedom as choice and endless fluctuation) is not being reflected in the very form of arguments that claim such universalizing systems no longer exist" (2002:3).

5. The story was taped by Juan Carlos Galeano, and he has given permission for its use here. The translation into English is my own, as are all the translations in this chapter.

6. For discussions of shape-shifting see Slater 2000; Uzendoski 2005a; Uzendoski, Hertica, and Calapucha 2005. I define shape-shifting as a somatic transformation involving the "power" or "soul-substance" of the body. Shape-shifters can be, for example, jaguar-humans defined by jaguar power that resides in their "flesh" and that gives them a different kind of body. The jaguar-human, however, does not necessarily have to turn into a jaguar in outward appearance. A shape-shifter can also be an animal that transforms into a human, as in the dolphin-man here.

7. The late Amazonianist Irving Goldman (2004) argued that Amazonian peoples are mostly concerned with metaphysical reasoning and a holistic, religious perception of the world. Goldman theorized that Amazonian religious thought is highly developed and incredibly complex, and that this tradition rivals our own commitments to science. In other words, Amazonian religious thought is a holistic theory that explains much more than simply "religion." Amazonian religious thought addresses questions the West has chosen to answer through many disciplines, including philosophy, biology, anthropology and sociology, and history, to name a few.

References

Appadurai, Arjun. 1986. Introduction: Commodities and the politics of value. In *The social life of things: Commodities in cultural perspective*, ed. Arjun Appadurai, 3–63. Cambridge: Cambridge University Press.

————. 1990. Disjuncture and difference in the global cultural economy. *Public Culture* 2:1–24.

————. 1996. *Modernity at large: Cultural dimension of globalization.* Minneapolis: University of Minnesota Press.

Bashkow, Ira. 2004. A neo-Boasian conception of cultural boundaries. *American Anthropologist* 106 (3): 443–58.

Chakrabarty, Dipesh. 2002. Universalism and belonging in the logic of capital. In *Cosmopolitanism,* ed. Carol A. Breckenridge, Sheldon Pollock, Homi K. Bhabha, and Dipesh Chakrabarty. Durham NC: Duke University Press.

Clastres, Pierre. 1989. *Society against the state: Essays in political anthropology.* New York: Zone Books.

Crocker, Christopher J. 1977. The mirrored self: Identity and ritual inversion among the eastern Bororo. *Ethnology* 16 (2): 129–45.

————. 1986. *Vital souls: Bororo cosmology, natural symbolism, and shamanism.* Tucson: University of Arizona Press.

Descola, Philippe. 1992. Societies in nature and the nature of society. In *Conceptualizing society,* ed. Adam Kuper, 107–26. London: Routledge.

————. 1996. Constructing nature: Symbolic ecology and social practice. In *Nature and society, anthropological perspectives,* ed. Philippe Descola and Gisli Pálsson, 82–102. London: Routledge.

Fausto, Carlos. 2000. Of enemies and pets: Warfare and shamanism in Amazonia. *American Ethnologist* 26 (4): 933–56.

————. 2004. A blend of blood and tobacco. In *Darkness and secrecy: The anthropology of assault sorcery and witchcraft in Amazonia,* ed. Neil L. Whitehead and Robin Wright, 157–78. Durham NC: Duke University Press.

Galeano, Juan Carlos. 2000. *Amazonia.* Bogotá: Editorial Magisterio.

————. 2005. *Cuentos Amazónicos.* Jalisco, México: Literalia Editores.

————. In press. *Folktales of the Amazon: Juan Carlos Galeano.* Translated by Rebecca Morgan and Kenneth Watson. Foreword by Michael Uzendoski. Westport CT: Libraries Unlimited.

Gleick, James. 1987. *Chaos: Making a new science.* New York: Penguin Books.

Goldman, Irving. 2004. *Cubeo Hehénewa religious thought: Metaphysics of a northwest Amazonian people.* Edited by Peter J. Wilson. Afterword by Stephen Hugh-Jones. New York: Columbia University Press.

Graeber, David. 2002. The anthropology of globalization. *American Anthropologist* 104 (4): 1222–27.

Heckenberger, Michael. 2005. *The ecology of power: Culture, place, and personhood in the southern Amazon, AD 1000–2000.* New York: Routledge.

Jackson, William J. 2004. *Heaven's fractal net: Retrieving lost visions in the humanities.* Bloomington: Indiana University Press.

Kelley, José Antonio. 2005. Fractality and the exchange of perspectives. In *On the order of chaos: Social anthropology and the science of chaos*, ed. Mark S. Mosko and Frederick H. Damon, 108–35. New York: Berghahn Books.

Lévi-Strauss, Claude. 1969. *The raw and the cooked: Introduction to a science of mythology.* Vol. 1. New York: Harper Torch.

Luna, Luis Eduardo, and Pablo Amaringo. 1991. *Ayahuasca visions: The religious iconography of a Peruvian shaman.* Berkeley: North Atlantic Books.

Mascia-Lees, Fran, and Jeff Himpele. 2006. Reimagining globality: Toward anthropological physics. *Anthropology News* 47 (5): 9–11.

Mosko, Mark. 2005. Introduction: A (re)turn to chaos; Chaos theory, the sciences, and social anthropological theory. In *On the order of chaos: Social anthropology and the science of chaos*, ed. Mark S. Mosko and Frederick H. Damon, 1–46. New York: Berghahn Books.

Mosko, Mark, and Frederick Damon, eds. 2005. *On the order of chaos: Social anthropology and the science of chaos.* New York: Berghahn Books.

Parameshwar Gaonkar, Dilip. 2001. On alternative modernities. In *Alternative modernities*, ed. Dilip Parameshwar Gaonkar, 1–23. Durham NC: Duke University Press.

Richards, Ruth. 2001. A new aesthetic for environmental awareness: Chaos theory, the beauty of nature, and our broader humanistic identity. *Journal of Humanistic Psychology* 41 (2): 59–95.

Santos-Granero, Fernando. 2002. Boundaries are meant to be crossed: The magic and politics of the long-lasting Amazon/Andes divide. *Identities: Global Studies in Culture and Power* 9 (4): 545–69.

Slater, Candace. 1994. *Dance of the dolphin: Transformation and disenchantment in the Amazonian imagination.* Berkeley: University of California Press.

———. 2000. *Entangled Edens: Visions of the Amazon.* Berkeley: University of California Press.

Taussig, Michael. 1987. *Shamanism, colonialism, and the wild man: A study in terror and healing.* Chicago: University of Chicago Press.

———. 1993. *Mimesis and alterity.* New York: Routledge.

Tsing, Anna Lowenhaupt. 2004. *Friction: An ethnography of global connection.* Princeton: Princeton University Press.

Uzendoski, Michael. 1999. Twins and becoming jaguars: Verse analysis of a Napo Quichua myth narrative. *Anthropological Linguistics* 41 (4): 431–61.

———. 2003. Purgatory, Protestantism, and peonage: Napo Runa evangelicals and the domestication of the masculine will. In *Millennial Ecuador: Critical essays on cultural transformations and social dynamics*, ed. Norman Whitten Jr., 129–53. Iowa City: University of Iowa Press.

———. 2004a. The horizontal archipelago: The Quijos Upper Napo regional system. *Ethnohistory* 51 (2): 318–57.

———. 2004b. Making Amazonia: Shape-shifters, giants, and alternative modernities. *Latin American Research Review* 40 (1): 223–36.

———. 2004c. Manioc beer and meat: Value, reproduction, and cosmic substance among the Napo Runa of the Ecuadorian Amazon. *Journal of the Royal Anthropological Institute* 10 (4): 883–902.

———. 2005a. *The Napo Runa of Amazonian Ecuador*. Interpretations of Culture in the New Millennium series. Bloomington: University of Illinois Press.

———. 2005b. The primordial flood of Izhu: An Amazonian Quichua myth-narrative. *Latin American Indian Literatures Journal* 21 (1): 1–20.

———. 2006. El regreso de Jumandy: Historicidad, parentesco, y lenguaje en Napo. *ICONOS* 26:161–72.

Uzendoski, Michael, Mark Hertica, and Edith Calapucha Tapuy. 2005. The phenomenology of perspectivism: Aesthetics, sound, and power in Napo Runa women's songs of Upper Amazonia. *Current Anthropology* 46 (4): 656–62.

Viveiros de Castro, Eduardo. 1998. Cosmological deixis and Amerindian perspectivism. *Journal of the Royal Anthropological Institute* 41 (4): 469–88.

Whitehead, Neil L. 2002. *Dark shamans: Kanaimà and the poetics of violent death*. Durham NC: Duke University Press.

———, ed. 2003. *Histories and historicities in Amazonia*. Lincoln: University of Nebraska Press.

Whitehead, Neil L., and Robin Wright. 2004. Introduction: Dark shamanism. In *In darkness and secrecy: The anthropology of assault sorcery and witchcraft in Amazonia*, ed. Neil L. Whitehead and Robin Wright, 1–20. Durham NC: Duke University Press.

Whitten, Norman E., Jr. 1985. *Sicuanga Runa: The other side of development in Amazonian Ecuador*. Urbana: University of Illinois Press.

Whitten, Norman E., Jr., and Dorothea S. Whitten. 2008. *Puyo Runa: Imagery and power in modern Amazonia*. Urbana: University of Illinois.

3. The Portrayal of Colombian Indigenous Amazonian Peoples by the National Press, 1988–2006

Jean E. Jackson

In this chapter I examine articles published in Colombia's two national daily newspapers on the country's Amazonian indigenous communities. I explore the ways the journalists and photographers working for *El Espectador* and *El Tiempo* construct the differences between indigenous Amazonians and the country's nonindigenous citizens, and between Amazonian indigenous communities (referred to here as *pueblos*, "people," "town") and pueblos located in other regions. The articles were collected as part of a larger, ongoing research project investigating these two newspapers' representations of indigenous Colombia during the period 1988–2006.

When conceptualizing this larger research project I assumed that the two dailies would offer a seriously distorted picture of the country's indigenous people. I envisioned uncovering the newspapers' participation in "opaque as well as transparent structural relationships of dominance, discrimination, power and control as manifested in language" (Wodak 2001:2). I hoped to "investigate critically social inequality as it is expressed, signaled, constituted, legitimized . . . by language use" (2), working to make such discourses more visible and transparent (Blommaert and Bulcaen 2000:448). I assumed such symbolic domination would be easy to document.

I certainly uncovered examples of bias, ignorance, insensitivity, and ethnocentrism in these two newspapers. Especially in the Amazonian corpus I found examples of texts that masked the effects of power and ideology in the production of meaning, so that unequal power relationships came closer to acquiring stable and natural forms and to being accepted as "given" (Wodak 2001:3). I found many instances of "othering," at times extensive. "Othering" refers to depictions that highlight alterity. Negative othering in its mildest form disparages; in its most blatant form it sends virulently racist, sexist, and xenophobic messages. I found that, overall, Amazonian pueblos are more othered than non-Amazonian pueblos, the contrast sharpest between representations of Amazonian and Andean pueblos. I also found much more pronounced othering of Amazonian women than men, some of it verging on negative othering. However, I found no case of clearly negative representations of pueblos or their members. (Some articles published prior to 1988 do contain negative stereotypes and at times exhibit shockingly biased attitudes.)

The absence of explicitly negative othering is surprising, especially when we take into account the fact that these two newspapers are by no means left-liberal; both are owned by families in the oligarchy. Nor are they especially good. *El Espectador* has challenged government policy more aggressively than *El Tiempo*, and its coverage of the nation's indigenous pueblos has been more extensive and favorable. (Financial problems eventually forced *El Espectador* to publish weekly, although it still publishes daily on the Internet.) The absence is even more striking when we consider the highly negative treatment of indigenous populations in the national press in several other Latin American countries, for example, Brazil (Ramos 1998) and Guatemala (Hale 2006).

Clearly, understanding the historical context is critical if we are to explain my main finding: the absence of truly negative images. The country's problems, among them poverty (see Ramírez, this volume), rampant corruption at all levels of government, and above all a conflict that has lasted half a century, are vital elements of this context. I argue that the manner in which indigenous Colombians appear in the press, ranging from neutral to positive and though often romantic or stereo-typical, is at times a means of critiquing nonindigenous Colombian society, in particular the various loci of power and authority where so many decisions harmful to the country are made. In this respect mainstream Colombian media continue a tradition that hearkens back to Montaigne's and Rousseau's enlistment of New World inhabitants in these philosophers' efforts to critique the European society of their respective eras. My findings fit within this volume's broader argu-ment—that constructions of Amazonian indigenous peoples, whether as nobly savage or ignobly savage, emerge out of specific historical contexts and cannot be understood in isolation from them.

To be included in the corpus being analyzed, an article had to either be about Amazonian pueblos or mention some variant of the word "Amazon."[1] I did not include articles about elections whose reference to the Amazon simply consists of listing candidates from the region. Also not included were articles about pueblos in other parts of the country illustrated with photographs of indigenous Amazonians, a frequently occurring practice. Colombia's politico-administrative units (called departments) do not correspond to Amazonia's bound-aries: Amazonian territory is found in the departments of Amazonas, Putumayo, Caquetá, Guaviare, and Vaupés, but only Amazonas consists entirely of lowland tropical forest (below 500 meters) that drains into the Amazon River and its tributaries. Colombia's Amazonia forms 35 percent of the national territory and 5.5 percent of the Amazon basin.[2] There are several ways of defining Amazonian Colombia; Ramírez's chapter in this volume provides an alternative scheme.

My more comprehensive project found three overlapping categories that receive extensive othering in the two newspapers in addition to Amazonian natives. The first is certain Colombian pueblos located in other regions of the country: the formerly nomadic groups in the eastern plains (*llanos*) in the Orinoco catchment area; pueblos in the Sierra Nevada de Santa Marta in the north of the country; the Wayu'u of the Guajira peninsula in the northeast; and the Emberá and Waunan in the Pacific region. Second, depictions of indigenous women contain far more othering than is the case for men. The third category consists of photographs that contain a far greater degree of othering than the texts they accompany. Quite often an editor has stuck in a photograph from the newspaper's archives that has no connection to the article's subject matter (apart from the common theme of indigeneity). For example, an indigenous woman breast-feeding a baby illustrates an article about guerrilla strategies for recruiting indigenous youth.[3] Sometimes even the caption has no relation to the photograph. Such photographs are excellent examples of what Shi-Xu (1997) terms "fossilizing," for they clearly have been chosen for their exotic, often sexualized nature. As expected, photographs of indigenous Amazonian women reveal the greatest amount of othering.

The chapter proceeds as follows: after a brief overview of the situation of Colombia's indigenous inhabitants, four of the most frequently occurring themes in the newspapers' treatment of indigenous Colombia as a whole are briefly discussed: the environment, lessons to be learned, the conflict, and gender. This contextualizing section is followed by a more in-depth analysis of these themes as they appear in articles about indigenous Amazonia. Discussion and conclusions follow.

Background

Colombia's indigenous people form ninety-four distinct pueblos and speak sixty-four different languages. The 2005 national census gives a figure of 1,378,884 natives, approximately 3.4 percent of the total population of about forty-four million (Meltzer, Rojas, and Camacho 2005:15).[4]

Living in exceptionally diverse habitats (mountains, deserts, vast plains, and tropical forests), Colombia's indigenous people have always been extremely marginalized socially, politically, and economically. Independence from Spain ushered in an ideology of nation building, which required forging a single national identity, a process that would eventually produce a homogeneous Spanish-speaking, Catholic, patriotic citizenry. As in other Latin American countries, the Colombian state espoused policies of *indigenismo*, which worked to incorporate the nation's pueblos into the general population through racial mixing and cultural assimilation. Indigenous communal landholding was especially inimical to the liberal nation-building project, and legislation intended to dismantle the Crown-established reservations (*resguardos*) was proposed. However, Law 89 of 1890 recognized the official status of the collectively owned *resguardo* and legalized the *cabildos*, the councils of respected authorities that govern the communities. Although the law's language was patronizing, participants who mobilized during the 1970s and 1980s came to appreciate the law's value in the struggle to reclaim communal territory. In 1988 Decree 2001 defined the *resguardo* as a special kind of legal and sociopolitical institution formed by an indigenous community or entire indigenous ethnic group (see Ramírez 2002). The 1991 Constitution even more definitively recognizes the *cabildo* as an indigenous community's governing authority, in accordance with its *usos y costumbres* (practices and customs), and recognizes the *resguardo* as a pueblo's communally owned territory.

The drive for constitutional reform in Colombia arose from awareness that the current social order, in which access to the government was gained exclusively through political parties (all other attempts being ignored or treated as subversion), could not adequately respond to changing social conditions (Van Cott 2000:63–89). The political and moral crisis resulting from the forty-year-long insurgency, the increase in violence as landowners and security forces attempted to stamp it out, and a pervasive distrust of a deeply corrupt state controlled by the oligarchy also strengthened arguments promoting constitutional reform (see Assies 2000:3).[5]

Indigenous political mobilizing during the 1960s and 1970s, which occurred mainly in Andean areas, eventually succeeded in getting the government to recognize the regional indigenous organizations that had arisen during this time (Jimeno and Triana 1985). The National Organization of Indigenous Colombians (Organización Nacional Indígena de Colombia, ONIC), founded in 1982, was also recognized. Largely due to pressure from these organizations and their nonindigenous allies during the 1980s, the government stepped up its program of creating new *resguardos* as part of a land reform that began in 1961. As of 2001 the country's pueblos collectively and inalienably owned 30,845,231 fully demarcated hectares (one hectare equals 2.47 acres), constituting 27 percent of the national territory (Arango and Sánchez 2004:50). Eighty-five percent of these lands are located in the country's plains and tropical forest. The two largest *resguardos* are in Amazonia. As of 2001 approximately 65 percent of the country's indigenous population lived in new *resguardos* (those created from 1961 on), and 22 percent lived in older *resguardos*, some of them established in the colonial period (Arango and Sánchez 2004:104). According to the economist Carlos Ossa Escobar, this "silent revolution," which resulted in pueblos owning 3,250,000 hectares more than the state (as of 1996), reflects a government policy intended to, first, return these lands to their ancestral owners, helping to avert a pattern of ever-increasing concentration of land, and, second, put the land into hands that would best preserve the forested areas and the environment in general (quoted in "Indígenas vuelven a ser dueños de la tierra," *El Espectador*, July 12, 1998).

The new Constitution changed the status of pueblo members from that of minorities without full citizenship to collectivities with full rights as citizens and special rights as distinct peoples. Indigenous leaders' influence during the drafting of the Constitution was far greater than the demographics would suggest (see Gros 2000; Jimeno Santoyo 1996; Laurent 2005; Roldán 1997). The reforms' original agendas had not included benefiting the country's minorities, but during the deliberations several political interests, not just indigenous and Afro-Colombian, realized that advocating pluralism would bring them closer to their own goals. Indigenous delegates to the Preconstitutional Assembly seemed to embody the hope the country's citizens were allowing themselves to express, for an almost euphoric mood was in the air during the early 1990s. The indigenous delegates' near celebrity status clearly was a factor in the media's overall favorable treatment of the country's indigenous people during that period and subsequently.

Despite these and other significant gains over the past thirty years, Colombian pueblos continue to face daunting challenges. In addition to the ongoing struggle for self-determination, autonomy, and justice, many communities are subjected to serious repression from armed actors, legal and illegal, operating in many areas of the country: two guerrilla armies (the Revolutionary Armed Forces of Colombia, FARC, and the National Liberation Army), paramilitaries, and public security forces (the army and national police; see Hunt 2006:98–107). Colombia's guerrilla armies have at best tolerated indigenous aims and at worst assassinated many individuals, leaders in particular. Unfortunately perpetrators of crimes benefit from a justice system estimated to have a 95 percent impunity rate (Aguilera Peña 2001:422, cited in Hunt 2006:100). Colombia's internally displaced citizens exceed three million (Amnesty International 2004:21, cited in Hunt 2006:109).

Overview of the Four Themes throughout Colombia

The background just sketched indicates some of the reasons why media treatment of Colombian Indians evolved the way it did in 1988–2006. I now present a brief countrywide overview of the four themes (which overlap somewhat) that appeared with regularity in articles published during this period: environmentalism, lessons to be learned, the conflict, and gender. (Other topics include politics, education, arts and crafts, religion and traditional culture, indigenous languages, and tourism.) These four themes were chosen because they provide the most useful clues for understanding the overall neutral to positive tone of the othering that appears.

Environmentalism

During the 1990s and the beginning of the new millennium the national press regularly discussed the important links between Colombia's pueblos and the need to safeguard the environment. For example, one article describes how much "greener" indigenous philosophy and practice are when compared to the West's. In a column titled "Fear of the Indian," Miguel Borja writes, "Indigenous models for using and conserving the more than 25 percent of the national territory, and their knowledge of Nature, ecology and biodiversity, are of great value to the country."[6] An article in *El Tiempo* ("Universidad Indígena," July 11, 1997) states that "all sectors of society" have environmental and ecological preoccupations and that "extremely varied kinds of damage occur daily with respect to proper and normal maintenance of the nation's environment." Everyone, therefore, should be supporting a proposed project to create "a kind of Indigenous University" that will develop a specific way to train Indians "as specialists in the protection of the environment, in the defense of their habitat." Obviously the Indians are the ones to do this "primordial task," because they "are so strictly associated with their environment."

Lessons to Be Learned

The examples above illustrate how indigenous values and cosmovision provide guidelines for safeguarding the environment, guidelines that all of the country's citizens would do well to follow. Articles about other topics also feature this "lessons to be learned" theme. An editorial titled "Arquímedes Vitonás: Symbol of the Year" praises the achievements of this Nasa leader, who was declared "Master of Knowledge" by UNESCO in 2004. The editorial praises Nasa organizations' "direct democracy" and "the admirable community independence" that reveals the Nasa community's cohesion and "collective ethics in their confrontations with the armed conflict." The Nasa clearly offer "not a few lessons and challenges . . . to the marked individualism characteristic of our society" ("Arquímedes Vitonás: Símbolo del año," *El Tiempo*,

December 19, 2004). Another journalist writes that indigenous people are "known for their strong sense of identity and for being carriers of a sharp knowledge of their diversity."[7] Other articles link the fate of Colombia's pueblos more directly to the country's future. Here is one discussing the slow progress in legislating the 1991 Constitution-mandated "indigenous territorial entities," a kind of collective land tenure that applies exclusively to pueblo landholdings: "Indigenous territories deserve much more attention, as does the demand for decentralization in general. Colombia cannot put the success of this process at risk, upon which, to a great extent, depend peace and national reconciliation" (*El Espectador*, January 10, 1994). An article about a Bogotá-based meeting of indigenous peoples from various countries comments, "Colombia ought to welcome the delegates to such an important encounter and wish for all possible success. It is to be hoped that their millenarian values and knowledge would not only be respected, but will be taken into account in facing a future that belongs to all of us" ("Encuentro indígena," *El Espectador*, January 21, 1999). Another article states that "[indigenous] territory is nature" and that defending nature has resulted in Indians finding themselves "in the middle of most intercultural conflicts, trying to stop development projects in the country" ("El territorio indígena es la naturaleza," *El Espectador*, July 2, 1997). However, groups that have recently designated themselves indigenous can receive quite critical treatment because they are not taken seriously. One article states that, although a group says its members are descended from the Muisca, a long-disappeared pueblo, their physical appearance shows them to be "wise guys" (*avivatos*) rather than *indígenas puros*. "Incredibly," it continues, this group received transferences from the state "as if they were a real, legally recognized resguardo" ("Resguardo de avivatos," *El Tiempo*, December 11, 2001).

The Conflict

One would expect sympathetic coverage of the plight of the nation's pueblos in so violent a country, and one finds it. Serious repression has been the norm in many locations. Pueblos are regularly described as caught in the cross-fire.[8] One article refers to them as a *colchón de resorte* (spring mattress), "primordial victims of the repressive campaigns of the Army, which often labels them 'collaborators with the guerrilla'" ("La política indígena, un acierto," *El Espectador*, July 27, 1988). Pueblos are especially targeted because they are in rural areas and because they are in strategic parts of the country, areas worth fighting over because, for example, they contain corridors for drug or weapons trafficking. Also, isolation and inaccessibility characterize some pueblo locations, which can attract narcotraffickers, and many pueblo territories have important natural resources such as minerals and oil or are targeted for large-scale development, like the huge Urrá hydroelectric project that flooded Emberá-Katío lands in the northwest of the country. Pueblos are poor and for this reason are sometimes suspected of having leftist leanings, and the pueblos' stance against all armed actors in their territories, including the army, is acceptable to none of these groups (ONIC 2002). Pueblos characterize their position in terms of autonomy rather than neutrality, for they want to be seen as ready to defend their communities rather than as passively neutral. Pueblos have thought long and hard about resistance: Avelina Pancha, a member of ONIC, reminds a reporter that Colombian pueblos draw on ample experience resisting armed actors: "We have been resisting for five hundred years" ("Indígenas no darán ni un paso atrás," *El Tiempo*, July 26, 2002). In the same article a Catholic missionary in one community voices the same idea: "This [resistance] isn't against only the guerrilla, rather, [pueblos] are protesting whatever form the violence takes."

Although indigenous protests (for example, large demonstrations against free trade agreements) do not always elicit praise in the press (especially when the Pan-American Highway is blockaded, which periodically occurs), unarmed confrontations with armed actors always inspire favorable write-ups. Whether the action is a mass demonstration, the takeover of a government office, or a confrontation with FARC,

indigenous participants will be unarmed. Following the demobiliza-
tion in 1990 of an indigenous guerrilla organization known as Quintín
Lame, the Andean Nasa (also known as Páez) resolved to oppose the
presence of all armed actors in their territory.[9] Beginning in the late
1990s they developed a campaign of pacific civil resistance, organizing an Indigenous Guard (*guardia indígena*) whose members are
unarmed, save for ceremonial staffs.[10] The Guard currently numbers
about seven thousand men and women (see Rappaport 2003). If FARC
warns a community that any kind of civil resistance—for example,
ignoring its commands—will not be tolerated, the response of *cabildo* authorities might consist of just that, even if brutal repression
follows. A number of articles discuss instances when members of
several Nasa communities have confronted armed actors with firm,
united actions. In 2001, when FARC began firing homemade mortars
on a police station in the Nasa community of Toribío, more than four
thousand unarmed community members flooded its streets, ending
the attack (Rappaport 2003:41). On another occasion a large contingent of community members traveled to a guerrilla stronghold to
obtain release of a kidnapped leader ("Indígenas rescatan su alcalde,"
El Tiempo, April 14, 2003). This ability to arrive at a consensus and forge
a collective will to act in the face of great danger has occasioned lauda-
tory commentaries in the media, church sermons, school lessons, and
everyday conversations, as does pueblo members' obvious respect for
leaders and traditional authorities. An example is the interest displayed
when governors of fourteen indigenous *cabildos* in northern Cauca
received the National Peace Prize for their Proyecto Nasa, a coalition
working to maintain community neutrality and autonomy in the face
of threats by armed combatants ("Más que neutrales, autónomos," *El
Espectador*, December 12, 2000).

Articles about the conflict often include critiques of the Colombian
government or Western civilization, a type of "lesson to be learned."
One journalist describes indigenous protests as "beginning a movement that could change the direction of the war. . . . Indigenous com-

munities seem to bring together the conditions that the rest of the country seeks in vain" ("Indígenas no darán ni un paso atrás," *El Tiempo*, July 26, 2002). Nonindigenous commentators believe that successful indigenous organizing is key, as well as pueblos' "strong identification with something, be it land, culture or a social or political project. . . . 'We're all owners of the indigenous project.' . . . Indigenous resistance doesn't consist of a show of force, but, rather, demonstrating cohesion" ("Indígenas no darán ni un paso atrás"; also see Espinosa 1998, Rappaport 2005). Pueblos' struggles are described as reclaiming "respect for life and co-existence" ("Indígenas no darán ni un paso atrás"). An editorial states that Nasa symbolizes two things that are seriously lacking in Colombia, which could "drastically change the equation of this unending war that bleeds the country: organization and independence. Indigenous power is synthesized in these." The year 2004 in particular offered the country "more than sufficient" demonstrations of this power to convince Colombians to take these lessons to heart ("Arquímedes Vitonás: Símbolo del año," *El Tiempo*, December 19, 2004). There is even an article about indigenous women's response to the violence (articles featuring indigenous women are very rare). This one describes how the women of one community are organizing "for autonomy and peace" ("Las indígenas, contra la violencia," *El Tiempo*, July 5, 2005). These indigenous responses, and the media's reports about them, resonate with Ramírez's discussion (this volume) of "perverse" and "productive" social capital. We see productive social capital being created when indigenous communities nonviolently resist the "perverse" capital that is so easily generated in "an institutional environment that favors opportunist and criminal behaviors" (Rubio 1997:805, cited in Ramírez, this volume). Such perverse illicit economies promote the abuses perpetrated on pueblos by both legal and illegal armed combatants.

Gender

With respect to the attention indigenous women receive in these newspapers, one would not conclude that they constitute 50 percent of the native population, for they appear very seldom in the texts themselves. This is especially true for the first years of the period under examination. The ratio of women's appearances in photographs as compared to text is much higher than the ratio for men. Indigenous women appearing in texts or photographs very rarely speak for themselves. Instances of orientalizing and naturalizing women in patronizing ways are especially found in human interest stories. Depictions of indigenous women in these two newspapers, I would argue, are intended to entertain (as opposed to inform) far more than are depictions of indigenous men. Despite what must be a substantial number of female readers, the two newspapers are clearly oriented to a male audience, resulting in Colombia's indigenous women and other minority women (e.g., Afro-Colombians) being doubly erased and "male-gazed" into what is at times a parody of themselves.

We should probably look to gender relations in Colombia in general, and within its indigenous communities in particular, to explain these gendered differences rather than lay most of the blame at the feet of biased journalists and editors. Articles about violence focus on men because men are more often its victims; so far as I have been able to find out, all assassinated indigenous leaders have been men, which is not surprising given the tremendous dearth of indigenous women leaders.[11] An occasional article will mention an indigenous female leader but, with one exception (see below), not in Amazonia. Of course, indigenous (and nonindigenous) women suffer tremendously from the conflict, but their suffering tends to be less newsworthy. The paucity of indigenous female leaders means that stories about indigenous leaders doing other newsworthy things will also be about men.[12]

Analysis of the Four Themes for Amazonia

As already noted, for the most part the two daily newspapers "other" Amazonian natives more than pueblos located elsewhere. Tourists are assured they will encounter "real" Indians (*indios de verdad*) there.[13] The indigenous Amazonian body, especially in ceremonial dress, signals a clear-cut, satisfying indigenousness that leads editors to choose photographs of Amazonians over, say, a member of the Andean Guambiano pueblo in traditional dress. Amazonian ceremonial dress is a powerful signifier that references the Amazon region itself and suggests such themes as the Primitive, Innocence, Harmony with Nature, Mystery and Adventure. The symbolic value of the Amazonian indigenous body is evident from the frequency with which photographs of Amazonians are used to illustrate articles about non-Amazonian topics. For example, a photograph accompanying an article about the opening of a photography exhibition on "Indigenous Colombia" in downtown Bogotá shows a shirtless, elderly indigenous Amazonian man using a traditional implement to scoop powdered coca leaf into his mouth. The caption reads, "An Amazonian shaman in communication with the higher spirits" (*El Espectador*, April 14, 1994). An article titled "Whites: Respect Indian Justice," about indigenous jurisdiction, is illustrated by a bare-chested Amazonian Indian with a feather crown. A large photograph of an Amazonian man in a feathered crown, loincloth, and jaguar-teeth necklace is the initial illustration for an article about racism throughout the country ("12 de octubre, Día de la Raza," *El Espectador*, October 12, 1997). We do not know for sure what such photographs are intended to communicate, nor how their message is in fact received by readers, yet we can conclude that although a significant degree of othering is apparent, these are not straightforward instances of symbolic violence. However, as Chaves's chapter in this volume describes, such exotic imagery can prevent members of communities that no longer use such signaling devices from being considered "really" (*de verdad*) indigenous people. If they respond to disparaging comments about their authenticity by reindigenizing, and this is their sole motivation, we have an example of self-orientalizing. While Chaves (2005) has demonstrated that such enactments can be performative, putting into play a much more profound reindigenizing process, in some cases petitioners are denied recognition because they do not look or act the part (for a non-Amazonian case, see Jackson and Ramírez 2009).

The adoption of a favorable tone toward the nation's pueblos by Colombia's national daily newspapers began in earnest with the coverage of President Virgilio Barco's 1988 trip to La Chorrera in the department of Amazonas to hand over more than five million hectares to the region's pueblos. The articles' positive tone clearly follows the lead of the chief of state; for example, Barco addresses the hundreds of assembled people in the Huitoto (also spelled Uitoto and Witoto) language: "Good morning, we are with you and we are here to give you your lands."[14]

Barco's speech to the crowd employs a rhetoric stressing the value of Amazonian indigenous citizens' contributions to nation building. The reporter comments, "The Head of State indicated that Colombians need to revalue the image that we have of Amerindian peoples, and the government proposes to inform everyone about their true value, as well as their contributions to the formation of our nationality." Upon departing Barco said, "Here are your lands, beloved compatriots. Continue loving them and taking care of them as you have until now . . . because only you know its secrets, its generosities, its weaknesses and its most subtle attitudes."[15] *El Tiempo* covers the occasion in a similar manner, with one article concluding, "Finally, after an incessant fight, these communities achieved an act of justice that will redeem the most vital component needed for their survival in the enormous Amazon. . . . Like a dream come true, those who were slaves will have enough land to work" ("De esclavos a propietarios de tierra," April 9, 1988). Interestingly the article in *El Espectador* describes Indians holding placards that read "Handing over what one owes is not generosity, it is scarcely doing what must be done."

The positive tone of these articles by no means indicates an absence of othering, an example being the description of Barco as the first president who visited *indígenas incrustados* (encrusted, inlaid) in the jungle.[16] A photograph of the president and his wife in feather crowns is captioned "Indigenous President."[17]

Articles in the two newspapers on Amazonian topics that might reasonably warrant a somewhat negative tone either are not negative or are so only indirectly, through criticism voiced by someone in the story. For example, several articles mention *saneamiento* (ethnic cleansing) of *resguardos*, which involves relocation of nonindigenous residents, usually poor *colonos* (settlers). A 1988 article simply mentions that the *saneamiento* of nonindigenous inhabitants from the new Predio Putumayo *resguardo* must occur within six months.[18] None of these articles contains any hint of sympathy for the plight of these *colonos*.

Nor do articles adopt a critical gaze with respect to the controversial issue of the "proliferation" of Indians, which refers to groups of reindigenized natives soliciting and obtaining official recognition of *cabildos* they have recently formed. Such solicitations increased especially after Law 60 of 1993 was passed, which enlarges indigenous authorities' sphere of action with respect to obtaining economic resources from the state. One year after the law was passed 80.4 percent of the country's *resguardos* presented projects to be funded (Laurent 2005:342).[19] The Putumayo is the site of much of this activity.[20] One article reports that the government office of Asuntos Indígenas (Indigenous Affairs, renamed Etnias, Ethnic Affairs, in 2003) estimates that about 350 communities throughout the country are seeking recognition as *aborígines*. The agency's director, Marcela Bravo, is quoted as saying categorically, "Indigenous pueblos that disappeared before the Spaniards arrived cannot reappear now."[21] Leaders from ONIC counter, "Communities that weren't indigenous are now recognizing themselves as such because for 500 years they were told that to be *índio* was a shame. But they now realize that this is not so and they are recovering their dignity. Nevertheless, this process is being delegitimized by the government." They go on, "We don't agree that the Ministry of the Interior should be the one to recognize who is and isn't indigenous. The community ought to define itself. What is really going on is a dispute over resources and lands."[22] The only criticism in the article comes from the mouth of the Etnias director. The contrast with the extremely negative tone of the article about the "wise guys" (*avivatos*) falsely claiming Muisca identity (see above) could not be stronger.

In cases involving clearly reprehensible behavior on the part of indigenous politicians and government appointees (corruption being the most frequent topic), criticism appears mainly in quotes from fellow Indians. (Note, however, that the well-known phrase *malicia indígena* [indigenous malice, mischief] appears in one article and in the title of an editorial.)[23] A story in *El Tiempo* reports that on September 21, 1994, Maximiliano Veloz was obliged to renounce his position as mayor of Mitú, the capital of the Vaupés, because a substantial number of indigenous "brothers," upset by the nonpayment of 150 million pesos the mayor's office owed the *resguardos*, took over his office and occupied it until he agreed to resign.[24]

Environmentalism in Amazonia

The theme of environmentalism and Amazonian pueblos appears in a major way in the newspapers. The notion of danger posed to both the environment and its inhabitants, who are described as closely linked to their surroundings, reflects themes found in media treatments of indigenous communities elsewhere in the country, but in Amazonia the connections are more tightly drawn. Settlers pose dangers to the environment, as do fumigation of coca fields and the conflict.

The far-sightedness of Colombia with respect to saving both the Amazon and its inhabitants is featured in numerous articles. President Barco describes his new policy goals as recognition of the rights of aboriginal communities and establishment of a "rational, balanced, and sustainable management of natural resources," to be achieved by turning over huge swaths of territory to the members of these communities.[25] Another article puts a nationalistic spin on Barco's policy, describing it as a model for other countries. The author, Edgar Cadena, writes that the new *resguardo* constitutes the largest indigenous reservation in the world, bringing the amount of Amazonian land "that has passed into the hands of its legitimate owners" to a total of almost twelve million hectares. These achievements demonstrate that "Colombia has authority: it is the most advanced country with respect to conservation of the environment, because it has not had to exploit this region. The Colombian Amazon is more preserved than other countries' Amazonian territories."[26] Barco states that even prior to handing over the Predio Putumayo, Colombia received "expressions of support and congratulations from the international scientific community. I consider . . . that this international recognition today is even greater due to the country's having doubled the area of protection and development for the indigenous communities and conservation of the environment."[27] An article published later that year discusses the favorable attention the *Miami Herald* was paying to Barco's Amazonia policies.[28] A 1989 article titled "The Key to Amazonian Success" praises the region's inhabitants, who are the answer to the problems that countries within the Amazon basin are experiencing with respect to management of the environment. The reporter claims that Colombians now understand that Indians utilize a large area around their longhouses; the idea of a virgin forest was erroneous because although the jungle surrounds Man, human culture extends through the jungle, regulating it ("La clave del éxito amazónico," *El Espectador*, May 13, 1989). By 1990 the number of hectares in Amazonia had increased to 18 million; Barco is quoted stating that these forty-two *resguardos*, along with the country's system of natural parks, show that Colombia is today one of the countries protecting the largest amount of tropical forest ("Colombia, el mayor protector de la selva tropical: Barco," *El Espectador*, April 24, 1990).

The theme of the Amazon as supplier of the world's oxygen also appears. One 1999 article about a "journey to the lungs of the world" reports on an international symposium in Leticia during which delegates traveled to a *maloka* (the traditional Amazonian longhouse) to hear indigenous leaders explain the significance Amazonia has for them. The article states that "within each maloka live the world's most efficient administrators [of the environment]" and quotes a Muinane leader: "We have demonstrated that we know how to carry out development without destroying nature. In this way we have always managed the environment" ("Viaje al pulmón de la Tierra," *El Espectador*, November 23, 1999; also see *El Tiempo*, December 9, 2005). Another article laments the negative impact of settlers on the ecosystem but speaks very favorably of indigenous Amazonians; after briefly recounting an origin myth and describing indigenous daily life, the author discusses the deleterious impact of the rubber boom and contemporary coca cultivation introduced by outsiders.[29] Another article describes the effect of illegal cultivation on indigenous Amazonians' way of life, in particular the negative impact on their ecosystems, which "is leading to extinction and displacement of these populations" ("Los indígenas también pierden," *El Tiempo*, May 18, 1998; also see *El Espectador*, April 27, 1994). In contrast, another article sympathetically describes indigenous Amazonians' need to cultivate coca for their own ritual consumption ("Queremos coca, no cocaína," *El Tiempo*, October 14, 2000). An article on a meeting in Bogotá of the National Congress of the Environment contains a photograph of an Amazonian man with feathers, necklace, and staff; the caption reads, "Indians were present in the congress to express their thinking about the fatal destiny of Mother Nature, and were radical in their opinions" ("Fin de semana verde," *El Tiempo*, July 27, 1998).

Amazonian "Lessons to Be Learned"

Although relatively little writing features Amazonian pueblos teaching "lessons to be learned," we have seen such suggestions indirectly mentioned in a number of articles described earlier. Here is a more direct example: "The elderly Uitotos talk about principles of peace, liberty, and abundance, because when speaking about traditional medicine they refer to the environment, to education and coexistence. Their knowledge is holistic and, like the universe, without fragmentation."[30] An article titled "Indigenous Wisdom, a Model for Peace" describes a workshop to discuss ways to end the conflict. A step forward was learning that those who dwell within the *maloka* respect their traditions, including myths and beliefs, as well as the environment. This is because the *maloka* represents the center of the community, where culture is born and knowledge, thoughts, and religiosity are transmitted ("Sabiduría indígena, un modelo para la paz," *El Espectador*, May 1, 1999).

The Conflict in Amazonia

Amazonian pueblos, many of whom find themselves extremely beleaguered (Jackson 2005), receive especially sympathetic treatment in the media. Extinction is mentioned more than once; because of their relatively small numbers, forced displacement and killings put many pueblos at risk of entirely disappearing ("Colombianos en peligro de extinción," *El Tiempo*, November 27, 2003). A 2003 article reports that twenty-two of the fifty-four pueblos are in danger of disappearing.[31] Three articles report on the massacre of seven Koreguajes in July 1997, which brought the total number of Koreguaje assassinations to forty-two (an additional four were "disappeared") in only four years.[32] This pueblo has only two thousand members. A Koreguaje leader concludes, "They want to violently obliterate us" ("Violencia contra koreguajes deja 42 muertos en cuatro años," *El Tiempo*, October 2, 1997). Another article quotes a Huitoto at a meeting: "Violence is the result of consumerism, of not wanting to share with others. From this comes hate." The reporter comments, "His words brought a message of hope, for he assured us that peace would be attained when Man comes to live harmoniously with Nature."[33] An article containing a photograph of three Amazonian indigenous men deep in the forest, where they have sought refuge, is captioned, "They are trying to conserve their tradition, despite the pounding of the West" ("El mapa no es el territorio," *El Espectador*, September 10, 2000).

89

Stories about Amazonian pueblos protesting guerrilla armies' forcible recruitment of their youth show another side of the conflict's negative impact.[34] Such forced recruitment is "against the philosophy of their communities, which support solidarity, respect and unity" (*El Espectador*, March 9, 2003).

Amazonian Gender

The overall higher ratio of photographs to text for women as compared to the ratio for men is especially true for articles on Amazonia. As already noted, indigenous women appearing in texts or photographs are quoted far less often than men, and this is particularly true of Amazonian women. Photographs of Amazonian women tend to embody sexual and "primitive" themes (see Pietikainien 2003:590); for example, a photograph illustrating an article titled "Indigenous Communities: Victims of 'Civilization,'" is captioned "Indigenous communities were persecuted in Colombia." But the photograph is a close-up of a bare-breasted young Amazonian woman flanked by two older women ("Comunidades indígenas, víctimas de la 'civilización,'" *El Espectador*, May 23, 1999). A photograph illustrating a story on special indigenous jurisdiction is captioned "The punishments handed down by the cabildos vary according to the crime and the community. They can stretch from the whip or communal labor all the way to banishment." But the photograph itself shows an Amazonian woman sitting in a chair with a hammock nearby and two boys in the background ("Ley de 'blancos' para indígenas," *El Espectador*, September 6, 1999). An article's photograph of three little Amazonian girls is captioned "The Indians of the region fight to preserve their culture" ("Amazonas, Cinco pasos por la selva," *El Tiempo*, November 9, 2006). In fact, only one of *El Tiempo*'s stories that feature photographs of Amazonian women shows a link between the text and the photograph (June 6, 1997), but only in passing: the text is about an arts fair in Bogotá. And only three *El Espectador* articles do so. The first, also only in passing, is found in a story about President Barco's visit to La Chorrera in 1988, which includes a photograph of a woman and an infant. The caption indicates that she resides in the *resguardo* that had received the large tract of land the previous day ("Barco, al rescate del Amazonas," *El Espectador*, April 24, 1988). The second, an article about the 1990 "Woman of the Year" prize given by the Fund for Family Compensation (Caja de Compensación Familiar), contains a photograph of the winner, the Huitoto María Encarnación Sukroque.[35] A captioned photograph was published the following day ("Figura de hoy," *El Espectador*, March 9, 1990). The third article that contains a photograph linked to both the caption and text features a Nukak-Makú high-fashion model in Bogotá (see below).

Although a few newspaper articles featured indigenous women, with two exceptions they live elsewhere in the country. The story about Sukroque describes her as an "authentic" leader who founded a women's community group that successfully pushed for better education and public health services. But the article also displays the familiar othering: she "embodies the authentic indigenous woman, working on a par with the man, barefoot, in the rain, cutting down trees with a machete in her little piece of jungle" in order to provide her husband and five children "with pineapples and other kinds of fruit."[36] No quotes are provided. The other article is about Francy Buitrago, a Nukak fashion model in Bogotá, "the model with nomadic blood." Although she is ostensibly "modern" and urban, this Amazonian native woman is the subject of a story whose main message is about a very exoticized other; for example, her totally plucked eyebrows receive serious attention.[37] Although clearly responding to feminist currents in the new millennium, both of these stories that feature Amazonian women are unmistakable examples of tokenism, both highly exoticized. The closest *El Tiempo* comes to such tokenism is a story published on Mother's Day titled "The Indigenous Woman: Authentic Mother through Tradition." A superficial survey based on an interview with the Colombian anthropologist Nina de Friedmann, the article mentions Amazonian women (described as "submerged in the jungle") three times.[38]

At this juncture I want to explore further what Colombia's indigenous Amazonians, especially women, symbolize for mainstream Colombian society. Familiar alterity signaling associated with the Amazonian native includes images of "the primitive," links to nature and the natural (the Amazon region itself), and tropes indicating child-like naïveté, ignorance, and inferiority. Contrasting images also appear that reference valuable attributes, such as authority vested in the elders, authentic spirituality, and possession of powerful esoteric knowledge used for the benefit of the community.

Amazonian women have often symbolized a mysterious and profound alterity, frequently of a sexual nature. A familiar image in earlier periods is the New World represented as indigenous female. She is a dusky, seductive, beautiful young woman ready for the taking, as in William Blake's famous etching of "Europe Supported by Africa and America" (see Nagel 2003) or Theodore Galle's "Vespucci 'Discovering' America," where America is depicted as a naked indigenous woman in a hammock (see Faery 1999). We also have Sir Walter Raleigh's famous characterization of Guyana as "a Countrey that hath yet her Maydenhead" (1997; Slater 2002:34; also see Faery 1999). Although in these earlier representations the attractive, inviting native woman represents all the Americas, the image fits stereotypes of Amazonian-like women far more than, say, Andean native women, for they are nearly nude and often portrayed in a supine, languorous pose. Clothing, work, children, and native men are nowhere to be seen.

As happens with the symbolics of the Amazonian native of unspecified gender, contradictions are easily found within the totality of symbols contained in representations of the Amazonian woman: a set of alternative, equally familiar images oppose the preceding set of images of the seductive and passive young native woman. These tropes reference power, most famously personified by the Amazons, the strong and independent women warriors of myth and explorer accounts. Literature about them, along with the literature that analyzes this literature, abounds (see, for example, Bamberger 1974; Murphy and Murphy 2004; Steverlynck 2003; Tiffany and Adams 1985). The message of power characterizing the warrior Amazon image is sometimes heightened by additional attributes that also signal power and authority, such as physical height and, occasionally, relative whiteness of skin (Slater 2002:89). These Amazons signify not only power and a will to violence, but independence from men and a renunciation of conventional (hetero)sexual and reproductive roles, symbolized by their willingness to cut off a breast to become more skillful archers. Or, if not renunciation, they indulge in a variety of sexual perversions that invariably challenge patriarchal authority. As Candace Slater (2002) points out, the powerful matriarch is also a member of this subcategory. We can conclude that ambiguity and ambivalence, at times profound, characterize the entire domain of warrior Amazon images. The nearly universal dictum that powerful women cannot be a good thing definitely characterizes this set of images.

Amazonian women are also recruited as symbols of the mysterious jungle and Nature herself. Representations along these lines include those in the Brazilian author Alberto Rangel's *Inferno verde* (Green Hell) and the Colombian author José Eustacio Rivera's *La vorágine* (The Vortex) and by the native woman in the Brazilian film *Como era gostoso o meu francés* (How Tasty Was My Frenchman, 1971). Slater cites Rivera's characterization of the Amazon jungle as "the wife of silence" and the "mother of solitude and mist" (*La vorágine* 99, cited in Slater 2002:252). A third trope, the Amazon region depicted as an elusive female, is exemplified in Lévi-Strauss's frustration at the Amazon forest's refusal to let him in on "the secret of its virginity" (Slater 2002:101, citing *Tristes Tropiques* 1964).

Clearly, the blatantly sexist and racist depictions of the sixteenth and seventeenth centuries are a thing of the past. However, it is important to note that the two newspapers' treatment of the country's Amazonian women makes use of only some of the tropes just described. The powerful Amazon warrior is totally absent, as is the powerful matriarch.[39] All depictions of indigenous power and wisdom appear in masculine form. The Amazonian woman, when she appears, is voiceless and, with the exception of "Woman of the Year" Sukroque and perhaps the Nukak Francy Buitrago, without agency, an object to be observed (and, of course, fantasized about). The Amazonian woman's frequent appearance as a type of exotic eye candy, as happens in photographs of young, often semiclothed women, recalls the earlier representations of the New World as seductive, passive, and, often, supine female native. The other, far less frequent type of representation in the two newspapers shows the indigenous Amazonian woman as an ordinary mother in tropical domestic surroundings, although the article about Sukroque does briefly mention her activities as a leader.

An article published in *El Espectador* slightly before the period under examination illustrates my point. Titled "God, Fertility and the Universe of Indigenous Longhouses" it describes the longhouse of the Murui-Muinane, a Colombian Amazonian pueblo. The article is illustrated with a large line drawing of a longhouse that encircles a naked indigenous woman with long hair and a fiber headdress. She has assumed a crouched position; the article describes this posture as the position for giving birth. Many of the symbols we have just examined are contained in this drawing: a young, enclosed, domestic, fecund, naked (save for a head ornament), crouched woman with her head lowered.[40] The fact that the Murui-Muinane do characterize their longhouses in somewhat similar terms (Carlos Lodoño, personal communication, September 8, 2008) does not alter this reading of the illustration, for I am analyzing the symbolic roles indigenous Amazonian women play for nonindigenous readers.

Discussion

Press coverage of Colombia's pueblos during the period 1988–2005 reveals a much more positive tone than I originally predicted. Favorable press attention to indigenous issues began in 1988 with stories covering the Barco administration's deeding large portions of the national territory to pueblos, especially in Amazonian departments. Of course at certain earlier moments during the 1970s and early 1980s pueblos received fairly positive media attention, for example, President Belisario Betancur's visit to Silvia, Cauca (an Andean department with a large indigenous population) in November 1982 to announce a new state policy addressing pueblos' territorial claims. But the most extensive and favorable coverage begins in 1988.

Obviously the phenomenon of increased and more positive media coverage during the 1990s was not simply due to a newly discovered perceived need on the part of the country's national newspapers to jump on the multicultural bandwagon. Several additional contributing factors played important roles. First, changes in the cultural politics of indigeneity over the past twenty years have been considerable; during this time Colombia witnessed all sorts of efforts on the part of its pueblos and their nonindigenous allies to achieve cultural revitalization. An example of self-indigenizing is the evolution of some indigenous leaders' speech, which showed a marked increase in indigenous words and phrases as well as allusions to indigenous values and cosmovision. Their choice of clothing and hairstyle also evolved over the period 1988–2005. Leaders such as the Tule (Kuna) Abadio Green and the Ingas Gabriel Muyuy and Antonio Jacanamijoy increasingly donned indigenous clothing.[41] The fact that many of the indigenous leaders described in the articles in the entire corpus are themselves very actively performing alterity needs to be considered when interpreting the degree of othering that appears in newspaper articles. To what degree are the journalists, photographers, and editors misleading readers through their choices of exotic images, and to what degree are these images appearing simply as the result of deliberate self-reindigenization through changes in clothing, speech, and nonverbal behavior?

An additional and related consideration is the significant change in the nation's imaginary of what I call Colombia's "jungle Indians," those pueblos found in the regions of Amazonia, the Orinoco basin, and Pacific lowlands. In previous eras everyone, not only nonindigenous Colombians but its natives as well (including lowland communities themselves), saw the lowland Indian as the stereotypical dirty, poor, ignorant, naïve *indio* who spoke a barbarous language. But as positive discourses of indigenous alterity came to the fore, pueblos whose members looked more indigenous found themselves becoming the standard-bearers in certain crucial symbolic respects, and these tended to be lowland pueblos (see Jackson 1991). Pueblos that retained their language, continued their traditional practices and customs (*usos y costumbres*), and wore some form of indigenous clothing had higher standing in the "authenticity" rankings. Because Amazonian natives in fact do differ from mainstream culture and society to a greater extent than most pueblos (even those retaining their language and traditional costume, as is the case for the Andean Guambianos), we cannot automatically conclude that the greater amounts of othering apparent in articles and photographs are due either to recent reindigenizing efforts on the part of Amazonian pueblos or to an excessive journalistic othering that misrepresents the actual situation.

Yet even in the case of extensive differences it usually is easy to spot media othering techniques. Media treatment of the Nukak-Makú pueblo offers a clear case of othering, their very real and visible differences notwithstanding. An unwilling poster pueblo for the category "jungle Indians," the Nukak-Makú would win any "authentic traditional Indian" contest hands down. Nomadic foragers who wear very little or no clothing, they are depicted as child-like and extremely naïve, effectively eliminating the possibility of their being viewed as intelligent, adult, and agentive people. Even the most sympathetic articles (the Nukak-Makú's very existence is imperiled by the conflict and infectious disease) almost invariably dwell on the most exotic items of their cuisine and almost always feature photographs of nearly naked and nearly bald Nukak-Makú women (all Nukak-Makú sport U.S. Marine-style haircuts).[42]

Over the past twenty years Colombia's indigenous communities have occupied a much larger space in the national media than their numbers would warrant. I have concluded that, to a greater degree

than happens in the national media of other Latin American countries, Colombia's indigenous people play the role of a messenger who
shows Colombians who they are by revealing what they are not, in
particular what they lack. (We must keep in mind that such "lessons
to be learned" are not always based on accurate or comprehensive
information.) Pueblos are seen to possess attitudes and practices that
Colombians would do well to take to heart. Pueblo members husband
the environment. They respect elders and traditions (e.g., shamanic
medicine). They maintain a less hectic pace, keep their spirituality
intact, and value their community, which they defend unarmed, save
for ceremonial staffs. Pueblos' traditional judicial systems are described
as functioning well, getting things done without either the long de-
lays or the endemic corruption found everywhere else. Pueblos are
also shown fighting transnational domination. For example, in contrast to a private Colombian university, which is depicted as having
sold out to powerful foreign scientific institutions and multinational
pharmaceutical companies, sympathetic stories show pueblos ac-
cusing these institutions of biopiracy.[43] Finally, pueblos are described
as having an enviable ability to collectively solve problems, internal
as well as external, without resorting to violence. Even extremely
divisive intrapueblo battles, some of them closely followed in the
media, merit positive media treatment, for these conflicts' peaceful
resolutions are seen as a lesson to mainstream society, which all too
often fails in this area.[44]

Although Amazonian indigenous leaders play such roles in the
press far less frequently than leaders from certain other regions of
the country (which is not surprising when we consider the small numbers and dispersed settlement pattern), when indigenous Amazonia
appears in the press the treatment is similarly positive. From Barco's
1988 La Chorrera speech to more recent depictions of indigenous
Amazonians as eco-friendly stewards of the forest and deeply wise
practitioners of traditional medicine, remarkably favorable coverage
continues to appear, along with portrayals of the Amazon region itself

as a unique source of pure and uncorrupted nature. The exception is press treatment of Amazonian indigenous women, which, although not overtly negative, cannot really be called positive. Even given the relative voicelessness of ethnic minorities that characterizes journalistic practice in general (Pietikainen 2003:595), press treatment of this minority is extreme in this regard, for they are, in effect, rendered mute.

Conclusion

As the title *Editing Eden* suggests, this book's main goal is to demystify the Amazon and its native inhabitants. The authors seek to engage with and analyze the dominant themes, stereotypes, and fantasies that work to create particular imaginings of the Amazon so as to reveal shortcomings and contradictions. In this chapter I have analyzed an extraordinary set of images and symbols found in articles about the country's indigenous peoples in Colombia's two national newspapers. The tone of the articles, which ranges from neutral to favorable, is unusual in Latin American media representations of indigenous communities. The nation's pueblos have played a pronounced hermeneutic role during the past twenty-odd years, in particular in those articles that invite nonindigenous Colombians to reflect on the nation's problems and to consider pueblos as role models pointing the way to solutions. Colombia's unfortunate position as a "façade democracy" (98 percent of crimes go unpunished, corruption is rife at every level, and the government is seen to be run by a coterie of elite, self-interested politicians) surely has played a part in bringing this role into being. The horrendous impact of the conflict is another key factor; not surprisingly, the disproportionate amount of the violence pueblos are subjected to educes sympathetic coverage, as do instances when unarmed communities resist domination by armed actors, legal and illegal. In short, press treatment will be favorable whenever pueblos are the underdog, no matter what the issue. This is not to say that the media always support pueblo positions. A columnist, for example, might wholeheartedly support oil exploration; however, even if the article discusses the U'wa pueblo's categorical rejection of seismic tests in their territory, they are not directly criticized. Instances of poorly planned and implemented neoliberal policies also inspire favorable narratives, as do cases demonstrating the negative side of globalization (e.g., biopiracy) or development projects that run roughshod over indigenous territories and desires.

Indigenous Amazonia inspires articles that continue the long tradition characterized by bell hooks as a "concrete search for a real primitive paradise, whether that location be a country or a body" (cited in Rodríguez-Mangual 2004:40). These denizens of an Edenic Amazon are portrayed as guardians of an imperiled ecosystem and practitioners of a shamanism characterized by an authentic and traditional spirituality. The two daily newspapers' treatment of indigenous Amazonian women constitutes the one glaring exception to positive portrayals. Although we have no definitive evidence of truly negative othering — in the sense of blatantly sexist and racist depictions — the fact that only two articles in my Amazonia corpus feature women, and that invariably when women appear (most often in photographs) they communicate very familiar and regressive messages, leads me to conclude that this is a case of "same old, same old." The way Amazonian women are depicted is all too recognizable; most often they are simply invisible, but when they are present they are almost always objects to be seen but not heard. This is especially so in the case of photographs, which at times offer up the Amazon woman as a kind of exotic eye candy to be savored by the male gaze. Insofar as we can infer the authors', photographers', and editors' intentions, the motivations and goals that led to these images being created and disseminated reveal a very distanced perspective, a need to objectify, and a disinclination to attribute agency to a collectivity that constitutes, after all, 50 percent of Amazonia's adult indigenous inhabitants.

Notes

An earlier version of this essay was presented at the 2006 Latin American Studies Association meetings in San Juan, Puerto Rico, in the session "De-essentializing Amazonian Social and Political Space." My thanks to Frank Hutchins and Patrick Wilson for organizing the session and subsequently providing very helpful editorial comments. *The first presentation of this research, "Documenting Ethnic Resurgence and Ethnocide: Representations of Indigeneity in the Colombian Press," took place in 2003 in the symposium "The Violence of Representation and Its Discontents: Creating Publics, Borders, and Bridges" at the* AAA *annual meeting in Chicago in November, organized by Charles Briggs.*

1. Pueblos include Andoke, Bora, Carijona (Karijona), Cocama, Coreguaje, Hupdu (Makú), Juhup (Makú), Kakua (Makú), Kofán (Cofán), Kubeo, Letuama, Makaguaje, Makuna, Matapí, Miraña, Muinane, Nonuya, Nukak (Makú), Ocaina, Tanimuka, Uitoto (Witoto), Siona, Tikuna, Yagua, Yukuna, Yuri, and the "Tukanoan cultural complex" (Bará, Barasana, Carapana, Desana, Kawiyarí, Piratapuyo, Pisamirá, Siriano, Taiwano [Eduria], Tariano, Tatuyo, Tukano, Tuyuka, Wanano, and Yurutí). In 2004 the vice minister of defense, Andrés Peñate Giraldo, said that fifty-six pueblos are in Amazonia (defined as including the departments of Amazonas, Caquetá, Guainía, Guaviare, Putumayo and Vaupés). "Militares, también a curso de indígenas," *El Tiempo*, July 13, 2004.

2. Winston Manrique Sabogal, "Tríptico de la selva," *El Espectador*, April 27, 1994.

3. Marisol Gómez Giraldo and Glemis Mogollón, "Seducción, arma de guerra contra indígenas," *El Tiempo*, July 31, 1998.

4. Carl Henrik Langebaek, "En busca del Colombiano Perfecto: El mestizaje se convirtió en una forma de exclusión social que aún perdura," *Semana*, October 30, 2006.

5. In 1990 *The Economist* named Colombia one of the world's five most corrupt countries (Buenahora 1991, cited in Van Cott 2000:49).

6. Miguel Borja, "El Miedo al Indio," *El Espectador*, May 8, 2000.

7. Blanca Lucía Echeverry, no title, *El Tiempo*, February 12, 1998.

8. Sixto Alfredo Pinto, "Sangre Indígena Bajo dos Fuegos," *El Tiempo*, November 1, 1998; José Navia, "Indígenas, entre fuego cruzado," *El Tiempo*, February 4, 1996.

9. Bibiana Mercado, "'Estamos en el centro de una guerra': Indígenas," *El Tiempo*, November 21, 1993.

10. José Luis Valencia, "Indígenas prohibirán paso a actores armados," *El Tiempo*, May 16, 2001.

11. Victoria Neuta, member of the ONIC executive committee in charge of women's issues 2005–2007, personal communication, November 2006.

12. But see Adriana Espinel, "6 mujeres asumen como gobernadoras," *El Tiempo*, January 19, 2005.

13. Alvaro López Pardo, "No hay que ser 'Rambo' para recorrer el Amazonas," *El Espectador*, April 11, 1989.

14. Orlando Henríquez, "Barco traza bases para política amazónica," *El Espectador*, April 24, 1988. Also see Lucy Nieto de Samper, "Martín von Hildebrand, un Antropólogo Dedicado a los Derechos de la Comunidad Indígena," *El Tiempo*, December 7, 2005.

15. Henríquez, "Barco traza bases para política amazónica."
16. Henríquez, "Barco traza bases para política amazónica." Also see Edgar Cadena, "Colombia: Líder de la cuenca amazónica?" *El Tiempo*, May 15, 1988.
17. Edmer Tovar, "Barco y García cumplieron una función social con los indígenas," *El Tiempo*, April 26, 1988.
18. Cadena, "Colombia: Líder de la cuenca amazónica?" See also Luzdary Ayala, "La tierra no está perdida," *El Espectador*, September 25, 1994.
19. In November 2006 I was told by an official in Etnias that as of October 2006 the office had received 150 formal petitions for recognition and knew of 250 others being prepared.
20. Andrea Linares, "Proliferación de indígenas," *El Espectador*, March 28, 2001. Also see Chaves 2003, 2005, and in this volume; Ramírez 2002 and in this volume; Jackson 2007.
21. Linares, "Proliferación de indígenas."
22. Linares, "Proliferación de indígenas."
23. Regina Matta, "No me condenen, soy indígena," *El Tiempo*, August 15, 1999; "Y la malicia indígena?" *El Tiempo*, September 19, 2003.
24. "Renunció ayer el alcalde de Mitú," *El Tiempo*, September 22, 1994. Also see María Ximena Godoy, "Maximiliano Veloz, Un indígena educando a más indígenas," *El Tiempo*, June 3, 1988.
25. Edmer Tovar, "Nueva política indigenista anuncia Barco," *El Tiempo*, April 24, 1988.
26. Cadena, "Colombia: Líder de la cuenca amazónica?"
27. Henríquez, "Barco traza bases para política amazónica."
28. Gerardo Reyes, "Barco indígena," *El Tiempo*, October 6, 1988.
29. Manrique Sabogal, "Tríptico de la selva."
30. Marta Morales, "Desalojan etnia del jardín botánico," *El Espectador*, March 17, 1998.
31. Álvaro Serra, "La Amazonia, asediada," *El Tiempo*, November 23, 2003.
32. "Asesinan a siete indígenas coreguajes en Caquetá," *El Tiempo*, July 26, 1997; "Masacrados 13 indígenas," *El Espectador*, July 26, 1997; "A punto de acabarse la comunidad Koreguaje," *El Espectador*, August 12, 1997. Also see Jorge Cardona, "El etnocidio de koreguajes," *El Espectador*, August 17, 1997; "El exterminio Koreguaje," *El Espectador*, October 2, 1997.
33. "La paz de los indígenas," *El Tiempo*, July 31, 1998. Also see Mauro Salcedo, "Indígenas sionas denuncian su extinción en el Putumayo," *El Espectador*, March 2, 1998; Bibiana Mercado, "Indígenas Buscan Refugio Antiaéreo," *El Tiempo*, September 22, 1997; Espinosa 1998; Consultoría para los Derechos Humanos y el Desplazamiento 2003.
34. "Asesinan a siete indígenas coreguajes en Caquetá," *El Tiempo*, July 26, 1997. Also see Luís Esnal, "Farc recluta a indígenas," *El Tiempo*, May 1, 2003.

35. Patricia Fajardo, "Una indígena, mujer del Año Cafam 1990," *El Espectador*, March 8, 1990.
36. Fajardo, "Una indígena, mujer del Año Cafam 1990."
37. Sonia Perilla, "Una Nukak se 'roba' la pasarela," *El Tiempo*, May 16, 2003.
38. Mónica del Pilar, "La mujer indígena: Madre auténtica por tradición," *El Tiempo*, May 4, 1998.
39. Another negative depiction of Amazonian women comes from a surprising source: Susan Kellogg's *Weaving the Past: A History of Latin America's Indigenous Women from the Prehispanic Period to the Present*: "To the extent that lowland women can be said to have an image either inside or outside their own nation-states, misogyny shapes how they are perceived" (2005:142). Unfortunately Kellogg herself has such a negative assessment of lowland women's status that a close reading reveals substantial bias. She consulted me about Tukanoan women and I happily agreed. I regret that my scholarship played a role in producing so distorted an image.
40. Claudia Cano, "Dios, la fertilidad y el universo de las malocas indígenas," *El Espectador*, February 15, 1987.
41. See *Actualidad Etnica*, no. 206 (February 14, 2006) for a photograph of Jacanamijoy. Also see Laurent 2005:249–50.
42. Diana Alexandra Mendoza, "Entre Dios y el demonio: Los Nukak siguen su peregrinaje por plena selva," *El Tiempo*, June 28, 1994. Such treatment can also be found in English-language publications on the Nukak-Makú; see, for example, "Colombia: Nukak Tribe — 'We are being wiped out,'" *Survival*, May 18, 2006, www.survival-international.org. An article by Juan Forero contains such copious amounts of egregious othering that we must describe it as negative. Juan Forero, "Leaving the Wild, and Rather Liking the Change: Driven from Jungle, and the Stone Age, by Amazon Strife," *New York Times*, May 11, 2006.
43. See, for example, Matta, "La biopiratería, el último saqueo?" *El Tiempo*, October 6, 1997.
44. An oft-cited example is a fierce, deeply conflictive battle in 1998 involving Jesús Enrique Piñacué, a Nasa senator in the national congress; ASI (Alianza Social Indígena), an indigenous political party; and various Nasa communities and factions. Piñacué had agreed to and then disregarded ASI's instructions with respect to the upcoming presidential elections. The dispute was resolved with Piñacué receiving a traditional Nasa punishment that was satisfactory to all actors, at least according to press coverage. Further discussion is found in Laurent 2005:45; Jackson 2007.

References

Aguilera Peña, Mario. 2001. Justicia guerrillera y población civil, 1964–1999. In *El caleidoscopio de las justicias en Colombia: Análisis socio-jurídico*, vol. 2, ed.

Boaventura de Sousa Santos and Mauricio García Villegas, 389–422. Bogotá: Siglo del Hombre Editores.

Amnesty International. 2004. Scarred bodies, hidden crimes: Sexual violence against women in the armed conflict. Available at http://web.amnesty.org/ library/Index/ENGAMR230402004.

Arango, Raul, and Enrique Sánchez. 2004. *Los pueblos indígenas de Colombia: En el umbral del nuevo milenio.* Bogotá: Departamento Nacional de Planeación.

Assies, Willem. 2000. Indigenous peoples and reform of the state in Latin America. In *The challenge of diversity: Indigenous peoples and reform of the state in Latin America,* ed. Willem Assies, Gemma van der Haar, and André Hoekema, 3–22. Amsterdam: Thela Thesis.

Bamberger, Joan. 1974. The myth of matriarchy: Why men rule in primitive society. In *Woman, culture, and society,* ed. Michelle Z. Rosaldo and Louise Lamphere, 263–80. Stanford: Stanford University Press.

Blommaert, Jan, and Chris Bulcaen. 2000. Critical discourse analysis. *Annual Review of Anthropology* 29:447–66.

Buenahora, Jaime. 1991. *El proceso constituyente: De la propuesta estudiantil a la quiebra del bipartidismo.* Bogotá: Cámara de Representantes/Pontífica Universidad Javeriana.

Chaves, Margarita. 2003. Cabildos multiétnicos e identidades depuradas. In *Fronteras: Territorio y metáforas,* comp. Clara Inés García, 121–35. Medellíin: Hombre Nuevo Editores.

———. 2005. "¿Qué va a pasar con los indios cuando todos seamos indios?" Ethnic rights and reindianization in southwestern Colombian Amazonia. PhD diss., University of Illinois at Urbana-Champaign.

Consultoría para los Derechos Humanos y el Desplazamiento. 2003. *Destierros y desarraigos: Memorias del II Seminario Internacional; Desplazamiento: Implicaciones y retos para la gobernabilidad, la democracia y los derechos humanos.* Bogotá.

Espinosa, Myriam Amparo. 1998. Práctica social y emergencia armada en el Cauca. In *Modernidad, identidad y desarrollo: Construcción de sociedad y re-creación cultural en contextos de modernización,* ed. María Lucía Sotomayor, 111–30. Bogotá: Instituto Colombiano de Antropologia.

Faery, Rebecca Blevins. 1999. *Cartographies of desire: Captivity, race, and sex in the shaping of an American nation.* Norman: University of Oklahoma Press.

Gros, Christian. 2000. *Políticas de la etnicidad: Identidad, estado y modernidad.* Bogotá: Instituto Colombiano de Antropología e Historia.

Hale, Charles. 2006. *Más que un Indio / More than an Indian: Racial ambivalence and neoliberal multiculturalism in Guatemala.* Santa Fe NM: School of American Research Resident Scholar Book.

Hunt, Stacey. 2006. Languages of stateness: A study of space and el pueblo in the Colombian state. *Latin American Research Review* 41 (3): 88–121.

Jackson, Jean. 1991. Hostile encounters between Nukak and Tukanoans and changing ethnic identity in the Vaupés, Colombia. *Journal of Ethnic Studies* 19 (2): 17–39.

———. 2005. Colombia's indigenous peoples confront the armed conflict. In *Elusive peace: International, national, and local dimensions of conflict in Colombia*, ed. Cristina Rojas and Judy Meltzer, 185–208. New York: Palgrave/Macmillan.

———. 2007. Rights to indigenous culture in Colombia. In *The practice of human rights: Tracking law between the global and the local*, ed. Mark Goodale and Sally Engle Merry, 204–41. Cambridge: Cambridge University Press.

Jackson, Jean E., and María Clemencia Ramírez. 2009. Traditional, transnational and cosmopolitan: The Colombian Yanacona look to the past and to the future. *American Ethnologist* 36 (3): 521–44.

Jimeno Santoyo, Myriam. 1996. Pueblos indios, democracia y políticas estatales en Colombia. In *Democracia y estado multiétnico en América Latina*, ed. Pablo González and Marcos Roitman, 223–36. Mexico City: Centro de Investigaciones Interdisciplinarias en Ciencias y Humanidades UNAM/La Jornada.

Jimeno, Myriam, and Adolfo Triana. 1985. *Estado y minorías étnicas en Colombia*. Bogotá: Cuadernos del Jaguar and Fundación para las Comunidades Colombianas.

Kellogg, Susan. 2005. *Weaving the past: A history of Latin America's indigenous women from the prehispanic period to the present*. Oxford: Oxford University Press.

Laurent, Virginie. 2005. *Comunidades indígenas, espacios políticos y movilización electoral en Colombia, 1990–1998: Motivaciones, campos de acción e impactos*. Bogotá: Instituto Colombiano de Antropología e Historia, Instituto Francés de Estudios Andinos.

Lévi-Strauss, Claude. 1964. *Tristes tropiques: An anthropological study of primitive societies in Brazil*. Translated by John Russell. New York: Atheneum.

Meltzer, Judy, Cristina Rojas, and Alvaro Camacho. 2005. Introduction to *Elusive peace: International, national and local dimensions of conflict in Colombia*, ed. Cristina Rojas and Judy Meltzer, 1–18. New York: Palgrave Macmillan.

Murphy, Yolanda, and Robert F. Murphy. 2004. *Women of the forest*. New York: Columbia University Press.

Nagel, Joane. 2003. *Race, ethnicity, and sexuality: Intimate intersections, forbidden frontiers*. Oxford: Oxford University Press.

Organización Nacional Indígena de Colombia, Consejo Indígena de Paz. 2002. *Los indígenas y paz: Pronunciamientos, resoluciones, declaraciones y otros documentos de los pueblos y organizaciones indígenas sobre la violencia armada en sus territorios, la búsqueda de la paz, la autonomía y la resistencia*. Bogotá: ARFO Editores e Impresores and Ediciones Turdakke.

Pietikainen, S. 2003. Indigenous identity in print: Representations of the Sami in news discourse. *Discourse and Society* 14 (5): 581–609.

Raleigh, Sir Walter. 1997. *The discoverie of the large, rich, and bewtiful empyre of*

Guiana. Transcribed, annotated, and introduced by Neil L. Whitehead. Norman: University of Oklahoma Press.

Ramírez, María Clemencia. 2002. The politics of identity and cultural difference in the Colombian Amazon: Claiming indigenous rights in the Putumayo Region. In *The politics of ethnicity: Indigenous peoples in Latin American states,* ed. David Maybury-Lewis, 135–68. Cambridge MA: David Rockefeller Center, Harvard University.

Ramos, Alcida Rita. 1998. *Indigenism: Ethnic politics in Brazil.* Madison: University of Wisconsin Press.

Rangel, Alberto. 1920. *Inferno verde.* 3rd ed. Tours: Typ. E. Arrault.

Rappaport, Joanne. 2003. Innovative resistance in Cauca. *Cultural Survival Quarterly* 26 (4): 39–43.

———. 2005. *Intercultural utopias: Public intellectuals, cultural experimentation, and ethnic pluralism in Colombia.* Durham NC: Duke University Press.

Rivera, José Eustacio. [1924] 1987. *La vorágine.* 2nd ed. Bogotá: Editorial Oveja Negra, Ediciones Lerner Ltda.

———. 1935. *The vortex.* Translated by Earle K. James. New York: G. P. Putnam's Sons.

———. 1953. *La vorágine.* 3rd ed. Buenos Aires: Losada.

Rodríguez-Mangual, Edna M. 2004. *Lydia Cabrera and the construction of an Afro-Cuban identity.* Chapel Hill: University of North Carolina Press.

Roldán, Roque. 2007. El régimen constitucional indígena en Colombia: Fundamentos y perspectivas. In *Derecho indígena,* ed. Magdalena Gómez, 233–51. Mexico City: Instituto Indígena and United Nations.

Rubio, Mauricio. 1997. Perverse social capital: Some evidence from Colombia. *Journal of Economic Issues* 31 (3): 805–16.

Shi-Xu. 1997. Discursive ideologies: Rationalizing cultural violence. In *Political linguistics,* ed. Jan Blommaert and Chris Bulcaen, 217–30. Amsterdam: John Benjamins.

Slater, Candace. 2002. *Entangled Edens: Visions of the Amazon.* Berkeley: University of California Press.

Steverlynck, Astrid M. 2003. *Encounters with Amazons: Myth, gender and society in lowland South America.* PhD diss., University of Oxford.

Tiffany, Sharon W., and Kathleen J. Adams. 1985. *The wild woman: An inquiry into the anthropology of an idea.* Cambridge MA: Schenkman Publishing.

Ulloa, Astrid. 2005. *The ecological native: Indigenous peoples' movements and eco-governmentality in Colombia.* New York: Routledge.

Van Cott, Donna Lee. 2000. *The friendly liquidation of the past: The politics of diversity in Latin America.* Pittsburgh: University of Pittsburgh Press.

Wodak, Ruth. 2001. What CDA is about: A summary of its history, important concepts and its developments. In *Methods of critical discourse analysis,* ed. Ruth Wodak and Michael Meyer, 1–13. London: SAGE.

4. Cannibal Tourists and Savvy Savages
Understanding Amazonian Modernities
Neil L. Whitehead

The ideological construction of indigenous peoples as obstacles to "progress" in public discourse, the media, and anthropological writings has served to enable and encourage violence against them. From the initial charges of cannibalism made against Amazonian peoples in the sixteenth century, there has been a continuous external discourse on native Amazonian savagery and wildness, particularly as evidenced in their supposed Satanic proclivities (shamanism) and demonic customs (cannibalism). This discursive production of "natives" continues to create a broad cultural framework in which violence against indigenous persons can be more easily obscured or justified.

In the region of my own ethnographic fieldwork in the Caribbean and northeastern Amazonia, *kanaimà*, a form of native assault sorcery, has become widespread in the cultural imagination of both national and indigenous populations as a violent marker of both tradition and indigeneity. In turn *kanaimà* practice itself has become closely attuned to the violence of the development frontier and thus symbolically, as well as materially, directly engages with this external discourse on savagery and development (Whitehead 2002a). In a similar way the notion of cannibalism, a term whose linguistic and historical origins are the same as those for "Caribbean," is an important historical part of this discursive construction of "savages" and likewise has been used to separate out the "good Amerindians" from the "bad," or the cooperative from the resistant to colonial development.

The idea of development in Western discourse alludes to forms of both material and spiritual redemption and advancement and should be understood as part of the colonial and national conquest and incorporation of indigenous communities under the power of the state and government. Amazonia is thus seen as the end point of exploration, the counterpoint of modernity, and so the necessary context for development. Accordingly the language of conquest and occupation still suffuses the national imagining of this region, and *kanaimà* comes to stand for that alterity, just as cannibalism did in earlier times.

Such ideological constructions thus were part of the program of conquest, and the fact that such ideologies are still sometimes part of the way national states and international agencies construe their indigenous policies and aid programs makes contemporary Amazonia and the Caribbean a significant region for analyzing how such constructions are rooted in regional histories and actively deployed today. One particularly fertile field for such analysis is tourism, which has grown significantly in the Amazon in the past couple of decades and is a critical part of the economy for certain Caribbean islands, such as Dominica, where Carib populations are still living.

Tourism is a relatively new and burgeoning topic in anthropology because of the vast growth in leisure travel and continuing education in the past twenty years or so. Given the millions of people who vacation each year in distant, if not exotic locations, the cultural phenomena of holiday travel and tourism is, for this reason alone, worthy of serious anthropological analyses (for example, see Brennan 2004; Desmond 2001; Smith 1989; Vivanco and Gordon 2006).

In other societies we do see patterns of movement that seem to reflect similar urges. In Amazonia a couple might well decide to take off on a hunting or fishing trip that will last one or two weeks, not just because more food is needed or because it is the season for a particular fish or game animal, although this may also be the case. Instead they may leave because of tensions in the home village or household, boredom with the dull grind of everyday routine, or simply to seek some intimacy and privacy. In other words the "tourist" urge is to a degree universal, and the value of exotic knowledge more generally seems to undergird this social proclivity, although the nature of Western tourism has of course specific origins that give it special characteristics and consequences. Some have suggested that the holiday, or holy day, should be considered in the light of its religious origins, whereby an explicit withdrawal from the things of this world was the aim of the saints' days and feast days that made up the bulk of the these holy days.

Indeed the medieval world of Europe was, perhaps as it is today, very much in love with its holy days such that they occupied some forty to fifty days per year and put a real limit on the productivity of the medieval economy. The religious upheavals of the sixteenth and seventeenth centuries might well be viewed as involving a battle over the social place of sacred and profane time, that is, to what extent the needs of this world should be allowed to overwhelm our preparation for the next. The pilgrimage to a holy shrine was an important forerunner of the idea of uniting travel with a holy day, and while those pilgrimages remained largely local—within a few days travel—they had few consequences for relations between peoples and cultures.

Nonetheless much of the panoply of the modern resort vacation can be seen in the early pilgrims' progress; various badges and votive objects purchased at pilgrimage sites have their equivalent in the fridge magnets and bumper stickers of today. Indeed the economic boost given to the sites of such pilgrimages was so considerable that the whole racket of false relics and the purchase of indulgences might be likened to the hypercommercialism of any resort location.

However, in the case of foreign or exotic pilgrimage sites issues of access or control of such locations might take on a different character. In the case of Jerusalem, for example, exactly these issues were part of the rationale for the Crusades. Whatever else the Crusades may have signified they certainly brought together the ideas of holy pilgrimage, foreign travel, and cultural encounter in a new way. This is not to suggest that the Crusades were simply some holiday jaunt, but rather that the same impulses that bring modern tourists face-to-face with exotic places and their inhabitants have a cultural continuity with those mass migrations of both the rich and the poor that were first seen in the twelfth and thirteenth centuries.

In any case, it is obvious that exotic travel was known to the elites of classical antiquity, so it is not foreign travel itself that is the key to unraveling the antecedents of modern tourism. Rather, it is the mass nature of this experience and the expectation that it should somehow be uplifting as well as restorative of body and soul, quite literally "re-creation" (see also Badone and Roseman 2004).

With the global spread of European colonial empires the contexts for this kind of travel expanded rapidly, and European travel literature amply reflects this. In that literature we find thematically a combination of the moral discovery of self and others, the possibility for a redemption and restoration of basic cultural values, and the possibility for some profit, be it spiritual or material. Such themes link colonial discovery to modern tourism and those early crusading expeditions via this exploding encounter with the distant and the different that was the experience of even the meanest ship hand in the years after 1500. In this sense, therefore, the way those visited receive and understand their visitors is conditioned by these wider meanings involved in cultural contact. It is for these reasons also that not all tourism, however well designed or intentioned, is welcomed by those who endure its consequences.

Moreover, those consequences themselves are an endemic part of human experience because the tourism industry is set to become one of the single largest economic forces on the planet, grossing in excess of 856 billion dollars in 2007 (World Tourism Organization 2009, www.unwto.org/index.php). In which case anthropology has a duty, as well as an opportunity, to offer comment on and understanding of the relationships that tourism sets up and how they might be optimally managed.

The Columbian Tour

In this light we might even cast Columbus himself as the first tourist to the Americas and in order to contextualize the arguments and observations made by the authors in this volume. I first want to offer a very brief discussion of the long trajectory of tourism by considering those who were the first to endure the redemptive travels of the Europeans, the Carib peoples of the Antilles, especially on the island of Dominica, where I conducted research in 1999.[1]

To these contemporary Caribs it often seems that millions of tourists searching for the wild and exotic set out from their urban lairs intent on eating up the culture and landscape of the last wild places. All the while these tourists think that perhaps not only strange plants and animals still exist there but also some vestigial trace of wild people themselves, tokens of a lost age of tribal harmony with nature and the free expression of untutored human instinct.

Of course such wildness must also have a scary edge, so that encounters with biting insects, snakes, or tropical parasites are a welcomed element of real adventure, just as is encounter with the original "cannibals" of the Caribbean (Hulme 2001). So it is that the great cannibal canoe of the tourists, the cruise ship, pulls up alongside the Dominican capital of Roseau, dwarfing not just the other boats but even the buildings along the shore line and docks. From here the tourists come ashore in their hordes, eating, consuming, absorbing, and capturing culture, just as Columbus did five hundred years ago. But five hundred years later there can be no real return to that aboriginal encounter, for the savages have since become quite savvy in the ways of the colonizer, who has relinquished a permanent presence on the islands, returning in person only for a few days a year. It is a vacation colonialism, a holiday in hell (see also Patullo 2005).

The Caribs are the descendants of the native people who first encountered Columbus, and despite continuing predictions of their demise over the past five hundred years they still stubbornly survive as an independent community in the modern island state of Dominica (Hulme and Whitehead 1992). At the time of first contact the Caribs were a powerful trading people whose canoes plied the waters of the Caribbean and coastal South America. But from the outset it was their wild, fierce, and cannibalistic nature that dominated European representations. During the colonial period this preeminence in sea and river traffic assured them a significant place within the colonial cockpit of conflict that was the Caribbean. This also led to an infusion of escaped black slaves and the eventual emergence of the black Caribs. Issues of "blackness" and Carib authenticity are still very much alive today.

By the middle of the nineteenth century, although severely reduced in numbers, the Caribs still persisted on Dominica, Martinique, and St. Vincent, but the stabilization of colonial regimes throughout the region meant that their special niche as interisland traders was severely curtailed. In this context they relied increasingly on agriculture and fishing as means of participation in the national cash economy. By the advent of the twentieth century their socioeconomic position was indistinguishable from that of the freed black slaves, who were their main economic competitors in the wage labor economy. However, their continuing cultural autonomy and economic exclusion led to a tradition of smuggling between Martinique and Dominica and also to their initial entry into the tourist market through the production of basketry.

Since independence from the former colonial power, Britain, in 1978 the economy of Dominica, as in other Windward islands, has been based on agricultural export, principally bananas, and tourism. However, as part of the independence package Dominica retained a special economic relationship with Britain that allowed the sale of bananas at well above the world market price. Following Britain's membership in the European Economic Community and pressure from the United States following passage of the North American Free Trade Agreement, that relationship was progressively phased out, and Dominican bananas are now sold at world market prices. The consequences of this for the island's economy as a whole have not been favorable, although the implementation of the post-NAFTA agreements between the United Kingdom and the United States proceed at a Caribbean pace.

For the Caribs in particular, who were heavily engaged as small-scale producers of banana crops, the effects have been potentially ruinous. Added to this change in external markets has been the physical destruction of the extremely powerful hurricanes of 1993 and 1995. It is very evident that the Caribs are facing these deep economic changes with little planning as to how the loss of this market will be offset by new kinds of economic activity. Among the projects planned are the production of aloe for cosmetics, investigation of the viability of producing for the "rainforest products" market (following the example of the Brazilian Kayapó and the Body Shop), and the possibility of marketing cultural heritage as eco- or ethnotourism. It is these initiatives that I am studying in my current research project. Such initiatives are certainly consonant with the development plans of the Dominican government itself, which has pushed hard to get Dominica into the club of Caribbean islands that host the huge tourist market. It is in this context that the Caribs are now deploying their cultural and historical heritage to ameliorate and improve their situation within the island's economy as a whole.

This marketing of cultural heritage in turn has fed debate on the nature of that heritage, particularly over who best exemplifies it. That idea of Carib purity has begun to be mentioned especially when such claims are also being used to negotiate between competing kin groups within the reserve lands of Salybia itself for leadership of the Carib Council. The Carib Council is the administrative body that oversees the territory. It is constituted in the same way as the rest of local government in Dominica and decides on land and resource issues, such as the use of reservation lands.

The suggestion is that the external marketing of their cultural and historical heritage rebounds on the internal politics of the Carib territory in unforeseen ways. The selling of culture thus takes a number of forms. First, culture is sold through the notion that the Caribs as aboriginal and "natural" occupiers of the island are perforce also "guardians" of its wildlife.[2] Second, culture is sold through the use of their savage, even cannibal image to promote the authenticity of their handicrafts in basketry and wood carving. Third, as savvy savages par excellence, there is a clear appreciation of the utility of a projection of themselves as viable and worthwhile recipients of external aid. Carib leaders are perfectly aware of the meaning that their culture can have to outsiders.

Contacts in the 1970s with the American Indian Movement in particular have meant that Carib political and social consciousness is far more akin to the activism found in the United States than the kinds of attitudes among Amazonian peoples. In the latter case the Save the Children Fund was persuaded to build a community center and small cultural resource center in the form of a traditional longhouse (*carbet*), though it was swept away in the 1995 hurricane. To add to the attractions of the territory a plan is currently under way to build a model village—that is, a re-creation of a traditional Carib village—and to populate it with twenty Carib couples "of pure blood."

Needless to say this intrusion of eugenic theory into debates on the territory are extremely unwelcome and a very good example of the negative impacts that responsiveness to outsiders brings with it. This issue also arises out of political traditions stemming from the earliest colonial times, when escaped slaves were absorbed into Carib society and culture. The colonial authorities at the end of the eighteenth century used these contrasts to defeat and expel large numbers of hostile Caribs, and that legacy is now played out in an effort to purify the territory so that the tourists will want to come. It is firmly believed that black Caribs do not sufficiently conform to the touristic ideal of the Indian and so should be hidden away, erased from the culture and history of the Caribs.

In less explosive ways the marketing of an authentic and pure Carib culture is implicit in the whole handicraft market. The central problem for craft producers is to try to anticipate the icons and symbols of indigeneity as they appear to the cannibal tourist, for if tourists will not buy the trinkets the effort will have been in vain. This leads not to a conflict between Carib producers over the ability of black Caribs to express Carib culture, but uncertainty over what should be the forms of craft production. Caribana Crafts is one outlet for producers in Roseau that seeks to ensure a relationship among producers, sellers, and consumers that highlights the cultural potential of craft production.

As ever, though, cannibal tourists are always on the search for the bargain and the "good deal meal," and so these aims are apt to be undermined by the economics of souvenir selling: location, price, and predictability. Carib crafts have few outlets in the capital, tend to be more expensive than the generics of key rings, bottle openers, and fridge magnets, and are not uniform in a way that is attractive to wholesale buyers. Such questions are by no means new; Caribs have produced handicrafts for tourists since the 1920s. What is new is the scale of potential markets and the lack of other viable economic alternatives at this time.

In sum, there can be little doubt that the need to develop viable economic alternatives to small-scale agricultural production dominates the immediate future of the Caribs. This is not to suggest that the matter of cultural survival and recuperation are not in themselves important projects. However, it is the conflicting pressure of commercialization and a search for authenticity that necessarily bedevil such exercises, and in this way the abstract cultural and historical claims people make can become material forces in the process of socioeconomic development. One might add that development, although often inimical to cultural autonomy and survival, is sometimes a precondition for the "primitive."

Amazonian Modernity

The chapters in this volume are particularly engaged with the peoples of Amazonia, and here tourism is a more recent phenomenon and indeed is often predicated on the idea that Amazonia itself is functionally untraveled or untouched. Of course the history of Western colonialism throughout the region belies this, although the image of a pristine, essentially still ancient Amazon has proved no less attractive to anthropologists than it has to tourists (Whitehead 2002c).

Anthropological fieldwork as a cultural phenomenon is imperfectly separated from the broader impulse to tourism, which, even in the Amazon, certainly predates professional anthropological fieldwork. When one considers the long list of self-styled travelers, explorers, and adventurers who have made this region their destination it becomes very evident that there is a guiding cultural metaphor of untouched primitiveness that has overhung all accounts of the Amazon since the first description of Orellana's descent of the river in 1540–41.

In this context the chapters gathered here pick up on a number of the themes discussed earlier in a highly illuminating way, as well as vastly increasing our appreciation of the complexity of issues involved. As Hutchins shows, indigenous communities are not simply "sucked naïvely into globalization, nor are they hurled back out as residue," rightly also referencing Sahlins's (1999:xvi) stress on the way the "experience" of capitalism is interpreted through "the schemata of a different cultural universe." Hutchins's chapter focuses on the production of culture as tourism commodity but importantly emphasizes that, for the Kichwa, this does not entail some wholesale dissolution of cultural autonomy. As in the case of the Caribs it undoubtedly poses a series of sharp questions for community leaders and most certainly entails unforeseen consequences since capitalist relations are not merely economic but necessarily affect the social relationships and ideological categories that guide them. In historical perspective, if not lifetime experience, there most certainly is "a general withering away of diverse possibilities for belonging in the world," but not necessarily a reduction in the rate at which new possibilities also open up. Uzendoski's chapter clearly shows this occurring in the case of "Techno-Kichwa," a form of Napo Runa music called Runa Paju. As Hutchins also argues, to some extent consciousness of precisely this process is a way of negotiating the episodic impacts of global capital, as has been the case for the Caribs since 1500.

Hutchins's field site of the provincial capital of Tena, Ecuador, has also long been a place of economic and cultural exchange, and while the modern scale of ecotourism represents an "intense market incursion" into participating communities, it also provides possibilities for participating in that market that may well serve as a vehicle to realize some existing wants and desires. But whatever the future trajectory, the inevitability of change is as present as it always has been, and the functionalist assumption of tradition = stability and modernity = instability has been superseded by a much clearer perception of the historicity of Amazonian peoples, as in Hutchins's chapter.

Moreover such a version of globalization as simply and always antithetical to the "traditional" is too simplistic and linear. There are histories outside the history of capitalist forms that continue to influence subjectivities and frame responses to the demands of the national state and global markets. Acknowledging these influences helps us understand how, according to Sahlins, "the world is also being re-diversified by indigenous adaptations to the global juggernaut" (1999:ix).

Hutchins perceptively connects this pluralization of the experience of capitalism and globalization to recent theoretical innovations with regard to the relationship between Marxist notions of the historical in Western cultural traditions and the recognition of the presence of historicity among non-Western societies, often in forms that are culturally opaque to observers searching for linear narrative and chronology- and text-based memory. Clearly also these forms of history address different issues and entail different notions of meaningful action and agency. In confrontation with the intrusion of powerful economic forces such alternative histories become a source of sustained autonomy, a collective experience that serves to sustain the lifeways of cultural minorities even in the face of the "global juggernaut." In the words of one Amerindian, "The white disturbs things because we have a plan, he arrives with another plan. So we drop our own plans and follow the thinking of the whites" (quoted in Whitehead 2002a:207). Hutchins also references Hannerz's work from the early 1990s to provide a framework in which the effects of this process might be analyzed. This allows Hutchins to outline "a story of socioeconomic hybridization . . . where . . . a 'global force' arrives via complex circuitry, [and] is refitted by particular histories and perspective."

In characterizing the way the global flows of information, commodities, and human labor appear to local actors, the notion of "fractal" relationships used by Uzendoski to describe just this experience of global capitalism through tourist markets seems very appropriate. The suggestion that fractal relationships are typical of Amazonian ideas of subjectivity and sociality offers another approach to interpreting cultural practice in the face of intensifying market penetration. Deriving from an established approach to the constitution of self and other in the literature of the past decade, Uzendoski avoids falsely opposing locality and globality, since people are embedded in myriad relationships with both the local and the global. This also reveals how the category of "indigenous" is inadequate to the realities of modern Amazonia, a point that emerges strongly from the more recent studies of *caboclos* and other *ribereños* (river people), whose complex cultural and historical heritage marks them as both indigenous and nonindigenous in a way that suggests the opposition of the categories is a real hindrance to better anthropological interpretation and ethnographic engagement. In this context Uzendoski's discussion of the case of Walter, who considers himself an Amazonian and easily moves between native and nonnative aspects of life, working for the military and living in an urban neighborhood, is exemplary of these processes. For these reasons, whatever the day-to-day relationships that are practiced in such contexts they also have a meaning for the wider national societies of the region.

Jean Jackson investigates the ways journalists working for Colombian media construct the differences between indigenous Amazonians and the country's nonindigenous citizens. Perhaps somewhat counterintuitively the prevalence of negative imagery is far less than might be expected, although the alterity of the indigenous is certainly emphasized, being part of its discursive power within the system of national self-imagining. Jackson focuses on three particular arenas where imagery of the indigenous has particular force: environmentalism, violence, and gender. Certainly the whole thrust of ecotourism relates to this identification of the indigenous with positive environmental values; more surprising is the way the indigenous is also seen as a counterpoint to the virulence of violence in Colombian self-understanding and as a source of more cohesive and even pacific values. Depictions of indigenous women in the two newspapers Jackson tracked were "orientalizing and naturalizing." At the same time a number of more generally familiar tropes of the "primitive," "infantile," and "natural" are regularly associated with the indigenous, but also positive values such as respect for elders, the capacity for "authentic" spirituality, and the possession of occult knowledge.

This kind of generalized imagery of "natives" can be traced right back to the initial encounters of the sixteenth century and through time have become deeply embedded in external cultural readings of the people of Amazonia. Such cultural readings in turn provide the backdrop against which the tractability of various native societies is evaluated, with regard to not only categories of mass cultural representation but also the policies of both the national government and international development agencies. For this reason such imagery is also deployed to discriminate the "good" from the "bad" indigene, creating (what I have termed elsewhere) a "demonology of development" (Whitehead 2002b).

A Demonology of Development in Amazonia

In Amazonia successive waves of spiritual and material development have pounded native communities, leading to the continuous ideological construction of indigenous peoples as obstacles to "progress." This is signaled by key cultural practices that have allowed the governmental regimes to separate out the "good" and the "bad" Amerindian. In Amazonia this has proceeded along a number of axes which all reference spiritual and ritual forms of action as ciphers for the political opposition that different native groups have showed toward these plans for their redemption and development.

Most notorious of these was a dualistic ethnic typology, originated in the Columbian tour, of "good" Arawaks and "bad" Caribs. However, this distinction became widespread across the region and in time a component of Amerindian identity itself. Colonial policy also enshrined this scheme in legal statutes, allowing plunder and enslavement of those populations considered Carib. Arawak populations, both through selective alliance and the involvement of key Lokono clan leaders, were then understood as basically tractable. Given a system of raiding and warfare between key Carib and Arawak populations, such as the Karinya and the Lokono, Arawaks were also considered to be self-interested, and so dependable, in their European alliances.

As missionaries began systematic evangelization in the seventeenth century along the Orinoco, this ready-made distinction became self-fulfilling because opposition to the missionaries was defined as Carib. In this way the Arawak, who accepted evangelization, were again seen as favorable to colonial development. But this distinction was, and still is, based on more than these competing representations of

Amerindian tractability and intractability, and refers also to spatial location and ritual proclivity. Consistent with the demonic nature of the colonial imagination of the space of Amazonia, the Caribs are pictured as interior bush-dwellers exemplifying the secretive, dangerous, and violent nature of the dark heart of the region. In contrast, the Arawaks, coastal dwellers and even urbanites, signal the possibility of indigenous redemption, reform, and development. These competing tropes of the indigenous can then be made to fit varying political and ethnic circumstances, using linguistics to bolster the idea of a fundamental difference in the cultural ontologies of Arawaks and Caribs.

The cultural production of cannibals thus served economic and political interests, given the legal provisions that allowed special violence against them. It is also a central issue for anthropological interpretation, since this is the original anthropological question. As a result the literary and ethnological production of the cannibal has gone hand in hand with the military and political domination of the native population in this region of South America. The violence of conquest in the region mimetically referenced cannibalism as its justification, and representations of the native population suppressed descriptions of Arawak torture and cannibalism, emphasizing only the barbarity of the Carib.

By the end of the eighteenth century, however, the figure of the cannibal had begun to fade away into that mist of nostalgia and remorse for the premodern. The conquest and control of native societies had led to the virtual extermination of most autonomous native polities, leaving only relatively isolated remnants in the deep interior and the emergent neoteric groups grounded in the social and cultural relations of the colonial world. As a result the violence and barbarity of the intractable Indian became occluded and hidden, a matter of inner orientation and belief, no longer an aspect of public culture. Thus, with the suppression of native warfare, and the loss of autonomy that implied, the uncontrolled and unknowable realm of spiritual and mystical assault emerges as the site of demonization.

Whereas before the warrior or cannibal-killer was the object of colonial nightmare, in the new world of nineteenth-century progress the infrastructure of native autonomy was absent, and so the mimesis of conquest became the skulking assassin, the vengeful and lone killer. In the demon landscape of Amazonia the prominence given to the shamanic practices in the colonial literature, as with *kanaimà*, also begins at this precise moment. But indigenous people are no less aware of the potential for a loss of tradition, a distinct way of "being Amerindian," which, paradoxically perhaps, the ritual skills of the *kanaimà* or *piya* (death or resurrection) best express. And so, in the face of modernity, *kanaimà* becomes a potent symbol of continuity with the past.

The experience of development and modernity in native Amazonia has largely been in terms of the spread of governmentality, the state apparatus by which we are all rendered citizens (Foucault 1991). However, despite Amazonians' being repeatedly surveyed, classified, and converted, the systems of law, education, sanitation, and economy, which were supposed to bring the Patamuna the fruits of development and progress, have failed to materialize.

As in other colonial and postcolonial contexts, industrial capital and Western democracy have appeared wearing the costumes and masks of evangelical redemption, medical services, schooling, economic development, and democratic rights—the full regalia of modernity, as it were. For the peoples of Amazonia, the experiences of such successive modernities have been highly episodic and fleeting, a series of one-night shows, short runs, and rapidly folding productions. Nonetheless the fact that the theater of development has been trying to establish itself over the past five centuries means that indigenous conceptions of the traditional and the modern are more complex and sophisticated than a simple opposition of, say, feathers and loincloths to trousers and shirts.

In these ways scientific tropes of evolution, literary and lyrical metaphors of wildness, and the anthropological categories of culture and society have eased the assaults of development by providing an intellectual framework for the comprehension and control of the native. This program is then made manifest in the policies of development, such as tourism, which become a material realization of this imagery of indigeneity. Development, whether or not it is driven by the "global juggernaut" of tourism, is not just about an end to the primitive and savage, but is necessarily also part of the violence of development and progress to be ended.

Notes

1. My project among the Caribs (Karipuna) of Dominica had a twin set of goals: to evaluate how the nature of cultural and historical claims by the Caribs changes and evolves under the lure of tourism, and to be an active program of the application of anthropological understanding, an exchange between extraneous and indigenous knowledge systems, between cannibal tourists and savvy savages, since the position of the ethnographer is not so far distant from that of the intelligent tourist.

2. This same canard is often found in ecotourist literature and represents a confusion of the idea of a systematic *indigenous knowledge* with the presumption that such knowledge must always be of a certain form that enjoins some kind of nonintensive, sustainable ecological practice.

References

Badone, Ellen, and Sharon R. Roseman, eds. 2004. *Intersecting journeys: The anthropology of pilgrimage and tourism.* Urbana: University of Illinois Press.

Brennan, Denise. 2004. *What's love got to do with it? Transnational desires and sex tourism in the Dominican Republic.* Durham NC: Duke University Press.

Desmond, Jane C. 2001. *Staging tourism: Bodies on display from Waikiki to Sea World.* Chicago: University of Chicago Press.

Foucault, Michel. 1991. *The Foucault effect: Studies in governmentality.* Chicago: University of Chicago Press.

Hulme, Peter. 2001. *Remnants of conquest: The Island Caribs and their visitors, 1877–1998.* Oxford: Oxford University Press.

Hulme, Peter, and Neil L. Whitehead. 1992. *Wild majesty: Encounters with Caribs from Columbus to the present day. An anthology.* Oxford: Oxford University Press.

Patullo, Polly. 2005. *Last resorts: The cost of tourism in the Caribbean.* 2nd ed. London: Monthly Review Press.

Sahlins, Marshall. 1999. What is anthropological enlightenment? Some lessons of the twentieth century. *Annual Review of Anthropology* 28 (1): i–xxiii.

Smith, Valene L., ed. 1989. *Hosts and guests: The anthropology of tourism.* Philadelphia: University of Pennsylvania Press.

Vivanco, Luis, and Robert Gordon, eds. 2006. *Tarzan was an eco-tourist … and other tales in the anthropology of adventure.* New York: Berghahn Books.

Whitehead, Neil L. 2002a. *Dark shamans: Kanaimà and the poetics of violent death.* Durham NC: Duke University Press.

———. 2002b. Magical modernities and occult violence in South America. In *Violence, globalisation and localisation,* ed. M. Bax et al., 33–51. Amsterdam: Free University Press.

———. 2002c. South America / The Amazon: The forest of marvels. In *The Cambridge companion to travel writing,* ed. Peter Hulme and Tim Youngs, 122–38. Cambridge: Cambridge University Press.

Part 2

Ethnopolitics, Territory, and Notions of Community

5. For Love or Money?

Indigenous Materialism and Humanitarian Agendas

Beth A. Conklin

The uneasy tension between friendship and material giving is an uncomfortable aspect of personal relations between native Amazonians and non-Indians who are sympathetic to indigenous people and causes. Do they like me, or do they just like what I can give them? is a recurring question for many of the aid workers, teachers, health personnel, anthropologists, activists, and others who approach native communities hoping not only to do some good, but also to make some deeper interpersonal, intercultural connection. Real friendships do develop. But even in close relationships there often are disconcerting moments when indigenous individuals seem to treat their non-Indian friends and associates as if they were valued mostly as a source of goods or money.

The British rock singer Sting is hardly typical of the outsiders with whom native Amazonians usually interact. But many of us who have lived or worked in native communities probably can identify with some of the frustration he expressed when his relations with the Kayapó of central Brazil hit a rough spot. Sting's involvement with the Kayapó began on a visit to the Xingu National Park in 1987, with a heady rush of personal experience with native village life, encounters that felt genuine, direct, and intimate. "It didn't take long for the varnish of civilization to leave us," he exulted at a press conference following his first visit. "After 48 hours, we were naked, covered in paint, and fighting snakes."

Sting began to use his celebrity to call attention to Kayapó land rights issues and the links between indigenous survival, rainforest protection, and the future of the global environment. In 1989 the Kayapó chief Rop ni (a.k.a. Raoni) accompanied him on a concert and fund-raising tour during which they met with world leaders, including President Jose Sarney of Brazil, President François Mitterand of France, and Pope John Paul II. The combination of rock star charisma and Rop ni's dramatic lip disk and feathered headdress guaranteed media attention and opened doors of power and pockets of funding. Sting's Rainforest Foundation, for which Rop ni served as honorary president, channeled funds and concert proceeds to help demarcate new boundaries for Kayapó reservations (Hemming 2003:275–76). The collaboration between Sting and the Kayapó seemed to embody the era's best hopes for productive new partnerships between conservationists and indigenous peoples (Conklin and Graham 1995).

By 1993 relations had soured. "They [the Indians] are always trying to deceive you," Sting complained to a journalist. "They see the white man only as a good source of earning money, and then as a friend." Rop ni was equally dismissive. "The Brazilian Indians do not need Sting," he said. "It would be better if we forgot him."[1]

Much can be said about the specific, in many ways unique circumstances of the Kayapó and the alliances they have forged with non-Indian supporters since the 1980s (cf. Fisher 2000; Turner 1993, 1995). The Rainforest Foundation continued to support the cause of Kayapó land rights, eventually contributing 1.3 million dollars to demarcate the Menkragnoti Indian Area (Hemming 2003:376). But the sense of disillusionment Sting expressed is a recurring dynamic in relations between native Amazonians and non-Indians who want to help or befriend them. Sting's desire to be seen *first as a friend* was, he felt, betrayed when Indian friends seemed to treat him *first as a source of money.*

Almost every non-Indian professional I know who has worked closely with native people has personal experiences that resonate with this sense of betrayal. Over the years that I have worked with the Wari', a group of native people in western Brazil, I have squirmed uncomfortably on numerous occasions at hearing a close friend introduce me to other Wari' by recounting our material history. Invariably my friends launch into a blow-by-blow recitation of consumer goods I have given them: "Her name is Beth. She brought us batteries, ammunition, fishhooks, fishing line," and so on. This has happened so many times that I have come to recognize it as a standard form of introduction. Still it bothers me. Why, I wonder, am I reduced to a list of commodities? What about my winning personality? What about all the time we've spent talking, laughing, working, joking together, confiding, feeding each other, caring for each other when we were sick? Flashlights and fishhooks mean more than friendship?

Why do Wari' do this, and why does it bother me? My hurt and disappointment contrast blatantly with the apparent glee Wari' take in emphasizing my role as a provider of goods. Though the circumstances in such incidents are personal and idiosyncratic, the pervasiveness of tensions around the balance between affective and material aspects of outsiders' relations with native people suggests something deeper is at stake. And the clashing expectations that Indians and non-Indians bring to their relations with each other play out not only in personal terms, but also in more public and political contexts, when Westerners expect "genuine" indigenous people to be disinterested in consumer commodities and moneymaking. The issues surrounding the differences in the meanings that indigenous and nonindigenous people associate with material transactions involving money and commodities are one facet of the tension at the heart of this volume: the disjuncture between tropical Edens of the imagination and the real-world Amazonia of flesh-and-blood people "editing" their lives with creative, flexible responses to cope with changing historical circumstances.

Eden was not a cash economy; money and merchandise came after the Fall. Those who cherish fantasies of natives flourishing in prelapsarian innocence, indifferent to the things that money can buy, inevitably are disappointed to meet real Amazonian Indians who dress in jeans and T-shirts, watch DVDs, and drink Coca-Cola (cf. Fiorini and Bail 2006). If that disappointment leads outsiders who are sympathetic to native cultures to categorize certain individuals or groups as "degraded," "acculturated," "corrupted," or "inauthentic," this negative stereotyping can have pernicious effects. At a minimum it blocks the understanding and cross-cultural communication on which effective support for indigenous rights needs to be based. More seriously judgments about authenticity have concrete political and economic consequences. In his chapter in this volume Patrick Wilson shows how conflicts between the views of NGOs and the views of local native communities regarding money, resources, and development projects influence which native leaders are considered legitimate and which groups do or do not receive NGO assistance.

In the dominant Western narrative of capitalist expansion into formerly nonmarket economies, there are only two story lines for indigenous cultures to follow: the well-trod narrative of alienation, cultural loss, corruption, and victimization, or a heroic narrative of rejection and resistance to capitalist domination. Yet as nearly every chapter in this volume shows, the paths forged by native Amazonians have been far more complex and heterogeneous. The historical paths forged by contemporary native peoples are seldom reducible to either/or visions of loss and corruption versus nobly pure resistance.

One key to developing more helpful and realistic understandings is the perspective emphasized in Frank Hutchins's chapter on ecotourism: to recognize that commodified encounters need to be viewed not only through a Western, capitalist gaze, but also through lowland Kichwa cultural lenses that may assign very different meanings to these encounters. This builds on Marshall Sahlins's point that there are numerous "cosmologies of capitalism," not just a single, relentlessly commodifying global process. Hutchins's case study and Wilson's chapter on NGOs and indigenous organizations in Ecuador's Napo region illustrate how irrelevant a simple capitalist/noncapitalist dichotomy is to describe the nuanced, culturally mediated ways that native groups interpret and transform consumer goods and "capitalist" economic relations.

In this chapter I explore the indigenous side of these dynamics and discourses around money and materialism in encounters between native people and outsiders who can offer assistance, highlighting conflicting cultural notions and historical experiences related to consumer goods in native societies. Of primary concern are the role of tangible exchange in affective relations (friendship, solidarity) and indigenous perceptions of the meaning of giving by humanitarian-minded outsiders.

"Real Indians Must Be Pure and Poor"

Since the earliest years of the European invasion of the New World, commodities have played a central role in non-Indians' relations with native peoples and in their evaluations of the worth of native cultures. On one hand European colonizers and their descendants have equated the material culture of the West with progress and treated native peoples' rejection or acceptance of specific commodities (such as clothing or salt) as a measure of their degree of savagery or civilization. The goal of spreading money and commercial goods has been part of many agendas for "improving" Indians by extending to them the benefits of Christianity, colonialism, or capitalism. Stephen Hugh-Jones notes that in Brazil's northwest Amazon, "each mission combines church with store, and even the cocaine dealers claim a civilizing mission as they barter coca leaves for Coca-Cola" (1992:42).

The flip side of this equation of commercial goods with acculturation and the negation of "savagery" is the long-running Western romance with images of pure, uncontaminated indigenous life. In the introduction to this volume Hutchins and Wilson note that in the past, anthropological research in Amazonia and other "peripheral" world regions often treated capitalism as a foreign, Western phenomenon, a modern intrusion into the timeless world of a tribal existence innocent of obsessions with material acquisition. To critics of Western culture, consumerism, and capitalist relations, the idea of a materially simple native way of life has enormous appeal. As Daniel Miller (1995:144) notes, this is a familiar symbolic dichotomy that has long structured many anthropological as well as popular representations of the Western "us" and the non-Western "them": the equation of capitalist society with asocial materialism, in contrast to a deeply social, nonmaterialistic indigenous value system.

Westerners sympathetic to indigenous cultural difference have a long history of seeing in native societies the virtues of nonacquisitiveness, egalitarian sharing, and the warmth of direct, unhurried human connections that contrast starkly (and appealingly) with the egocentric individualism, competitiveness, and cold impersonality of capitalist relations. As Hutchins and Wilson note in their introduction to this volume, "Indigenous peoples become moral foils for the malaise of modernity and the ills of Western society." Small-scale tribal societies in particular tend to be credited with amaterialism or even antimaterialism.

When the absence of commercial goods and commodity relations is taken as a sign of indigenous cultural purity and virtue, the use of Western goods becomes a ready symbol for cultural corruption and the loss of authentic, distinct, exotic indigenous identity (Conklin 1997). Hugh-Jones (1992:42) traces this theme in intellectuals' writings disparaging indigenous peoples' desires for Western goods from Jean-Jacques Rousseau's *Second Discourse on Inequality* to twentieth-century anthropologists' lamentations about the pitiful or injurious effects of Western commodity desire on indigenous communities. This oppositional construct that equates indigenous authenticity with lack of Western goods lives on in contemporary public attitudes. In this deeply entrenched Western symbolic construct, native individuals who participate in consumer culture and moneymaking become easy targets for criticism, cynicism, and allegations of illegitimacy. As Alcida Ramos comments, Kayapó leaders' economic success "offended those people for whom *real Indians must be pure and poor*" (2001:14, emphasis added).

Popular notions that equate authentic indigeneity with purity and poverty acquired fresh force in the cultural politics of the 1990s, when indigenous people emerged as global icons of anticapitalist resistance. Throughout the world local struggles for land and control over natural resources historically have pitted native communities against corporate mining and logging interests and state policies favoring nonnative economic interests. This oppositional indigenous positioning acquired new voice and visibility in 1994, when the Zapatista movement in Chiapas, Mexico, burst onto the headlines with militant Maya protests against the North American Free Trade Agreement. The Zapatistas' brilliantly poetic communiqués and media savvy made them an inspirational magnet for left-of-center solidarity. Their articulate critiques of neoliberal policies reinforced popular expectations for Indians to be critics of capitalism.

As many scholars have noted, indigenous people who fail to live up to outsiders' expectations tend to be devalued and dismissed as inauthentic and illegitimate (cf. Conklin 1997; Jackson 1995; Ramos 1994, 1998). The categories organizing expectations are numerous and salient. As Jean Jackson's (this volume) case study of Colombian media images shows, "traditional" clothing and body decorations or, better yet, nudity are widely treated as the most visible symbol of "real" Indianness (Conklin 1997). The nearly naked Nukak-Makú foragers, Jackson notes wryly, "would win any 'authentic traditional Indian' contest hands down."

Ecologically oriented criteria that define indigenous identity through ties to land and ancestral territories are another salient symbolic construct that can work against the interests of legitimate indigenous people. In her chapter in this volume Margarita Chaves shows how this emphasis de-legitimizes the identity claims of native people who have been displaced from their homelands by war, poverty, and migration. Lacking a geographic base, they may be "de-Indianized" according to state definitions of indigenous status and denied the material benefits and respect accorded groups that assert territorial claims. Assumptions about territorially based indigeneity also conflict with the deep cultural orientation to mobility and migration among native Amazonians such as the Guarani, who for centuries have moved across the South American landscape in search of the mythic Land without Evil.

Along with expectations that genuine Amazonian Indians should look exotic and be rooted in the land, outsiders also commonly measure native authenticity by distance from consumer culture. Hugh-Jones (1992) observes that those who expect indigenous people to be icons of spirituality uncorrupted by commodity desire are often unpleasantly shocked to discover that many native Amazonians seem to have an obsession with Western consumer goods and how to get them.

In the past anthropologists tended to treat native concerns with commodities as evidence of acculturation, corruption, and loss of tradition (Miller 1995:144–46). Recently ethnographers such as William Fisher (2000) have begun to grapple with more nuanced questions about the meanings and roles of commercial goods within contemporary indigenous societies. Fisher's study of the Xikrin Kayapó emphasizes how commodities fit into indigenous sociality and reinforce internal relationships and cohesion within Kayapó society. As in many other Amazonian societies, Kayapó leaders' legitimacy is tied to their ability to obtain material goods for their communities.

Wilson's chapter explores the double bind that indigenous leaders confront in dealing with NGOs that fund development projects for local communities. Native leaders who use and distribute NGO resources in accord with NGO policies are considered incompetent by their indigenous constituents, and they lose their leadership positions. Yet when leaders deploy NGO resources in accord with indigenous cultural principles the NGOs interpret this as nepotism, corruption, and financial mismanagement. To get past this plethora of intercultural double binds, Hugh-Jones emphasizes that we need to "disentangle our own views as to whether or not Indians *should* want consumer goods, from an understanding of why they *do* want them" (1992:70). The need to engage with the market economy is a fact of life for the vast majority of indigenous people in Amazonia today. Loss of land and resources to non-Indians, the introduction of cosmopolitan infectious diseases, and other environmental, social, and political changes make it impossible for most native people to live in a strictly "traditional" manner. In addition, in Brazil since the 1970s there has been a demographic upturn in many (though certainly not all) native communities as a result of better access to Western medical care and other factors (McSweeney 2005). With population growth, greater literacy, and more participation in regional and national politics since 1988, when the new Constitution made indigenous people Brazilian citizens, have come shifts in indigenous activism. Ramos observes that whereas the 1970s and 1980s were a "charismatic era" in which native activists "focused on calls for legitimacy of their ethnic otherness," in the 1990s the focus shifted to development projects oriented to resource management and increased involvement in the market economy (2001:15). For most contemporary native communities some of the biggest challenges are to generate income, market their commodities, and find jobs in order to have access to the medical care, education, goods, technologies, and other things they need to operate effectively as citizens of the nation-state and defenders of their own rights and livelihoods. Hugh-Jones cautions:

The tendency to blame Indian "consumerism" on outside pressures, to dwell upon the more "traditional" aspects of Amerindian exchange, to draw sharp and sometimes morally loaded lines between two economies signalled by "gift" and "commodity," and to underplay the Indians' active involvement in trade with white people . . . all stem from a misguided liberalism. These views do not accurately reflect the past history and present circumstances of the Indians of Amazonia, nor will they help them in their future struggles, and they run the risk of presenting them as passive victims rather than as active agents in their own destinies. (1992:70)

The unrealistic expectation that native people should be pure and poor—the assumption that "real" Indians should not want commercial goods in the first place—is one contributor to the disillusionment outsiders feel when native Amazonians foreground economic transactions in interpersonal relations. Differences in interpretations of the assistance outsiders provide are another factor.

Wari' Histories of Humanitarian Agendas

The Wari' (pronounced *wah-REE*) are a Chapakuran-speaking population of nearly three thousand people who live in the rainforest of western Rondônia, Brazil, near the border with Bolivia. They have been in sustained contact with non-Indian Brazilians and others since the late 1950s and early 1960s, when Wari' were first contacted by government expeditions sent to "attract" them to stop defending their territory against rubber tappers and gunmen employed by local business-men who wanted access to rubber trees (*Hevea brasiliensis*) on Wari' land. From the 1960s to the 1990s Wari' received assistance from three major outside sources: employees of the national government Indian agency, missionaries from the conservative Protestant New Tribes Mission, and Catholic priests and lay workers with relatively liberal orientations. In the early 1990s new sources of aid became available through nongovernmental indigenous rights organizations.

Representatives of these various groups have approached Wari' with offers of assistance based on very different priorities and intentions. Over the years outsiders have provided medicines, blankets, mosquito nets, clothing, pots and pans, machetes, axes, chain saws and other tools, new crops, boats and motors, and, at times, commercial foods such as sugar, salt, cooking oil, and powdered milk. Nonmaterial forms of aid have included numerous agricultural and economic development projects and projects to train indigenous health workers and bilingual teachers, create internal leadership structures, and teach Wari' skills in reading, writing, and mathematics.

In some cases this help has turned out to be decidedly *unhelpful*. There is a long history of failed development projects and assistance schemes that disrupted local communities and families' food security (Conklin 1989). But from their own perspectives, the missionaries, priests, and NGO representatives, as well as many government employees, have seen themselves as humanitarians, as morally motivated helpers of Indians trying (in some case at the cost of considerable self-sacrifice) to improve the lives of the Wari'. And in fact Wari' do recognize in many of these individuals positive differences that distinguish them from the shopkeepers and other local individuals who denigrate, cheat, and exploit them.

When I set out to write about how Wari' describe the past half-century of their relations with Protestant and Catholic missionaries, government workers, and activists, I thought the story would be about how they represent differences among these groups. Wari' are aware of their distinct institutional affiliations and the antipathies and competition between Protestants and Catholics and between missionaries and anti-missionary activists. If one asks, any Wari' can explain something about how these groups differ in their rhetoric and ways of relating to Indians. These differences in ideology and policy have been a major focus of the local histories written by me and other scholars, journalists, and activists. We tend to highlight how the Protestants' policies have differed from the Catholics', how government policies have changed over time, how new discourses of indigenous empowerment and partnership differ from older models of subordination, dependency, and patronage. Our outsider histories take account of the political squabbling and history of power plays among these groups.

This is not how Wari' tell the tale. In their accounts of the history of their relations with the more humanitarian brand of outsiders, they tend to talk about all of them in remarkably similar terms. They do not try to explain much about where these outsiders come from or why they differ from each other. Wari' accounts of what "helpful" outsiders have done over time revolve around one salient theme: the material goods that they have and have not given to indigenous communities.

In these indigenous narratives interethnic relationships that involve large amounts of nonmaterial forms of interaction are described primarily as a series of commodity transactions. Over and over the stories of individual and group relations with government employees, religious workers, and NGO staff are reduced (in the first telling) to a recitation of lists of goods and material assistance given and received, narratives of commodities delivered or promises broken. Wilson's account (this volume) of development projects in the Napo region of Ecuador shows a similar focus on material aid as the central concern of indigenous communities in their relations with NGOs. Wilson makes the important point that in many cases the practical, economic value of such aid is of less concern than its social value, what it says about the connections, influence, and commitments that leaders and groups can mobilize.

If we ask Wari' why they focus so heavily on material goods in representing their relations with non-Indians who provide assistance, an additional dimension of this problem emerges. Wari' focus on material goods not just because they are needy (although they certainly are in many ways), nor because they are greedy. Rather, these local "material histories" are strategic tools that Wari' employ to cope with aspects of these relationships that the outsider helpers downplay or deny. Indigenous narratives about gift-bearing foreigners are configured in a series of overlapping ideas associated with the categories of "strangers" and "gifts," symbolic fields that reflect both indigenous values and recurring experiences in past dealings with would-be friendly outsiders. In their historical experiences gifts received from outsiders have been sources of both agency and anxiety.

Material Sociality

Wari' emphasize the material bases of individual and group identities in all their relationships. Kinship comprises body substances (blood, breast milk, semen, and vaginal secretions) shared among family members, and kin ties and commitments are affirmed and made visible through acts of feeding and being fed (Conklin 2001a:111–31; Conklin and Morgan 1996). Among Wari' individuals, as in many other native communities, positive relations with nonkin also are expressed through exchange, marked in material flows of the giving and receiving of food, drink, labor, parties, and tangible assistance (Conklin 2001a, 2005). The idea of a friendly relationship that does not involve material exchange is unthinkable.

History and histories of relations with other people are experienced in material forms, not just through oral narratives and representations that associate memories with tangible things, especially animals, plants, foods, and landscapes (cf. Whitehead 2003:60). When Wari' talk about their relations with others and whether they can or cannot depend on them, they refer to specific histories of tangible giving and receiving.

The salience of materiality as a conceptual basis of sociality comes out clearly in the context of death, when mourners must terminate and transform their relations with the dead person. At funerals relatives eulogize the deceased, singing of their memories. The imagery revolves especially around food produced and things given by and to the dead person: "My grandfather, my grandfather who killed fish for me to eat," "My sister whose *chicha* I drank," "My husband who bought sandals for his children." The history of an individual life, its value and meanings to others, is told largely through an account of material giving and receiving.

Thus when, as mentioned earlier, Wari' introduce me to others by listing things I have given them, part of what is going on is that they are framing my role in terms of this indigenous value system. These commodity-identity performances, as I have come to think of them, happen when Wari' I know well introduce me to other Wari', especially people from distant communities. Listing things I have given conveys a degree of amity and time depth in our relationship and indicates that those who have received these things have some claim on me. In other contexts, in more intimate conversations and in contexts in which they wish to affirm companionship rather than commodity relations, the same individuals emphasize our fictive kin connections and other, no less tangible events in our relations. They reminisce about times when they fed me well or I fed them, about memorably large quantities of honey or fruit we harvested, work we have done together, herbal medicines exchanged. A favorite story is about how my American doctor-father delivered my Wari' "mother's" tiny, premature baby, who survived and grew up to become a tall, strong teenager. The material basis of sociality runs through these representations as well, but in these contexts it is not so much the flow of commercial commodities but the tangible materiality of feeding, nurturing, and caring for the bodies of others. And although I prefer to think of my relations with Wari' in these terms rather than the crasser reality of my role in accessing commercial goods, Wari' apparently see little conflict between these different kinds of material sociality.

If the presence of exchange defines Wari' persons and positive relationships, the absence of exchange is what traditionally located non-Wari' others outside the category of real persons. Until 1956 Wari' lived in a self-contained social universe, with no trade, no intermarriage, and no peaceful contacts with other human populations. The lack of an exchange relation defined the ethnic Other (Conklin 2001a; Vilaça 1992). In that precontact world Wari' categorized all non-Wari' people as *wijam* (pronounced *wee-YAHM*), enemy outsiders. Relations with *wijam* were categorically hostile.

The division between Wari' and *wijam* was a fundamental principal of the Wari' social universe before the contact. But oral histories describe some precontact relations of an intermediate nature, in which Wari' encountered individuals or groups of strangers who, although initially unknown and potentially hostile, eventually became remote friends (*tatirim*, a term for members of other Wari' subgroups, sometimes extended to other Indians; cf. Vilaça 2006:103).

In his classic essay *The Gift* Marcel Mauss (1950) emphasized how gift exchanges create and legitimize social relations. Among Wari', as in many other native societies, the ritualized transformation from enemy stranger to remote friend involved establishing a formal exchange relation in which an initial gift of maize *chicha* (a drink symbolically associated with blood and kinship; Conklin 2001a:140) or food was followed by ongoing, loosely reciprocal exchanges of parties that included musical performances and sometimes small gifts (Conklin 2005; Vilaça 2006:107–39). In these cycles of party giving, like was exchanged for like: similar performances, drink, food, and gifts flowed in two directions, between givers and receivers who, over time, exchanged the roles of host and guest in cycles of reciprocity that continued until something disrupted the exchange.

The Foreigner as Natural Resource

Warfare was another distinct context in which Wari' engaged in material exchange with non-Wari'. Like many other native Amazonian peoples, Wari' believe that when a man kills an enemy foreigner elements from the victim pass into the killer's body. These elements are conceived differently in different cultures, as the enemy's blood, spirit, vital energy, or other qualities. This exogenous enemy element in the killer's body is dangerous at first, but the killer can expel, neutralize, or transform it by performing proper rituals. The process of accomplishing this ritual expulsion or transformation of the incorporated enemy enhances the warrior's spiritual state or physical capacities, endowing him with superior strength, longevity, or immunity to disease. By incorporating and transforming an enemy foreigner's spirit substance a Wari' man attained the highest state of physical-spiritual perfection. These benefits were not limited to individual killers, but also passed to women with whom they had sexual intercourse (Conklin 2001b).

Among earlier generations of Wari' such rituals were highly elaborated and the most important and honored event in a man's life. Killers of enemies went into ritual seclusion for a period of many weeks, during which they observed strictly controlled bodily disciplines aimed at taming and transforming the dangerous enemy spirit blood in their bodies. By consuming large amounts of maize *chicha* the killer "fed" the enemy spirit, transforming it from enemy to kin, so that the enemy spirit blood lost its foreignness and "became Wari'," the spirit child of the warrior in whose body it resided (Conklin 2001b). This is another expression of the pan-Amazonian principle through which certain kinds of material exchange establish positive and identity-transforming relations with strangers (see Fausto 1999 on the principle of "familiarizing" transformations).

Among Wari' the idea of warfare as a way to acquire a valued resource from foreign outsiders was a salient theme and stated motive for attacking enemies. Foreigners were seen as a kind of natural resource that could be appropriated and transformed to enhance health, fertility, knowledge, and social reproduction in the indigenous community. Similar principles underlay many historical practices of warfare and raiding in other native Amazonian societies, such as taking trophy heads, women, and orphans. The foreigner-as-resource extended also to relations with less hostile non-Indians. Michael Brown observes that "as the new breed of rainforest activists and NGO advocacy groups appeared on the Amazonian horizon, Amazonian Indians approached them in much the same spirit as they had approached earlier generations of missionaries, traders, and other outsiders: as sources of money, trade goods, and political advantage that are useful only until they begin to threaten native autonomy" (quoted in Conklin and Graham 1995:706).

Strangers Bearing Poisoned Gifts

How to engage with outsiders and their resources without slipping into danger or dependency has been a central challenge in Wari' history. Before the contact they confronted real risks from participating in parties and visits with other Wari' from distant communities. These contacts were a major channel through which fevers and infectious diseases spread even before Wari' had direct contact with non-Indians (Conklin 1989). Wari' attributed a number of precontact epidemics to poison that visitors left behind or that party hosts put into the beer. To this day a degree of wariness and suspicion attaches to any party or gathering between nonkin from different communities.

Since long before they had direct contact with non-Indians, Wari' associated Western commodities with disease. There is a story, probably dating to the nineteenth century, of a Wari' man who moved away, married a Brazilian woman, and began to wear Brazilian clothes, use Brazilian tools, and eat Brazilian foods. Relatives who visited him returned home carrying strange new goods that subsequently made them sick and started an epidemic in which several people died. Other Amerindian peoples also recognize associations between disease and Western commodities. The Wakuenai of northwestern Amazonia, for example, associate metal tools and white peoples' goods with exogenous diseases and epidemics (Hill and Wright 1988:93).

For Wari' the link between disease and Western commodities intensified in the 1950s and 1960s, when several teams composed of men employed by the Indian Protection Service (a national government agency) and Protestant New Tribes missionaries or Catholic priests made expeditions into the forest with the goal of establishing contact with the "wild" Wari'. Following the agency's time-honored methods of "attraction" (to convince "wild" Indians of whites' peaceful intentions and entice them into direct, peaceful contacts that will eventually bring them under government control), these teams left large numbers of presents—machetes, axes, knives, mirrors, and food—along forest trails and in clearings where they hoped Wari' would find them.

These "presents" were the wedge that cracked Wari' autonomy, for soon after they began to take items directly from the hands of outsiders people got sick. After each of the first contacts in different regions in 1956 and 1961–62, one epidemic after another swept through the immunologically semi-virgin population: measles, malaria, whooping cough, polio, influenza. Sixty percent of the population died within two or three years after these first contacts. Constantly sick and traumatized the survivors were forced to depend on missionaries and government agents for food and medicine during much of the 1960s.

Exchange Relations in Humanitarian Aid

The strategy of using gifts to lure Indians into amicable relations with outsiders is most explicit in the methods of first-contact "attraction," but commodities play similar roles in other interethnic relations as well. Throughout Amazonia missionaries, government officials, traders, and local entrepreneurs use their privileged access to goods, pharmaceuticals, money, and credit to make friends and influence native people. Ethnographers also participate in commodity relations, for "an exchange of goods for hospitality and information also forms part of the anthropological enterprise," and goods received from outsiders often carry prestige within indigenous communities (Hugh-Jones 1992:49–50).

Western societies draw sharp distinctions between gifts and things given for payment, as exemplified by Mauss's (1950:47) interpretation of Malinowski's distinction between calculated commerce and the spontaneous gift. In theory gifts are supposed to be free of calculation, with no requirement for the recipient to reciprocate, or at least no requirement to give anything one does not want to give or would not give otherwise. This no-strings-attached image of the gift as an expression of noneconomic, noncalculating personal ties fits into the Western symbolic dichotomy in which affective relations (love, friendship) are (in theory) antithetical to monetary or commodity relations.

In Wari' experiences of their relations with outsiders, flows of gifts freely given inevitably have turned into calculated (and from their point of view, often disadvantageous) exchanges. After the period of epidemic disease, death, and social disruption in the 1960s the demographic situation stabilized. From the 1970s onward missionaries and administrators dedicated themselves to weaning Wari' away from their dependency on outside assistance. In place of material aid (food, medicine, clothing, tools) provided in response to indigenous need, the flow of commodities shifted to a basis of calculated exchanges, with outsiders giving Wari' goods in payment for indigenous labor or products. Over the years Wari' have seen most of the outsiders who have come to help them (government agents, missionaries, nursing aides, teachers) as more friendly and less exploitive than many other local Brazilians with whom they have dealt. But still they treat all non-Wari' with a degree of distance that in some ways is closer to the traditional category of enemy-as-resource than the category of remote friends because they do not sustain balanced exchange relations over time.

A characteristic common to all the competing groups of Protestants, Catholics, government administrators, and NGOs is that after using presents and aid of one sort or another to gain entree and acceptance among Wari', they subsequently decrease the flow of aid, with the goal of discontinuing it entirely. Economic self-sufficiency and freedom from dependency—helping the Indians stand on their own two feet—are the goals of all these organizations. To Wari' this looks like reneging on the relationship, for even after the distribution of free gifts stops the outsiders continue to demand that Wari' do certain things.

In the case of humanitarian assistance, any organization that provides goods or services on a sustained basis inevitably wants something in return. They want the Indians to change their behavior, or participate in the organization's projects, or give their loyalty or friendship, or at least express gratitude and appreciation. Material goods and aid may be repaid in different forms, but the relation between native recipients and humanitarian givers is implicitly an exchange to which strings *are* attached.

Missionaries, whose agenda for changing Indian behavior is explicit, are often more open about acknowledging the exchange dynamics in their work than are many anthropologists and activists. Notions of calculated exchange are at odds with the commitment to indigenous self-determination that has become a baseline principle in much of the rhetoric of contemporary indigenist advocacy. Yet hidden behind the idea of indigenous self-determination is often an implicit, unexamined assumption that Indians (at least the "good," uncorrupted ones) will want what their well-meaning, better educated supporters think they should want.

A classic example surfaced in a meeting between representatives of the GAIA Foundation, a London-based environmental advocacy organization, and representatives of the Xavante of central Brazil. Laura Graham reports that the anthropologist Catherine Howard, who was translating for the NGO, described how the GAIA staff member asked the Indians to tell the foundation what they needed. "You can trust us," said the GAIA representative. "We are not like other whites who have betrayed you. We want to help you and we are here today to hear what you natives want. We are videotaping so we have a record of what you want, directly from you" (Graham 2002:199).

The Xavante men talked among themselves and (having learned the power of written words) wrote lists of what they needed. With the camera rolling, "one by one the elders stood in front of the camera, held up their pieces of paper, and stated their requests. . . . They requested tractors, trucks, and generators, and each reiterated that he would return to his people trusting that the GAIA Foundation would not betray them" as the government Indian agency had in the past. "As the requests came in, one after another, the GAIA representatives exhibited greater and greater discomfort. After the eighth or ninth one, they shut the camera off. Realizing the bind they had gotten into, the head of their team turned to Howard and asked with exasperation, 'Don't they understand what we want them to do? The things they are asking for destroy the environment!'" (Graham 2002:200).

In the shift from the promise "We are not like other whites who have betrayed you.... We want ... to hear what you natives want ... directly from you" to her exasperated "Don't they understand what we want them to do?," the GAIA representative confronted the contradiction of the hidden agenda that coexists with the rhetoric of indigenous self-determination in much progressive pro-Indian advocacy: the purpose is not to help Indians do what they want to do, but to help them do what outsiders think they should do.

Mauss (1950:65) quoted Emerson on the idea that charity is wounding for those who accept it. The moral sensibilities of Western liberalism try to mask the injurious patronage of the rich almsgiver. Contemporary NGOs that value the idea (if not the practice) of indigenous self-determination cannot represent the flow of presents and aid as simple charity because this would put native people in the subservient position, as recipients of charity or patronage. Conversely, to recognize an exchange relation in which Indians reciprocate with actions the giver desires would undermine the fiction that the do-gooder and Indians share the same interests.

Critical Commodity-Giving Discourses

When indigenous people insist, as Wari' do in their "material histories," that relations with "helpful" outsiders are primarily valued for access to goods or money, this negates the cherished self-narrative of humanitarian assistance in general, and progressive contemporary indigenism in particular. Rather than recognize a natural alliance of interests in which outsiders are altruists dedicated to facilitating native people's own goals, the Wari' version casts these relations in the uncomfortable light of exchange and calculation.

147

Wari' emphasize the contrast between the unbalanced, ungener-
ous, conditional patterns of giving practiced by outsiders with their
ideal of more balanced, continually renewable flows of goods in the
indigenous society, in patterns of reciprocity that reinforce egalitarian
relations. By relentlessly emphasizing how outsiders use commodity
gifts in stingy, inconsistent, un-Wari' ways, Wari' mark their distance
from even friendly individuals, relegating them to the category of
wijam or, at best, *tatirim*: others still, outsiders always.

Framing narratives of outsiders' assistance around a critique of the
flow of commodities serves as a tool in the politics of interethnic relations. By portraying outsiders first and foremost as channels through
which to access commodities, Wari' carve out a conceptual zone of
autonomy for themselves. Representing local histories of relations to
humanistically minded outsiders as "material histories" consisting of
little more than a flow of commodities reinforces the claim that outsiders' power over Wari' is limited: outsiders are good only as long as
they are materially useful. Such discourses obviously create pressure
on outsiders to keep providing the kinds of tangible aid that Wari'
define as useful. And they stake out moral grounds for terminating
the relationship if what the natives demand is not forthcoming.

By adhering to a resolutely pragmatic politics of measuring obligations in material terms Wari' seek to shape the terms of their relations. As in their precontact relations with the enemies whose spirits
and vital substance they absorbed and tamed, Wari' use discourses
framed around commodities as a way to appropriate resources from
the external world while marking and reinforcing the separateness
of their own identity and autonomy.

Notes

1. Suzanne O'Shea, "Bitter Sting Learns Laws of the Jungle," *The West Australian*,
May 3, 1993.

References

Conklin, Beth A. 1989. *Images of health, illness and death among the Wari' [Pakaas
Novos] of Rondônia, Brazil*. PhD diss., University of California at San Francisco
and Berkeley.

————. 1997. Body paint, feathers, and VCRS: Aesthetics and authenticity in Amazonian activism. *American Ethnologist* 24 (4): 711–37.

————. 2001a. *Consuming grief: Compassionate cannibalism in an Amazonian society.* Austin: University of Texas Press.

————. 2001b. Women's blood, warriors' blood, and the conquest of vitality in Amazonia and Melanesia. In *Gender in Amazonia and Melanesia: An exploration of the comparative method,* ed. Thomas Gregor and Donald Tuzin, 141–74. Berkeley: University of California Press.

————. 2005. Intercambio fractal en una cosmología caníbal: Dinámicas de oposición y amistad en las fiestas de la Amazonía. *Boletin de Arqueologia PUCP* (Lima) 9:45–66 [published in 2008].

Conklin, Beth A., and Laura R. Graham. 1995. The shifting middle ground: Amazonian Indians and eco-politics. *American Anthropologist* 97 (4): 695–710.

Conklin, Beth A., and Lynn M. Morgan. 1996. Babies, bodies, and the production of personhood in North America and a native Amazonian society. *Ethos* 24 (4): 657–94.

Fausto, Carlos. 1999. Of enemies and pets: Warfare and shamanism in Amazonia. *American Ethnologist* 26 (4): 933–56.

Fiorini, Marcelo, and Christopher Bail. 2006. Le commerce de la culture, et le Coca-Cola: Le commerce des cultures. *Gradhiva* (Paris) 4:97–114.

Fisher, William H. 2000. *Rainforest exchanges: Industry and community on an Amazonian frontier.* Washington DC: Smithsonian Institution Press.

Graham, Laura R. 2002. How should an Indian speak? Amazonian Indians and the symbolic politics of language in the global public sphere. In *Indigenous movements, self-representation, and the state in Latin America,* ed. Kay B. Warren and Jean E. Jackson, 181–228. Austin: University of Texas Press.

Hemming, John. 2003. *Die if you must: Brazilian Indians in the twentieth century.* London: Macmillan.

Hill, Jonathan D., and Robin M. Wright. 1988. Time, narrative, and ritual: Historical interpretations from an Amazonian society. In *Rethinking history and myth: Indigenous South American perspectives on the past,* ed. Jonathon D. Hill, 78–105. Urbana: University of Illinois Press.

Hugh-Jones, Stephen. 1992. Yesterday's luxuries, tomorrow's necessities: Business and barter in northwest Amazonia. In *Barter, exchange, and value: An anthropological approach,* ed. Caroline Humphreys and Stephen Hugh-Jones, 41–74. Cambridge: Cambridge University Press.

Jackson, Jean E. 1995. Culture, genuine and spurious: The politics of Indianness in the Vaupés, Colombia. *American Ethnologist* 22 (1): 3–27.

Mauss, Marcel. 1950. *The gift: The form and reason of exchange in archaic societies.* London: Routledge.

McSweeney, Kendra. 2005. Indigenous population growth in the lowland neotropics: Social science insights for biodiversity conservation. *Conservation Biology* 19 (5): 1375–84.

Miller, Daniel. 1995. Consumption and commodities. *Annual Review of Anthropology* 24:141–61.

Ramos, Alcida Rita. 1994. The hyperreal Indian. *Critique of Anthropology* 14:153–71.

———. 1998. *Indigenism: Ethnic politics in Brazil*. Madison: University of Wisconsin Press.

———. 2001. *Pulp fictions of indigenism*. Série Antropologia 301. Brasilia: Universidad de Brasilia.

Turner, Terence S. 1993. The role of indigenous peoples in the environmental crisis: The example of the Kayapo of the Brazilian Amazon. *New Perspectives in Biology and Medicine* 36:526–45.

———. 1995. An indigenous people's struggle for socially equitable and environmentally sustainable production: The Kayapo revolt against extractivism. *Journal of Latin American Anthropology* 1 (1): 98–121.

Vilaça, Aparecida. 1992. *Comendo como gente: Formas do canibalismo Wari'*. Rio de Janeiro: Editora UFRJ.

———. 2006. *Quem somos nos: Os Wari' encontram os brancos*. Rio de Janeiro: Editora UFRJ.

Whitehead, Neil L. 2003. Three patamuna trees: Landscape and history in the Guyana highlands. In *Histories and historicities in Amazonia*, ed. Neil L. Whitehead, 59–77. Lincoln: University of Nebraska Press.

6. Alternative Development in Putumayo, Colombia

Bringing Back the State through the Creation of
Community and "Productive Social Capital"?

María Clemencia Ramírez

In July 2003, when I was conducting fieldwork in the department of Putumayo in Colombia's Western Amazon, I was invited by the director of Vida y Futuro, an NGO headquartered in the Andean region, to visit "the biggest and most high-tech alternative development project, an agro-industrial project that has become a model to be replicated." This project was run in the rural settlement (*vereda*) of El Espinal in the municipality of San Miguel. San Miguel is in lower Putumayo, near the Ecuadorian border. The project involved the intensive raising of pigs. Twenty-five campesinos were working together under the umbrella organization Asociación Porcícola El Espinal (Association of Pork Producers El Espinal, APES). The NGO had formed APES as a for-profit business to replace a nonprofit livestock and dairy cooperative that had been formed the previous year by sixteen campesinos whose coca crops had been sprayed. Vida y Futuro had convinced the campesinos to drop their livestock and dairy production cooperative, arguing that it was not economically competitive. Wilfran Fraidel, the legal representative of the peasant association, explained that the sixteen members of the previous association undertook the pig-raising project unenthusiastically because the NGO had given them little choice: "Accept the project or we'll take our money elsewhere." The project continued for two years, during which the NGO was able to hire both a technician and an administrative staff (an accountant and a secretary) to coach the members. In the meantime members had begun to leave for various reasons. In 2005, when only four members were left and the NGO had ended its contract, the project was suspended. In Wilfran's words, "It was the beginning of a change in people's lives and in their economic condition, but they weren't prepared for the business world." This encapsulates one of the central paradoxes posed by the neoliberal international development agenda, an agenda transplanted to a marginalized coca-growing region in Colombia that seeks to "produce rational citizens who will be entrepreneurial and competitive" (Ong 1999:52).

Vida y Futuro was one of six Colombian NGOs contracted by Chemonics International Inc.,[1] a well-established international development consulting company based in Washington, founded in 1975 "to promote meaningful change around the world," with projects in five continents. By 2003 it had "launche[d] an initiative to help agricultural producers in developing countries increase their competitiveness through better understanding of international grades and standards."[2] Chemonics was contracted by the U.S. Agency for International Development (USAID) under the budget for Plan Colombia to carry out alternative development programs in Colombia (initially in the departments of Putumayo and Caquetá) as a "reparation" to campesinos after aerial spraying had taken place, a strategy seeking primarily to eliminate coca crops rather than to establish a comprehensive rural development plan in this region. Accordingly Chemonics International measured success by the number of coca hectares eradicated.

The Western Amazon of Colombia (comprising the departments of Putumayo, Caquetá, Guaviare, and southwestern Meta) has historically been a marginal area. Today coca cultivation is the principal economic activity, and nonstate armed actors such as paramilitary groups and the Revolutionary Armed Forces of Colombia (FARC) are also present and regulate the coca market. Under the guise of the war on drugs, millions of dollars have been channeled to the region in the name of alternative development. The main policy for this area is focused on fighting coca cultivation as the source of financing for nonstate armed actors. The policy complicates both the representation of the inhabitants of the area by the central government and multilateral institutions and the definition of who or what should be developed and in what way. The development agenda that has been implemented in Western Amazonia reflects a neoliberal emphasis on economics, individual entrepreneurship (to counter poverty as a "subjective condition"), and good governance as synonymous with economic development, disregarding the structural causes that lead campesinos to cultivate coca. Thus the alternative development projects that have been executed in this region reflect a selective definition of development imposed from the outside and conditioned by the war on drugs.

I argue that as the neoliberal development agenda conflates the war on drugs with the long-term armed conflict in the Western Amazon region of Colombia, instead of contributing to resolve the problems in this area through economic alternatives that take into account local society and politics, it legitimizes and confirms the existence of a criminal peasant class that is allegedly responsible for its own marginality and economic exclusion.

Between 1998 and 1999 coca production decreased in both Bolivia and Peru, while in Colombia it increased by 66 percent and the country consolidated its position as the major grower of coca in the Andean region. Thus a large percentage of coca growing in Colombia goes directly to the narcotraffic market. In contrast with Bolivia and Peru, all coca cultivation was declared illegal in Colombia through the Narcotics Law of 1986, criminalizing all coca producers, no matter how small. Coca cultivation is mostly carried out in Colombia by *colonos* (nonindigenous settlers) in Western Amazonia, a condition that exacerbates the national imaginary that portrays *colonos* as the source of environmental degradation and social problems. The Colombian Antinarcotics Police (DIRAN) claims that one hectare of coca entails the destruction of three hectares of forest;[3] this contradicts the representation of the indigenous people as noble protectors of the forest. Moreover, as Jean Jackson argues in this volume, the image of the noble Indian circulates in national media as a foil for critiquing the malaise of the nation in terms of violence, drug trafficking, and lawlessness, while it can be argued that *colono* coca growers are portrayed not only as promoters of violence and lawlessness because they live in a region where coca growing and armed conflict are conflated, but as criminals in search of easy money, with no attachment to the region, and as such are subject to repressive antidrug policies. To get a sense of the *colono* population it is necessary to give a short account of the colonization history of the Western Amazon region of Colombia.

The colonization of the Colombian Amazon began in the late nineteenth century, mainly by inhabitants of the Andean highlands at that time, and has continued since.[4] This colonization has responded to social, political, and economic upheavals in central Colombia. It has evolved during this time, incorporating frontier areas into the economic sphere of the centralized Colombian state in order to resolve structural social, political, and economic problems occurring elsewhere. These include the high concentration of land ownership that has characterized Colombia's rural structure (1.3 percent of the population owns 48 percent of the best land); violent confrontations in the interior of the country (in the 1950s) between the dominant Liberal and Conservative political parties in their struggle to gain and maintain power, and today as result of the conflict between guerrillas, paramilitaries, and the armed forces; and the conversion of Colombia into a major coca producer since the 1980s. When drug trafficking rose to prominence land appropriation was the preferred way for drug traffickers to launder money (International Crisis Group 2005), and a "reverse agrarian reform" was generated by this large-scale purchase of land by drug traffickers. Rocha (2000:33) estimates that drug traffickers own 4.4 million hectares. This land is generally used for cattle ranching, affecting productive agriculture. From 1996 to 2004 between two and three million people were internally displaced (United Nations High Commissioner for Refugees 2005). The Consultancy on Human Rights and Displacement reported in December 2004 that between 1997 and 2003 paramilitaries took control of five million hectares (12.35 million acres) using three methods: (1) appropriating abandoned lands as a result of campesinos being caught in the cross-fire between irregular armed groups, (2) forced dispossession, and (3) forced purchase of lands ("ONG revela que Paramilitares se han quedado con 5 milliones de hectáreas de tierra entre 1997 y 2003," El Tiempo (Bogotá), December 21, 2004). Each of these contributed to enhancing the "reverse agrarian reform" initiated by the narcotraffickers. Low international prices for agricultural products, particularly in the case of Colombian export coffee, and the general crisis in the rural agricultural sector have also driven growing numbers of small campesinos to plant coca and poppies for lack of viable alternatives.

As a result, Western Amazonia is now densely populated and colonos are culturally dominant. Of the entire population of the Colombian Amazon, 86.3 percent is concentrated in the west at a density of 2.5 inhabitants per square kilometer. In contrast, Eastern Amazonia (Amazonas, Vaupés, and Guainía) is characterized by its low demographic density of 0.1 inhabitants per square kilometer, a predominantly indigenous population, and significant urbanization. The guerrilla and paramilitary presence as well as the coca farming are mostly found in colonization areas of Colombia such as Western Amazonia.

In this chapter I analyze the outcome of the implementation of development programs in the context of Plan Colombia, guided both by the war on drugs and a neoliberal agenda in the marginal and conflictive region of the department of Putumayo. First I examine

the place of alternative development as a strategy to counter narcotrafficking in the context of Plan Colombia. Second I discuss the
diagnosis of the area made by the international development company Chemonics, a diagnosis in accordance with the representation
above. Third I analyze how this diagnosis has been contested by the
small coca growers in the region. Fourth I examine the meaning of
implementing good governance, a central aim of USAID, strengthening civil society and promoting social capital in such a marginal and
conflictive context. Finally I discuss the implications and contradictions entailed in the implementation of certain community enterprise
associations and agro-industrial development in relation to existing
communal organizations.

Alternative Development as Part of Plan Colombia

Plan Colombia was first launched in December 1998 "as a policy of
investment for social development, the reduction of violence, and the
construction of peace" (Observatorio para la Paz 2000:167). President
Andrés Pastrana (1998–2002) described it as a Marshall Plan for the
economic and social development of southern Colombia, hoping
that the international community would respond to the devastation
caused by drug production and trafficking as it had to the devastation
of Europe in World War II.

Originally described as Pastrana's national development plan, Plan
Colombia was substantially transformed as a result of U.S. pressure;
a year after the initial proposal, President Pastrana presented Plan
Colombia as a Plan for Peace, Prosperity and the Strengthening of
the State: "to ensure order, stability, and compliance with the law; to
guarantee effective sovereignty over the national territory; to protect the state and the civilian population from the threats of illegal
armed groups and criminal organizations; and to break the existing
ties between these groups and the drug industry that supports them"
(Contraloría General de la República 2001). By 1999 Colombia was
already the third largest recipient of U.S. military assistance in the

world; for the first time, that year the United States provided a small amount of alternative development assistance.

Thus Plan Colombia was a response to U.S. security needs, seeking to maintain a secure southern border, prioritizing counterinsurgency and counterterrorism operations, and breaking the link between drug trafficking and the guerrillas and other nonstate armed actors. However, U.S. national security policy also "remains firmly committed to the interdependent regional objectives of democracy and free-market economic progress," an aim that implies the "expansion of the concept of security from maintaining military defenses against external threats to include internal political, economic and social concerns."[5] Accordingly the "new" Andean Regional Initiative launched by President George W. Bush and the U.S. State Department in May 2001 established three overarching goals:

1. To promote and support democracy and democratic institutions.
2. To foster sustainable economic development and trade liberalization.
3. To significantly reduce the supply of illegal drugs to the United States at the source, while simultaneously reducing U.S. demand.

The first two goals constitute the foundation of the socioeconomic policies included in the part of Plan Colombia that is executed in the Andean Region, and specifically in Colombia, by USAID. In Colombia the goal of reducing the drug supply at the source has entailed the increase of aerial spraying where coca and poppies are cultivated (USAID 2000).

The six-year budget for Plan Colombia was set at U.S.$7.5 billion. Colombia would provide $4 billion and the international community, including the United States, would provide $3.5 billion. To support Plan Colombia the U.S. Congress approved and President Bill Clinton signed into law on July 13, 2000, a special supplemental appropriation of $1.3 billion. The bill included $860 million for Colombia, $180 million for several of Colombia's neighbors, and $260 million for the antidrug efforts of several U.S. agencies (Ramírez, Stanton, and Walsh 2005).

Of Colombia's share, 60 percent ($519.2 million) went to the armed forces and 14 percent ($123.1 million) went to the national police.[6] The centerpiece of Plan Colombia, which administration documents called the "push into southern Colombia" (in other words, into the departments of Putumayo and Caquetá), was the addition of two counternarcotics battalions to the one created in 1998–99 to form a new Counternarcotics Brigade within the Colombian Army to ease the way for the massive fumigation of coca crops in Putumayo. The remaining 26 percent of Plan Colombia, $217.7 million, was allocated for measures promoting peace (1 percent) and the following programs administered by USAID: for alternative development (8 percent), for the provision of services to the displaced population (4 percent), for human rights protection and to fight corruption (6 percent), for judicial reform (2 percent), and for strengthening the rule of law (5 percent).[7] It must also be emphasized that Plan Colombia economic and social aid has been provided through the International Narcotics Control budget at the State Department, underscoring the aid's link to drug control objectives, which poses a significant paradox. The security focus of the aid package has been maintained; in any given year between 68 percent and 75 percent of Colombia's Andean Counterdrug Initiative aid has gone to the military and police. But though the composition of the aid has not changed, the counterinsurgency and counterterrorism objectives have become more and more explicit in both U.S. and Colombian policy. President Álvaro Uribe (2002–present) has wholeheartedly embraced the discourse of counterterrorism and has implemented the aid package he inherited with its counterinsurgency logic.

Putumayo became the epicenter of Plan Colombia beginning in July 2000. The region contained 54 percent of the area used for coca cultivation in Colombia (66,022 hectares), 30,000 small producers with from one to five hectares each, and a floating population of 50,000 people who worked in coca production and commercialization (National Association of Campesinos 2001). This department, where FARC had been present since the early 1980s, saw the arrival of paramilitaries beginning in 1998, and the two groups began to compete for territory, the power to regulate the coca market, and the ability to collect the illegal taxes, or *gramaje*, paid by the local population. All of these circumstances combined to make Putumayo an ideal setting for the central mission of Plan Colombia as presented by President Pastrana.

Since the beginning of fumigation the government's attitude toward small cultivators has been ambiguous. On the one hand, Law 30 of 1986 specified that the cultivation of marijuana, coca, and opium poppies in excess of twenty plants was a crime. Law 599 of 2000, which revised Colombia's penal code, reaffirmed that growing these crops is illegal and increased the penalties for violations. On the other hand, policy initiatives throughout the 1990s differentiated between "industrial" or "commercial" production (three hundred hectares or more, directly controlled by drug traffickers) and "small coca growers" or "coca cultivators" (peasant and indigenous people cultivating coca on parcels of land between two and five hectares).[8] In this order of ideas, the agreements signed by government representatives following the 1996 coca growers and collectors protest marches was achieved when the recently created (1995) National Program for Alternative Development (PLANTE) agreed to focus on assisting small campesinos and indigenous communities who hold less than three hectares of coca with programs of crop substitution and alternative development, in recognition of the economic, social, and political conditions that foster reliance on illicit crops.[9]

However, under the guidelines for fighting the war on drugs, alternative development programs are implemented only as compensation after fumigation and forced eradication. As such, they do not occupy a central place, either financially or politically, in the strategy to combat coca cultivation through the promotion of a comprehensive rural development plan. Consequently a report from the U.S. General Accounting Office on USAID's alternative development activities in the Andean region states that "alternative development interdiction and eradication efforts must be carefully coordinated to achieve mutually reinforcing benefits" (2002:2).

Along these lines the place of alternative development in the Colombian government's antidrug strategy is also unclear. On the one hand, it is part of the component to reduce the supply, along with spraying, interdiction, and strengthening of the military. On the other hand, it is a component on its own that seeks to promote social development and the economic restructuring of an illicit into a licit economy, an aim that goes beyond just reducing the drug supply to the United States.[10]

In April 2001 USAID channeled $87.5 million of Plan Colombia funds into a five-year contract with Chemonics to implement, administer, and supervise alternative development activities, primarily in the departments of Putumayo and Caquetá. Eighty million dollars of USAID funds were invested in Putumayo. On his visit to Villagarzón, Putumayo, in December 2004 U.S. Ambassador to Colombia William B. Wood stated, "Those dirty profits [from coca cultivation], as I am sure you would all agree, did not produce good living. Quite the contrary. That illicit drug money led to corruption, drove out legitimate economic activity, and attracted the worst kind of newcomers. Neighbors lost confidence and trust in each other, in local organizations, and in the state. Crime and violence were rampant; personal and collective welfare suffered, and only the illegal armed groups gained" (U.S. State Department 2004).

These declarations sum up the representations that the central government of Colombia and the U.S. antidrug officials have jointly created for the marginal areas of Colombia, where the conflation of coca cultivation, nonstate armed actors, and an absentee state has become the norm. Central government policies targeting the Amazon region are the outgrowth of this region's marginality, a condition that stems from long-term historical processes.

Constructing the Existence of a
Perverse versus a Productive Social Capital

In 2004, after three years of implementing alternative development plans in Putumayo, Chemonics presented the construction of "social capital" as one of the main achievements of its intervention in the area. A section title in a Chemonics news bulletin on alternative development in Putumayo reads, "*Putumayenses*: Happier, More Organized and Living in Peace" and the article states, "From a Perverse Social Capital that included illegal armed groups, illicit crops, attacks against the state and non-acceptance of the state, a transformation leading to Productive Social Capital has ensued. This has strengthened the collective spirit and promoted legal social and economic development, contributed to the social fabric, and involved communities in government policies geared towards the final eradication of illicit crops" (Chemonics Inc.-CAD 2004:3).

Chemonics understands social capital "as the degree of trust existing between actors in society, practiced civil behavior norms and the existing degree of association building" (Chemonics Inc.-CAD 2004:3). When the existence of "practiced civil behavior norms" is heralded as a factor of social capital, the component of "civility" is added to the way the multilateral aid agencies currently understand social capital.[11] Following Putnam, the accepted definition of social capital mainly consists of "social networks and the associated norms of reciprocity and trust" (2002:xxi). The historical period in which the Spanish conquistadors described the Amazon region as inhabited by savages is re-created to represent this marginal region as inhabited today by migrants and criminals under the control of the guerrillas and, as a consequence, by the existence of a perverse social capital. Both during the colonial period and today an "indomitable" and "uncivil" people must be brought under control, dominated, "normalized," and "civilized."

Referring to juvenile delinquency in Colombia and contesting the theories that explain delinquency as the result of deficiencies in social capital, Mauricio Rubio introduces the concept of perverse social capital "as detrimental to economic efficiency and the welfare of society" (1997:805). Rubio stresses the existence in Colombia of "an institutional environment that favors opportunist and criminal behaviors." Youth become involved in illegal activities as a result of an environment that "inspires" their participation. And although Rubio recognizes that "the incentives are monetary and of such magnitude that they become attractive in comparison to almost any legal activity within reach of a young Colombian" (807), he stresses that Colombians make these decisions "consciously and rationally" and without the condemnation of their families, alluding to the lack of moral social principles and sanctions. Moreover, he states, "well-educated segments of the juvenile population . . . who have 'adequate' social capital including those from the elite, in other words, members of an undoubtedly 'civilized class,' who, it can be assumed, consequently behave according to the norms, have been attracted by the organized crime in Colombia." He maintains that perverse social capital is created by guerrilla movements, criminal organizations, and drug cartels "through the takeover of existing institutions or by creating their own contacts, networks, information systems and power relations" (808). One of the main points that Rubio is making in his analysis is that the criminal environment in Colombia leads to individual and subjective decisions to get involved in illegal activities. This idea has been taken even further by Francisco Thoumi (2003); discussing why narcotrafficking became more central to the Colombian economy than to other Andean economies, Thoumi has argued that there is a long-term structural tendency in the collective identity of Colombians to choose illegality over legality. Historically Colombians have been recognized smugglers; now they are narcotraffickers, experts in laundering money. Moreover

Thoumi maintains that poverty or the lack of economic opportunities or even of agrarian reform does not explain the predominance of illegal activities in Colombia. Instead of considering the structural economic, social, and political causes that lead campesinos to resort to illicit crops, Thoumi refers only to what he calls the "structural social causes," and although he takes into account the incapacity of the state to enforce laws and norms in marginal regions and to include these regions in the nation-state, overall he emphasizes the lack of social capital and of moral social sanctions to individual behavior and corruption in search of individual profit. Both Rubio's and Thoumi's analyses respond to the way that poverty under advanced liberalism is cast as a "subjective condition" (Rose 1999:265). In these contexts poor people are being held responsible for their own poverty, while wealthy people with "adequate social capital" are excused for getting involved in narcotrafficking activities only because criminals take over the existing institutions.

In the case of the Putumayo region the establishment of the existence of "perverse social capital" is rooted in several assumptions. First, small coca growers are part of the "criminal" networks created not only by the drug cartels but now by the guerrilla groups, who have been characterized as narcoguerrillas and now as terrorists, negating their political stance. When Colombia's guerrilla groups became narcoguerrillas—so termed in 1984 by U.S. Ambassador Lewis Tamb—they became legitimate targets of antidrug policy. At first, to defeat the guerrillas meant eliminating their source of funding, not attacking them directly. To enforce the distinction between counterdrugs and counterinsurgency, the Clinton administration issued an executive order banning the U.S. military from sharing non-drug intelligence with its Colombian counterparts. After 9/11 Colombia's guerrillas became "narcoterrorists," and the overemphasis on a military response was reinforced with the authorization given by Congress and signed by President Bush in August 2002 (in a supplemental appropriations bill) to use counterdrug assets for counterterrorist purposes, reversing the Clinton executive order banning the sharing of non-drug intelligence. Thus counterterrorist objectives have become more and more explicit in U.S. policy toward Colombia. Second, it is assumed that coca growers have consciously decided to become involved in this illegal activity, and so they are designated by the government and the paramilitaries as "guerrilla collaborators" attacking the state, while the guerrillas designate them as "paramilitary collaborators." As the war on drugs has become a war on terrorism, campesinos are expected to take sides in the conflict. A third assumption is that the cultivation, processing, and sale of coca promotes violence, individualism, the desire for easy money (the so-called narcomentality), and the loss of values. Fourth, the nonexistence of peasant organizations, or the disruption of the so-called social fabric (*tejido social*), is a consequence of choosing illegal activities. This is a stereotypical view of the people of coca-producing regions, mainly campesinos who have migrated from the heartland of the country (*campesino colonos*), described as fortune hunters, rootless and violent people who act outside the law and have their own divergent set of rules, and moreover are prone to criminality.

Indeed in Chemonics' argument for the importance of constructing "productive" social capital as part of the alternative development strategy, the following factors are stressed as being problematic: first, "the difficulty to consolidate associative projects because of the priority given to individual interests backed up by individual profit" due to coca cultivation; second, "the lack of trust of the campesinos towards public institutions, their organizations and their neighbors"; and third, "the lack of trust in an economic restructuring of the region, based on competitive and profitable agricultural projects or agribusiness, as proposed by the multilateral agencies and official institutions" (Llano 2004:11).

Underlying the argument made by Chemonics is the assumption that "social networks and the associated norms of reciprocity and trust" that define social capital have to be constructed through external intervention, denying the long history of colonization in Amazonia and therefore not accounting for populations whose presence there predates the arrival of coca and who had their own forms of community organization, as I analyze below. Although there is a sector of the population that arrived in Putumayo in the 1980s and 1990s in response to the coca boom, there are three generations of Putumayan residents. One generation arrived with children born outside the zone who then grew up there and formed a second generation. The third generation comprises the grandchildren of those original migrants. When Chemonics states that the lack of trust exists not only toward public institutions but also toward peasant organizations and neighbors, it is prioritizing the illegal and criminal condition of coca growers and overlooking the social, political, and economic causes that make campesinos resort to illicit crops or, even more, their situation within the armed conflict.

Contesting the Existence of Perverse Social Capital

In contrast to the Chemonics perspective, small growers see coca as a means to improve their standard of living. They report that coca provides them with "sustenance and work," and they stress causative social and economic reasons for its cultivation. They relativize its illegality, although that is the central factor in Chemonics' analysis. Among the economic conditions that the campesinos provide for their participation in coca growing are low levels of employment and income, poverty, the availability of agricultural inputs, and a guaranteed market for the crop. This makes coca a more profitable crop than other agricultural products such as manioc and maize. Insufficient road infrastructure is fundamental for the low profitability of other agricultural products, as a campesino explains:

There are some veredas six kilometers from the road that you can't even see if you go by in a car. What they need is access roads to get to those communities from the main road. What happens is there's a lack of these access roads to all these human settlements that are on fertile land where you can grow plantain, maize, soybeans, but there's no road to get to town. It's not the same to get a hundred loads of manioc out [without a road] or to carry two hundred or three hundred sacks of maize out by mule on a rough path. . . . When they talk about the lack of roads that's what they mean. (Interview in Orito, July 2004)

Growing coca is also the only means by which the campesino *colonos* have been able to gain access to basic services. For example, during coca booms in some remote *veredas* campesinos were able to repair roads and hire a rural teacher and pay her when the government had not assigned one; most important, they've been able to send their children to departmental capitals such as Cali to study in high school or college. The absence of the state is the metanarrative that explains the presence of both coca growing and the armed conflict in the region. When asked why coca came to Putumayo a campesino in Orito answered, "Many people say it's to make easy money, but before coca came in the state never paid us any attention. Actually it was the absence of the state that encouraged coca, that encouraged the guerrillas and other armed groups. This place turned violent and became a coca-growing area because there was no state here" (interview in Orito, July 2004).

Coca cultivation is not a lucrative crop, as has been depicted. Small coca growers (with less than three hectares) are the weakest link in the narcotrafficking chain and earn only slightly more than the official minimum monthly salary of about U.S.$166 (December 2005 figure).[12] Although campesino *cocaleros* assign responsibility for the expansion of coca cultivation to the state, they also demand the commitment of the state to the substitution process: the state is expected to fulfill campesino expectations to provide needed services to the population. Another campesino reflected on his experiences in alternative projects sponsored by Chemonics and by the state: "The programs that have been coming here are good. It's too bad they arrived when we were already overwhelmed with fumigation and all that. If they [government representatives] thought that coca was going to do so much damage they would have come with something before, something better, like medium- and long-term projects" (interview in Orito, July 2004).

Although the lack of confidence in the government has been exacerbated by the frequent fumigation, not only of coca crops but of legal crops and established alternative development projects, and although fumigation operations overshadow other aspects of government presence, coca growers continue to demand a state presence rather than resist that presence, contradicting the idea that they belong to networks of armed actors and as such act against the state. This very call for state action has become a central demand in the context of the armed conflict between guerrillas, paramilitaries, and the army in Putumayo. When popular organizations define themselves as a "civil society," they are presenting themselves as civilians affected by the armed conflict who do not want to be identified with any of the armed groups confronting each other. Thus the new forms of collective citizenship being constructed define an emerging local civil society in opposition, not to the state, but to the armed actors.[13]

This affirms the social representation of the state as a provider of services crucial to the people of this marginal region who feel abandoned by it and are treated as fifth-class citizens (Ramírez 2001). However, as the antiterrorist struggle took priority coca came to be viewed by Álvaro Uribe's government solely as a source of financing for terrorism, and the social, economic, and political problems of small growers that impelled them to cultivate coca were given no further consideration. Moreover campesinos are considered supporters of the armed actors without realizing that the activities of the illegal armed actors in the region and the degree to which they actually control territory have affected the access of campesinos to alternative development projects because these projects were frequently withdrawn due to breakdowns in public order. Furthermore it can be argued that the hegemony exercised by armed actors in different areas has limited even further the implementation of a comprehensive alternative development plan.

The Deployment of Good Governance, Social Capital, and Civil Society in Putumayo

Under advanced liberalism, as Rose has pointed out, the relationship between the state and the people changes, and "the image of the social state gives way to that of the facilitating state." This means that the state maintains "the infrastructure of law and order," and the people or civil society are expected to "promote individual and national well-being by their responsibility and enterprise" (1999:139). Thus under the neoliberal framework of the free market *good governance* is "simply a means to development" (Stirrat 1992:205, 209), so that it is expected that a good government will provide the conditions for effective and efficient markets. Both civil society and social capital are central to development and good governance. Civil society is depicted as harmonious, monitoring the activities of the state, controlling its expansion, and advocating for good government in the terms defined above. It is presumed that at the local level citizen participation is more effective. Moreover decentralization of government is assumed to facilitate the governmental process. In sum, development from below is prioritized and communities are said to be the main actors. Thus under the new development agenda strengthening civil society becomes central and is "understood to mean the sphere of association [voluntary rather than ascriptive] situated between the state on the one hand and family and kin groups on the other" (Harriss 2002:111). This approach is "locked into a dichotomy of civil society versus the state" (Howell and Pearce 2001:7).

This is a problematic perspective in the context of Putumayo, as discussed earlier, mainly because achieving a strong civil society requires, first of all, autonomy from the armed actors, and the state represented by local government representatives is participating in this endeavor. It is worth bringing attention to the fact that when the employees of Chemonics talk about civil society they are referring fundamentally to the members of the NGOs, the sectors of civil society "whose behavior is 'acceptable' according to governmental standards" (Dagnino 2003:4), in contrast to the "criminal behavior" of coca growers. As a result of the stigmatization of the coca producers as criminals and guerrilla collaborators, it is implicitly assumed that in Putumayo there is no civil society. However, Chemonics defines itself as committed to the aim of strengthening civil society through the creation of a network of the ten national and local NGOs with which Chemonics has established contracts, as well as by promoting the creation of producers associations, a central purpose of this NGO network. Various authors have called attention to the regulatory functions that NGOs have assumed under the neoliberal policy of minimizing the role of government. Whitehead (2007:81–84) emphasizes that NGOs and civil society organizations "are viewed as more effective deliverers of social services than the state" and as a result become part of a "civic governance." Gupta and Ferguson (2002:990) take this argument even further when they see emerging a "system of transnational governmentality" as a result of this "outsourcing of the functions of the state to NGOs." As NGOs assume government functions they intervene to shape the behavior of their project's recipients (Li 2007), an aspect that is analyzed in depth by Wilson's chapter in this volume for the case of the Federation of Indigenous Organizations of Napo in Ecuador, where leadership traits have been recently reshaped as a result of the interaction between indigenous peoples and NGOs.

A February 2002 report by USAID, *Foreign Aid in the National Interest: Promoting Freedom, Security, and Opportunity*, establishes the focus of international development assistance in accordance with this neoliberal mandate. The report states that USAID's first strategy is promoting democratic governance. Governance is defined as "a broad concept encompassing the capacity of the state, the commitment to the public good, the rule of law, the degree of transparency and accountability, the level of popular participation and the stock of social capital. Without good governance, it is impossible to foster development. No amount of resources transferred or infrastructure built can compensate for—or survive—bad governance." This definition stresses popular participation and a stock of social capital, which implies an emphasis on "communities," in order to achieve good governance and overall economic development. It does not call for a strong civil society. Wilson's chapter in this volume alerts us to how NGOs seek to work with well-built grassroots organizations to implement their projects because these organizations are expected to guarantee their work based on the previous evidence of social capital. In contrast to Wilson's analysis of NGOs attracted to strong indigenous organizations in Ecuador, in the case of Putumayo the central issue for NGOs is to tackle the lack of social capital. As Wilson points out, social capital is not necessarily a condition possessed a priori by grassroots organizations and it can be either strengthened or dismantled by NGOs.

But what about the role of NGOs in the strengthening of the capacity of the local state and its institutions in a conflictive area? It is worth clarifying that Chemonics has contracted Colombian NGOs with both national and local agendas to implement alternative development programs in the field. Chemonics pointed to "the bad institutional management of economic resources by state agencies" due to inefficiency and corruption as a problem that impeded gaining the trust of coca growers in the alternative development projects (Llano 2004:11). Chemonics also argued that NGOs "open doors, offer security, establish credibility with local communities and help in management of inherent difficulties that arise from the presence of a U.S. organization operating in a highly volatile environment," the last of which refers to the security problems resulting from Chemonics personnel working in a conflictive area (Chemonics Inc.-USAID 2006:32). This diagnosis justified Chemonics' direct contracting of NGOs, and no USAID resources passed through government bodies such as the Peace Investment Fund, created to administer Plan Colombia's resources, or PLANTE. Chemonics was able to develop projects autonomously. Moreover mayors did not participate in designing the alternative development policy conducted by the NGOs in the municipalities they governed, and they complained that the amount of resources invested by the development agency in each municipality was three times the municipal budget, which fundamentally comes from central government transfers. A local official explained, "The final blow for the region came from the executing NGOs and from Chemonics. These institutions implement their projects with an enormous amount of money compared to our municipal and departmental budgets, and they work without any relation to the needs and expectations of the communities. They ignore the development plans and the insti-tutional projects of the [local and departmental] governments and state agencies working in the region" (interview with the director of Corpoamazonía, July 2003).

Chemonics claimed that although "the participation of local authori-ties is highly desirable because it offers legitimacy to local projects, enhances community acceptance and helps with effective dissemi-nation of key information," local governments were not capable of implementing or managing financial resources because they not only lacked local legitimacy and administrative efficiency, but risked po-litical manipulation due to the department's insufficient tradition of governance (Chemonics Inc.-USAID 2006:32). The role that official local institutions have played or can continue to play in the region work-ing together with the coca growers to construct a comprehensive development plan for Putumayo is discarded in the name of building community, constructing social capital, and restoring the "social fabric." Thus instead of strengthening state institutions to achieve governance competence, the initial central strategy of the development agency was to work directly with volunteer organizations and promote com-munity associations based on trust, a process I analyze in the next section. Moreover the community associations that Chemonics and NGO functionaries promoted were expected to generate not only social capital but their own economic development. As DeFilippis has pointed out, analyzing what he calls "the myth of social capital in community development," "The benefits of social capital and cIvIl society extend beyond simply promoting and supporting democratic institutions of government to generating and sustaining economic growth" (2001:787).

It can be argued that in Putumayo the procedures adopted by the development agency to combat corruption and increase efficiency have in practice decreased state legitimacy, bypassed state agencies, further eroded public confidence in the state, and effectively reduced the already minimal state presence in the region. Local governments are in fact undermined, contradicting the promises of neoliberal reform to strengthen the local state as a result of decentralization and state restructuring. In addition, the role of the central state as a provider of services in the region and as an interlocutor with the small campesinos is limited. In December 2002, four months after Álvaro Uribe came to office, PLANTE was eliminated and regional offices were closed.

The Construction of Social Capital, Peasant Enterprise Associations, and Implications for Communal Organizations

When *colonos* from the heartland of the country arrived in Putumayo they founded rural settlements called *veredas* composed of a number of nuclear families separated from each other by thirty to fifty meters. In many cases members of these nuclear families also formed extended families. Each *vereda* has a Junta de Acción Comunal (JAC), a Communal Action Committee, which in rural Colombia has become a basic unit of social organization at the community and village levels. Each JAC has a president and a number of other officers called "dignitaries" (*dignatarios*), all elected for three-year terms, as well as many "affili-ates" (*afiliados*), in this case the *vereda* residents. The president and the board members are in charge of establishing relations, demanding services, and proposing projects to improve the living conditions in their *vereda*. Once a JAC is created, its main project is to construct a school building and demand a primary school teacher. In many cases a JAC splits and another is created when the *vereda* expands and the school is too far away for some of the children to attend. The JAC and the school are always associated, and together they mark the beginning of a colonizing process.

The JAC is a political institution representing the interests of the communities under its jurisdiction that emerges as a peasant form of governance and has been part of the rural organizational landscape for a long time in other parts of the country. As the visible political body of almost every peasant community, JACS are the government's main interlocutors with the members of these communities. The government has also established mechanisms to incorporate the JACS into the governmental structure through the requirement of a *personería juridical,* which gives each junta a registration number in the Chamber of Commerce of its department, in order for each JAC to be recognized as legally constituted. To be elected a board member implies social recognition as a political leader, and as such it is expected that board members will defend the communities' rights. This has led the JACS to confront government policies and to become the main promoters and leaders of peasant movements in rural areas that demand services from the government. On the other hand, guerrilla groups, as is the case with the FARC in Putumayo, control the campesino population through the JAC. The 1996 coca growers and collectors protest marches were promoted both by the FARC and a civic movement that worked with the JAC network to coordinate the marches. The marches are remembered for their extensive territorial coverage and coca growers' participation, clearly showing that at the local level the organization of the campesino population was in the hands of the civic movement and JAC leaders.

Using the discourse of promoting participation and modernizing the organization, but mostly as a response to the general political stance of JACS in the rural areas, in 2002 and 2003 a new law and decree were enacted by the government to establish tighter regulations controlling

JACS, including delimiting the number of members, causes of suspension, and type of participation.[14] From the government's perspective JACs are entities that perform social control functions.

When alternative development projects were initiated in 1995 by PLANTE in Putumayo, the JACS were seen as the main interlocutors with the state agencies in charge, and individual credits were prioritized. By 1999, however, a new development model began to be implemented based on collective credits and the promotion of "peasant enterprise organizations." The JACS were viewed as too political. Development required technical associations. In the words of an official from the National Plan for Alternative Development, "Negotiation for an alternative Project is conducted with the JACS as the political representative organizations, but the economic alternative project has to be implemented through the creation of an 'entrepreneurial' association. This doesn't mean that if I become a partner of an association the JAC has to disappear. On the contrary, I am constructing social development and human capital" (interview with Arturo Ospina of PLANTE, April 4, 1999). Ospina was describing the first stages of the new development agenda. He referred to human capital rather than social capital because there was still concern related to the well-being of the communities as a result of promoted state development programs. But he made explicit the depoliticization of development that has been described by various authors (DeFilippis 2001; Fine 1999, 2001; Foley and Edwards 1996; Harriss 2002; Harriss and De Renzio 1997; Putzel 1997; Tarrow 1996; Tilly 1991). By 2001, when USAID under Plan Colombia took over alternative development in Putumayo, this was the model that was being implemented.

Chemonics initiated activities in Putumayo through the Program on Local Initiatives for Alternative Development and Early Eradication (PILDAET), guided by the need of the U.S. government to evaluate the success of the alternative development program quantitatively through the number of hectares fumigated or eradicated. Although it was supposed that the early eradication initiative should arise from within the community, a participating *vereda* had to commit to eradicate 100 percent of its coca in order to receive project financing. The PILDAET agreements were signed by the whole *vereda*, not individual residents. The eradication was to be carried out in "representative and verifiable areas" (PLANTE 2001). The JACS, as the political representatives of the *vereda* community, were indispensable for accomplishing this objective, and the NGOs contracted by Chemonics began to work with them. As a Chemonics report explains, "The first phase of the Colombia Alternative Development Program (CAD) between 2001 and 2003 was geared toward building a platform for change." This meant eradicating coca and establishing "licit activities through the introduction of new agricultural alternatives with modern technology" and contributing "to the creation of institutional conditions necessary for a licit economy by means of social capital formation and strengthening with community and regional-level organization" (Chemonics Inc.-USAID 2006:20).

Rose has pointed out that under advanced neoliberalism "it is through moral reformation, through ethical reconstruction, that the excluded citizen is to be re-attached to a virtuous community" (1999:139). He further explains that it is "through the political objectification of 'this community' and its culture that government is to be re-invented," and he emphasizes that this idea of community building becomes "governmental when it is made technical" (172–75). The conduct of individuals "is made intelligible in terms of the beliefs and values of their community." In an illegal environment, with people depicted as "rootless," without cultural identity, and lacking a "social fabric," community building becomes even more significant, as it is assumed by the development agency that a redemption of the population from the armed actors and the coca mentality is also achieved when the sense of belonging to a community is restored and a kind of social capital is constructed. As Margarita Chaves discusses in her chapter in this volume, in Putumayo the mobility of urban and rural populations challenges the normative discourse that fixes identity to territory and bounded communities. However, the imaginary of the community as a natural foundation of social interaction in rural areas continued to haunt Chemonics officials, who diagnosed a "crisis of community and/or of government" in this colonization area, and as a consequence experienced "a fascination with and desire for community," in the words of Creed (2006:12).

By 2003 Chemonics was working with fifteen thousand families, 25 percent to 30 percent of Putumayo's population (interview in Puerto Asís with Chemonics' manager of agribusiness, March 2003). Once coca was eradicated in a *vereda* the NGO in charge of the municipality presented the campesinos with a proposal for projects to be carried out through community organizations, emphasizing that agribusiness requires collective work for the projects to be competitive in the market. Chemonics proposed raising fish, pigs, and chickens; the campesinos wanted to raise cattle, arguing that they had more experience in this field and that there was already good pasture. They proposed to raise cattle in an intensive way that would not threaten the forest. Raising cattle did not require a central location for the animals, as a pig farm does, so each owner would be able to have cattle on his own property. Chemonics' plan was to implement twenty-two commercial pig farms in Putumayo, so this project was prioritized by the different NGOs, as explained by the legal representative of APES in the quote that opens this chapter. Campesinos complained that although they were asked by NGO officials what they wanted to produce and with whom they wanted to work (in accordance with NGOS' idea of trust), the NGOs actually constrained them and imposed their own judgments about such matters.

Once the campesinos accepted a project, a community association was created to carry it out. In some cases the whole *vereda* would work to develop a project and the JAC became the legal representative for project management, although this was not the rule. For example, in any *vereda* you could find eight people working on fish farming, ten people growing sugar cane and producing *panela* (brown sugarloaf), and eleven people raising chickens for meat. In some cases campesinos were able to negotiate raising cattle under ecological systems that included silviculture. Each association had to register with the Chamber of Commerce to be legally constituted and eligible to open a joint bank account with an NGO representative to coadminister the project. To be approved, every expense had to pass through a Support and Oversight Committee that was composed of the board of directors of the association, a technician, and a representative of one of the NGOs. Three signatures were required on any check: those of the president and treasurer of the association and an NGO representative. Campesinos resented this, saying that they were treated as either corrupt or incapable of managing funds.

As a beneficiary of the program stated, "The culture of the JACs has been disrupted and you can find four associations of producers under one JAC." He added, "These associations have no future because they are born spontaneously in response to a specific interest in a project, not because the members have an interest in making progress [meaning a broader comprehensive goal], and when the project is over those associations end, while our organization that had other reasons to start is still and will continue to live" (interview in Orito, August 2003). Whether decisions to set up an organization are autonomous helps determine if an enterprise association has long-lasting durability. As Creed points out, this "[fascination] and desire for community may be inadvertently generating disappointment, alienation, fragmentation and segregation" (2006:13). These are all unintended consequences that took place in Putumayo.

As alternative development projects began to be implemented, internal conflict and dissension as well as differing levels of commitment began to undermine the notions of naturally homogeneous and functional communities. Most of the campesinos in the area had migrated from the Andean region, where small individual property is the norm and there is little tradition of extrafamilial collective production. Autonomous nuclear families may work collectively on specific tasks with others but usually only with their extended families and some neighbors, who may also be related. Having to work together on an ongoing basis became one of the main concerns of the campesinos on Chemonics projects. One campesino compares his work before and after the arrival of Chemonics:

When you're going to do a project with the municipality, like a school for example, then you do contribute your labor, but the community just meets no more than one day and the next week another day and no more. In these projects, though, it's very different because you have to spend every day of the week on the project. How can I explain it? [With Chemonics] we were planting sugarcane so we had to work every day on planting cane. We couldn't say you would plant for two days and then the other three days you were going to work somewhere else to make money. No, because when they got the project going that was the problem. So I told them [the NGO officials] that we would have to see, that they could pay us for our labor, say 10,000 pesos per day so you could work, and with that 10,000 pesos you could buy food for the week while you were working in the cane, and if there wasn't any more work in the cane then there was time for you to go work somewhere else for another day's wages. That's what I argued for, but they said absolutely not because that wasn't what was stipulated. I wanted to be in the project so much that I had to give in, but that was very clear to me. (Interview in Puerto Caicedo, July 2004).

A number of other problems emerged in the campesino associations. It was difficult to agree on how to organize different tasks and who would take them on. Financial and technical reports were a burden on the board of directors; they didn't have to write such reports for their own businesses, and if they made a mistake they were accused of mismanagement. Not everybody invested the same amount of work and time, and some didn't go to work every day; this affected those who did. They didn't know how to administer a business and felt that they needed more training than they were receiving from the NGO. They were not making a profit so members not only had to invest their labor without receiving any payment, but also had to make periodic payments just for the association to continue. Above all, campesinos claimed they were not "accustomed" to this type of agribusiness because they were "simple campesinos or peasants." As members began to leave the association the need to hire workers arose. This was not easy because people were making more money harvesting coca. In several cases pigs or chickens were distributed among the members of the association at the beginning of the project. Technicians on the project frequently commented, "It's difficult to make campesinos work as members of an association." Sometimes this difficulty was attributed to the origin of most of the campesinos in the Andean department of Nariño, where individual small property and the nuclear family unit of production is the norm.

Frank Hutchins (this volume), analyzing RICANCIE, a network of indigenous community-based organizations that promotes ecotourism in the Upper Amazon of Ecuador, engages in this debate when he examines how these organizations fight to be "owners of their development" through a process of "democratizing the economy," how they challenge state regulations that impede their full involvement in the tourism industry, enabling them to run a community-based business inserted in a global-scale market system. This outcome questions Chemonics' assessment of the paradox it faced in implementing its development agenda in Putumayo: "It appears that the processes that underlie the successful strengthening of social capital (based on broad and democratic participation) do not coincide with what is needed to create businesses or to establish value chains, which involves processes that are centrally organized, less democratic and include far fewer people" (Chemonics Inc.-USAID, 2006:30).

The second phase of CAD, between 2003 and 2006, was focused on promoting agro-industrial development through implementing "several agro-industrial chains to facilitate the commercialization of products both within and outside the alternative development areas." This new focus was viewed as reflecting "a legitimate concern to promote more sustainable regional development, which implies a greater presence and participation of the private sector in alternative development" (Chemonics Inc.-USAID 2006:20–22). Chemonics characterizes the two phases as an extensive versus intensive strategy, and evaluating the results points out that the major difficulty in the transition from the first to the second phase "Is the gap between the large number of families participating in voluntary eradication and the far smaller number that are involved in subsequent activities (for example, of more than 28,000 families that participated in the first phase of CAD, only 4,477 were involved in the second part)." The Chemonics report adds, "This situation inevitably creates expectations that cannot be fulfilled, affecting the credibility of all institutions involved in AD [alternative development]" (28). Chemonics officials attributed the lack of confidence local people had in the institutions to alternative development program management. It is worth recalling that over the years the lack of follow-through on development aid has left many farmers skeptical that the Colombian government will actually provide aid once their coca is eradicated, and doubtful that aid programs that are established will be sustained long enough to make a difference. This lack of confidence was exacerbated by the frequent fumigation of legal crops and the disruption of already established alternative development projects. This explains the lack of trust in institutions unrelated to the existence of the so-called perverse social capital. Paradoxically this same aerial spraying added to the presence of guerrillas and paramilitaries in the area fighting for the control of the territory and its population in order to gain the coca revenues, and encouraged the campesinos to accept the alternative development projects that Chemonics was offering them.

Although the development agency talked of strengthening community organizations already present in the area, it implemented market-oriented projects to generate economic growth as one of the main benefits of constructing social capital. These projects required "enterprise associations," and Chemonics demanded that campesinos in the area create these types of associations in order to receive funding. The associations were a response to "a context in which the state is gradually withdrawing from its role as guarantor of rights [and] the market is offered as a surrogate instance of citizenship . . . as the incarnation of modernizing virtues and the sole route to the Latin American dream of inclusion in the First World," in the words of Dagnino (2003:14–15). But we must remember that the final objective is to guarantee control of the population in order to achieve good governance, a goal that becomes even more important in the context of the war on drugs, in which narcotrafficking has been declared a threat to U.S. security. Improving the welfare of the most excluded sectors is not a priority. The population is left to compete in the market in what is called the "best situation," that of "socially responsible capitalism," which fosters "partnerships and dialogue among civil society, business and government" in order to "provide a new means of regulation [of the market] that simultaneously injects a degree of morality into the working of capitalism" (Howell and Pearce 2001:8). This is the situation with regard to three plants Chemonics constructed in Putumayo in 2004, two for the dehydration and processing of tubers and grains and one for the production of feed concentrate for fish, fowl, pigs, and cattle, as well as other industrial products.

The three plants were consolidated into a single legal entity and the company's stock was distributed in the following manner: 52 percent to the private sector, 15 percent to the public sector, and 33 percent to agricultural producers (Chemonics Inc.-CAD 2004:1). The campesinos who belong to the third group are better off than those who grow manioc and maize independently for sale to the company. The latter group complained that the company was paying just one-third of the price paid in the regional market.

Power relations, property rights, and inequality regarding access to resources by these local enterprise associations are washed out of the concept of social capital, as is the importance of political movements, parties, and labor unions as interlocutors with the state or any development agency. As an employee at Chemonics stated, "The state should be able to invest in the businesses that we create, that we organize, so that the business can provide the technological services and the consultancy that are necessary to the campesino so he can produce under the conditions that the market demands. So the state, the private sector, and the community have to collaborate to create that intermediary. This is not the kind of thing that can be done in one or two years. It's not just like a meeting with the mayor to make a list of community needs; it's much more complicated" (interview, August 2004).

The people of the region feel "assaulted" (in the words of a campesino leader in Orito) by this new scheme of enterprise associations. They were not prepared for it, and although they really wanted to participate, they complain that the organizations have not functioned well due to a lack of training. They themselves assume their incompetence is to blame for their inability to achieve better living conditions (interview with community leader, August 2004). The demand for a way to develop skills is made repeatedly, and its lack is seen as an obstacle to campesino organization: "Why do I say that illiteracy is part of this? Because suppose we look at the rural population. I think that eighty percent of the campesinos are uneducated. We're illiterate if not worse ... we don't understand what we're supposed to do; we go to one of these forums and we're afraid to speak. Sometimes we're afraid to speak even in front of a group of fellow campesinos" (remarks of a community leader at a May 1997 forum).

Chemonics accepts that "many potential partners come with limited business know-how and capability." However, "training and technical assistance to strengthen their management ability and consolidate their market knowledge requires considerable time, which in many cases can easily reach the five year mark" (Chemonics Inc.-USAID 2006:36). As a result, external private partnership was privileged.

In its fourth report, the Contraloría General de la República concludes that the design of the program Campo en Acción, promoted by the government through Plan Colombia, "is not the most appropriate to confront the problems of peasant agriculture, especially in conflict zones. Its programs seem more oriented to the strengthening of entrepreneurial organizations that are structurally very different from 'peasant enterprises'" (2003:47). Although the enterprise association has been privileged, evidenced by the increase in the number of associations of producers in the region, other forms of communal organization already present in the area have had to be integrated, including the JACs, because of the power they have as legitimate community representatives in the more marginalized areas of the Putumayo department, which coincides with high amounts of coca cultivation. Such is the case with the municipalities of San Miguel and Valle del Guamués. As a politically recognized entity, these JACs were able to negotiate with the guerrillas so that the NGOs would be able to work in these areas. In a recent interview the governor of Putumayo, Carlos Alberto Palacios, strongly suggested that USAID and its contractors should consult the JAC: "Consult closely with communities in the elaboration of their own development and business plans. Make existing local organizations, particularly the JACs, central actors in this process. This in turn will strengthen democracy, local participation and the social fabric."[15]

Even Chemonics recognized that "there is a strong sense of democracy among the social organizations in Putumayo, reflected in various initiatives to form community groups, the election of local leaders by consensus, and the legitimization of their administration" (Chemonics Inc.-USAID 2006:30). But under the new neoliberal market-oriented development agenda, Chemonics asserts, "The biggest challenge is to overcome the inherent contradiction between an enterprise culture and the social objectives of the association" (36).

Conclusions

Six months before the departure of Chemonics from Putumayo, a project to consolidate the economic and social capital of the beneficiaries of CAD was funded with the remaining money as a strategy to guarantee continuity of the PILDAET program in the department. The objective was to support social initiatives presented by the communities. This project was implemented with the participation of the official and private institutions in the area that were invited to cofinance the community proposals. The Fund to Support the Social Initiatives of the Veredas was created with U.S.$400 million; it involved eight municipalities and forty-two institutions. The program was executed by three NGOS; 141 projects were funded (Chemonics Inc.-CAD 2005:13). Importantly, only when Chemonics was preparing to leave did both the JACS and the institutions in the area suddenly become important resources to guarantee continuity of the projects. Moreover, in the final report of the Development Program CAD, Chemonics states that one of the important lessons was "to gather solid evidence that, a) social capital exists; b) people can feel it and express it; c) it is possible to measure it; and d) there was clearly a positive change in social capital in Putumayo in the period 2000–2004" (Chemonics Inc.-USAID 2006:29). If social capital exists, can it be developed and promoted? Or is this process of promoting social capital disguising or disregarding, intentionally or otherwise, structural issues of inequality as well as the local associations and institutions that are working together to resolve structural problems in the region?

Chemonics states that it is open to debate whether the agroindustrial chains will be able to "survive the rigors of competitive markets without donor subsidies" and maintains that conditions in the majority of the regions where illicit crops are produced create major disincentives to investment (Chemonics Inc.-USAID 2006:22, 20). The mayor of Orito has already closed the animal feed plant; its monstrous building was left behind by Chemonics as testimony to what happens to an external enterprise that does not include the local population in its design. We must ask whether the promotion of programs to include Putumayan campesinos in the free market is undermining

ALTERNATIVE DEVELOPMENT IN PUTUMAYO

their existing strengths, augmenting exclusion, and disempowering the poorest and the already excluded and marginalized.

In response to the situation analyzed, coca growers continue to protest and seek to become visible political actors. As the second phase of Plan Colombia was about to begin its implementation in 2006, peasant associations of different municipalities of the Putumayo department organized a departmental assembly with the assistance of the governor, the mayors of the thirteen municipalities, and public officials, as well as the peasant associations, to discuss an Integral Development Plan for Putumayo, recalling the marches of 1996 and the proposals presented to the government at that time. One of the campesinos' objectives is to establish a direct relation with the Presidency Alternative Development Program and USAID without the intermediation of the NGOs, arguing that the contractors instead of the campesinos were benefiting, and claiming their capacity to define policies and alternative programs for the Putumayo, supported by local government representatives. After four years of alternative development projects and NGO activity in the region, campesinos have catalogued the language, skills, and methods of NGOs and seek to use a similar language to assert their capacity to engage in alternative development without NGO guidance, an unintended consequence of a new development agenda under neoliberal guidelines, concurring with Postero's argument that "subjects of neoliberalism find in it a number of resources and tools" (2006:18). Can this be considered an example of productive social capital?

Notes

The fieldwork informing this chapter was carried out in the department of Putumayo, Colombia, between 1999 and 2004 as part of an ongoing research project funded by the Colombian Institute of Anthropology and History and the Colombian Institute for the Advancement of Development Science and Technology (Colciencias). The project focused on the impact of Plan Colombia on local peasant and cocalero organizations and the construction of citizenship in the context of the international war against drugs and terrorism. This chapter was written while I was the Santo Domingo visiting scholar at the Rockefeller Center for Latin American Studies and was delivered as a paper at the 2005 AAA annual meeting in the panel Creating the Present in the Past: Violence,

Memory, and the Community in the Study of Latin America, organized by Kimberly Theidon from Harvard University and Andrew Canessa from the University of Essex. I want to thank Patrick Wilson and Frank Hutchins for their comments on this chapter, which not only pointed out inaccuracies but made me improve my analysis.

1. The NGOs contracted by Chemonics Inc. to administer resources and implement projects in the campesino sector were Fundaempresa (Puerto Asís and Puerto Leguízamo), Restrepo Barco (Puerto Caicedo and Villa Garzón), Vida y Futuro (San Miguel), Huairasachac (Orito), Comfamiliar (Valle del Guamués), and Maloca (Mocoa, Orito).

2. Chemonics website, www.chemonics.com/AboutUs/OurHistory.asp (accessed July 15, 2005).

3. Dirección Nacional de Estupefacientes website, www.dne.gov.co/index.php?idcategoria=738 (accessed September 30, 2008).

4. The area of Colombia is 1,138,388 square kilometers, and its Amazon region is 423,473 square kilometers. This is 37 percent of Colombian territory and 6 percent of the South American Amazon. The Colombian Amazon is made up of the following departments: Caquetá, with 88,965 square kilometers; Putumayo, with 24,885; Guaviare, with 53,460; Amazonas, with 109,665; Vaupés, with 54,135; Guainía, with 72,238; and the southwestern part of Meta, with 10,125.

5. The rationale is "the realization that U.S. security is inextricably tied to the stability, prosperity, and well-being of the interdependent hemispheric and global communities" (Manwaring 2001:10).

6. See Center for International Policy, "The Colombia Aid Package by the Numbers," Washington DC, July 5, 2000, available online at http://ciponline.org/colombia/aidcompare.htm.

7. The appropriation allocated, in millions, $3.0 for peace, $68.5 for alternative development, $37.5 for aid to the internally displaced, $51.0 for human rights, $13.0 for judicial reform, and $45.0 for rule of law.

8. Different Colombian agencies have used different definitions of "small." Consejo Nacional de Estupefacientes (National Narcotics Council) and Dirección Nacional de Estupefacientes (National Directorate of Narcotics) have used two hectares, while Colombia's development agency PLANTE, founded in 1995 but eliminated under President Uribe, referred to three to five hectares (National Program for Alternative Development 2001:47).

9. In 1996 more than 200,000 small coca growers and collectors gathered in one of the largest mobilizations in Colombian history as a result of the first large-scale fumigations in Western Amazonia of Colombia to protest the government failure to comply with earlier development agreements.

10. Government antidrug strategies include the following:

    1. The reduction of supply, or the war on drugs, through aerial spraying,

interdiction, the strengthening of the military, and alternative development.

2. Institutional strengthening through the confiscation and administration of properties acquired through money laundering and other illicit activities.

3. Reduction of demand.

4. Alternative social development.

11. he issue of civility recalls its earlier definition. During the eighteenth century, when the creation of a modern civil society was at stake, "incivility was the ghost that permanently haunted civil society. Civilization therefore denoted an ongoing historical process, in which civility, a static term, was both the aim and the outcome of the transformation of uncivil into civil behavior" (Keane 1998:117). This civilizing process was in the hands of the privileged classes of Europe because it was assumed that it was among the unprivileged that violence was reproduced.

12. In June 2004 the United Nations Office on Drugs and Crime estimated that "93 percent of all coca fields [in Colombia] were smaller than 3 ha (8.1 acres), accounting for approximately 69 percent of the total cultivation." The highest concentrations of coca crops can be found in departments with especially high poverty indicators; for example, 45 percent or more of the population without access to safe drinking water, electricity, sanitary, and educational services (United Nations Office on Drugs and Crime and Government of Colombia 2004:27).

13. For an analysis of the armed conflict in Putumayo, see Ramírez 2009.

14. Law 743 of 2002 and Decree 2350 of 2003.

15. "Gobernador contra las fumigaciones," *El Tiempo*, July 16, 2004.

References

Chemonics Inc.-Colombia Alternative Development Project. 2004. *Alternativas.* Bulletin 3. Bogotá.

———. 2005. *Informe mensual de monitoreo y evaluación.* October. Bogotá.

Chemonics Inc.-U.S. Agency for International Development. 2006. *Toward a licit economy: Colombia Alternative Development Program final report.* March. Bogotá.

Contraloría General de la República. 2001. *Plan Colombia: Primer informe de evaluación.* August. Bogotá.

———. 2003. *Plan Colombia: Cuarto informe de evaluación.* July. Bogotá.

Creed, Gerald. 2006. *The seductions of community: Emancipations, oppressions, quandaries.* Santa Fe NM: School of American Research Press.

Dagnino, Evelina. 2003. On confluences and contradictions: The troubled encounters of participatory and neo-liberal political projects. Paper presented at the Twenty-third Congress of the Latin American Studies Association, Dallas, Texas, March 27–29.

DeFilippis, James. 2001. The myth of social capital in community development. *Housing Policy Debate* 12 (4): 781–806.

Fine, Ben. 1999. The developmental state is dead—Long live social capital? *Development and Change* 30:1–19.

———. 2001. *Social capital versus social theory: Political economy and social science at the end of the millennium.* New York: Routledge.

Foley, Michael, and Bob Edwards. 1996. The paradox of civil society. *Journal of Democracy* 7 (3): 38–52.

Gupta, Akhil, and James Ferguson. 2002. Spatializing states: Towards an ethnography of neoliberal governmentality. *American Ethnologist* 29 (4): 981–1002.

Harriss, John. 2002. *Depoliticizing development: The World Bank and social capital.* London: Anthem Press.

Harriss, John, and Paolo de Renzio. 1997. "Missing link" or analytically missing? The concept of social capital. An introductory bibliographic essay. *Journal of International Development* 9 (7): 919–37.

Howell, Jude, and Jenny Pearce. 2001. *Civil society and development: A critical exploration.* Boulder CO: Lynne Reiner.

International Crisis Group. 2005. *War and drugs in Colombia.* Latin American Report No. 11, January 27. Washington DC.

Keane, John. 1998. *Civil society: Old images, new visions.* Stanford: Stanford University Press.

Li, Tania Murray. 2007. *The will to improve: Governmentality, development and the practice of politics.* Durham NC: Duke University Press.

Llano, Gregorio. 2004. *Construcción de capital social en zonas de conflicto e inmersas en la reducción de cultivos ilícitos: Resultados de la encuesta sobre Capital Social Programa CAD-Departamento de Putumayo-Colombia.* Bogotá: Documento del Proyecto CAD, Chemonics Inc.

Manwaring, Max G. 2001. *U.S. security policy in the Western Hemisphere: Why Colombia, why now, and what is to be done?* Carlisle PA: U.S. Army College, Strategic Studies Institute.

National Association of Campesinos. 2001. *Putumayo: Seminario taller seguimiento y monitoreo Plan Colombia,* August 11–12. Santiago, Putumayo.

National Program for Alternative Development. 2001. *Estrategia de desarrollo alternativo y pactos voluntarios para la sustitución de los cultivos con fines ilícitos.* December 5. Bogotá.

Observatorio para la Paz. 2000. Plan Colombia: Juego de máscaras. In *Cultivos ilícitos, narcotráfico y agenda de paz,* ed. Darío Posso. Bogotá: Mandato Ciudadano por la Paz, la Vida y la Libertad.

Ong, Aiwha. 1999. Clash of civilizations or Asian liberalism? An anthropology of the state and citizenship. In *Anthropological theory today*, ed. Henrietta L. Moore, 48–72. Cambridge and Oxford: Polity Press and Blackwell.

Postero, Nancy. 2006. *Now we are citizens: Indigenous politics in postmulticultural Bolivia*. Stanford: Stanford University Press.

Putnam, Robert. 2002. Foreword to *The role of social capital in development*, ed. Christian Grootaert and Thierry van Bastelaer, xxi–xxii. Cambridge: Cambridge University Press.

Putzel, James. 1997. Accounting for the "dark side" of social capital: Reading Robert Putnam on democracy. *Journal of International Development* 9 (7): 939–49.

Ramírez, María Clemencia. 2001. *Entre el estado y la guerrilla: Identidad y ciudadanía en el movimiento de los campesinos cocaleros del Putumayo*. Bogotá: Instituto Colombiano de Antropología e Historia-Colciencias.

———. 2009. Negotiating peace and visibility in Putumayo as a civil society in Putumayo amidst the armed conflict and the war on drugs. In *Colombia: Building peace in a time of war*, ed. Virginia M. Bouvier. N.p.: U.S. Institute of Peace.

Ramírez, Maria Clemencia, Kimberly Stanton, and John Walsh. 2005. Colombia: A vicious circle of drugs and war. In *Drugs and democracy in Latin America: The impact of U.S. policy*, ed. Coletta Youngers and Eileen Rosin, 99–142. Boulder co: Lynne Rienner.

Republic of Colombia. Law 30 of 1986. Narcotics statute. Estatuto Nacional de Estupefacientes. January 24. Bogotá.

Rocha, Ricardo. 2000. *La economía Colombiana tras 25 años de narcotráfico*. Bogotá: PNUD.

Rose, Nikolas. 1999. *Powers of freedom: Reframing political thought*. Cambridge: Cambridge University Press.

Rubio, Mauricio. 1997. Perverse social capital: Some evidence from Colombia. *Journal of Economic Issues* 31 (3): 805–16.

Stirrat, Roderick. 1992. "Good government" and "the market." In *Contesting markets: Analyses of ideology, discourse and practice*, ed. Roy Dilley, 203–13. Edinburgh: Edinburgh University Press.

Tarrow, Sidney. 1996. Making social science work across space and time: A critical reflection on Robert Putnam's *Making democracy work*. *American Political Science Review* 90 (2): 389–97.

Thoumi, Francisco. 2003. *Illegal drugs, economy and society in the Andes*. Baltimore: Johns Hopkins University Press.

Tilly, Charles. 1991. Review essay: Individualism askew. *American Journal of Sociology* 96 (4): 1007–11.

United Nations High Commissioner for Refugees. 2005. *International protection considerations regarding Colombian asylum-seekers and refugees*. March. Geneva.

United Nations Office on Drugs and Crime and Government of Colombia. 2004. *Colombia coca cultivation survey for 2003*. Bogotá: Government of Colombia.

U.S. Agency for International Development. 2000. *Strategic plan*. FY 2000–FY 2005. Bogotá.

———. 2002. *Foreign aid in the national interest: Promoting freedom, security and opportunity*. Washington DC.

U.S. General Accounting Office. 2002. *Efforts to develop alternatives to cultivation of illicit crops in Colombia have made little progress and face serious obstacles*. GAO/01-26, February. Washington DC.

U.S. State Department. 2001. *Fact sheet on United States policy toward the Andean region*. Washington DC.

———. 2004. Ambassador William B. Wood's remarks at the Villagarzón Agro-Industrial Center. http://usembassy.state.gov/posts/co1/wwwsww44.shtml# English.

Whitehead, Judith. 2007. Anatomy of disaster: The neo-liberal state in Mumbai's 2005 flood. *Focaal-European Journal of Anthropology* 49:81–98.

7. Normative Views, Strategic Views

The Geopolitical Maps in the Ethnic Territorialities of Putumayo

Margarita Chaves

> *Space is a social construction, and in turn,*
> *all social processes occur in a spatial*
> *dimension, whether conscious or not.*
> *However, the relationship is not unequivocal.*
> *Societies rarely relate to unique and coherent spaces.*
>
> Manuel Castells, *The Power of Identity*

In Putumayo, a colonization frontier in the southwestern Amazon of Colombia, the proliferation of demands for ethnic recognition propitiated by multicultural policy has posed a challenge for the institutions that handle state ethnic policies. These institutions attempt to maneuver in the midst of three related circumstances: the constant increase of populations defined as "ethnic"; the differential access to rights and services, such as health, education, and land allocation; and the conflicts generated among ethnic constituents (groups, collectives, individuals) due to competition for land. To confront this situation and to limit the reach of the groups that seek ethnic recognition, the state has demanded that the groups demonstrate ethnic authenticity by reference to cultural singularities and attachment to an ancestral territory. But despite the fact that ethnic identity and territory are not intrinsically connected, the conflation of the two is at the center of identity discourse and politics. Who benefits from this conflation? How does this change in time and space? How does this vary even within a single region? In this chapter I examine the consequences of inscribing ethnic identity into space from contrasting perspectives: the discourse of re-ethnicized and indigenous migrants and that of the legal state apparatus and its functionaries. The analysis is based on my recent work on identity politics in diverse areas of Putumayo, where indigenous and re-ethnicized peasant colonists coexist.[1] I use the term "re-ethnicized" to refer to processes of reconstruction of ethnic identity on the part of *mestizos* and indigenous people who only recently refused ethnic singularity for self-identification. Much of this process is linked to the rights and benefits that the Colombian state now confers under its multicultural policies. This reconstruction of ethnic identity combines the instrumental enunciation of the powerful artifice of difference with cultural productions associated with the revival of past things. Throughout this chapter I seek to explore the spatial dimension implicit in processes of re-ethnicization, which I have partly alluded to in other works (Chaves 2003a, 2003b, 2005).

Upon closer inspection, in the spatial and ethnic mobility characteristic of displaced populations and related to re-ethnicization converge complex economic, political, social, and cultural dynamics whose motion is dictated not only locally, but also in state and global arenas. Two of these dynamics are particularly relevant here. One is the constant spatial displacement of an important segment of indigenous and peasant populations within and outside of regional boundaries generated by the search for viable economic alternatives. Included in this type of forced mobility is the process of colonization of the Upper Amazon originating in the Andean highlands, a consequence of land expropriation that Andean peasants and indigenous populations underwent throughout the twentieth century. Forced displacement resulting from the threats represented by armed struggles between guerrillas and paramilitaries, who since the late 1990s have struggled to control key areas for coca production and commercialization, must also be taken into account. Unlike what happens in other regions in which the paramilitary presence has come hand in hand with a counteragrarian reform, that is, the expulsion of peasants and indigenous populations from their land for private appropriation, paramilitary intervention in Putumayo has focused on controlling coca producers by means of intermediaries who extort a percentage of their profits from producers of coca paste. (For an excellent analysis of these relations, see Jansson 2006.) The state military apparatus, as the main agent behind the conflation and implementation of antiterrorism and antinarcotics policies, has also played an important role in this struggle (see Ramírez, this volume).

The second dynamic relates to the way state intervention geared to controlling space and populations has generated processes of identity mobility. In particular it is important to understand the state's need to administer urban and rural re-ethnicized dwellers as well as displaced communities. Specifically the state seeks to regulate their demands over civil rights and the benefits associated with ethnic recognition (land, health services, education, and economic incentives) in a context in which all are sorely lacking.

These two dynamics coincide in time and space in Putumayo, where peasant and indigenous populations have redefined their territorial and ethnic boundaries following state parameters. The recent history of these processes, along with the complex context in which they are taking place, call for an analysis and comparison of concrete cases as a step toward a general characterization of the spatial dimension. It also allows us to understand debates related to the conceptualizations of space and ethnic claims by indigenous and peasant populations vis-à-vis state normativity crystallized in "ethnic codes," "geo-graphic" control, and institutions for territorial administration. To decipher these conceptualizations of the territory, or as Lefebvre (1991) would have it, the "representations of the space" (see Oslender 1999),[2] is my goal in this chapter. After delineating some regional dynamics, I explore visions of space and its production among the aforementioned regional actors.

The Regional Context

The 1990s in Putumayo were marked by the constitutional reform of 1991 and its implications for the redefinition of the political, territorial, ethnic, and social relations in the region. More recently, as the importance of supranational governance institutions grew in the late 1990s, state social policies toward the region were inscribed in the context of Plan Colombia (now Plan Patriota), sponsored mainly by the United States. Plan Colombia was conceived to assist small farmers who grow coca to make the transition to legal economic activity. By the time of its implementation in 2000 it had become an integrated strategy to combat the expansion of guerrilla forces and drug trafficking in many areas of the country. This reorientation of its initial goals was a result of pressure from the United States as the Plan's major donor (see Asociación Latinoamericana para los Derechos Humanos [Latin American Human Rights Association] 2000). Since then the state has deployed a strategy against insurgent groups, now labeled terrorists, and against coca cultivators through the combination of aerial fumigation and manual eradication programs, all supported by a military buildup.

With little success in fighting the consolidation of coca production as the most important component of the regional economy, Plan Colombia has also attempted to promote subsidized agro-industry projects as an alternative to coca cultivation and processing (see Ramírez, this volume). Paradoxically, however, instead of revitalizing the peasant rural economy these projects have allowed agriculture and cattle suppliers to profit from the state's social investments. Meanwhile, at least until 2006, the presence of diverse armed forces and the intensification of armed conflict due to the geopolitical strategy and competition for the control of coca production, as well as to the increase of extractive development (mainly oil) and extensive cattle ranching, has resulted in a complex social and political scenario for the civil population. Indigenous peoples and peasant colonists have been subjected to considerable socioeconomic tension and armed violence, and thus have been obligated to modify their lifestyle and to redefine their participation in the main political and economic processes in the region.

Historically the indigenous and peasant populations in the region could opt for settling in rural areas in two different ways. Indigenous people could choose to gain the fragile security offered by the *resguardo* system at the expense of restricting their geographic mobility.[3] Peasant colonists sought to consolidate their rural living through productive activities on their farms and to resist land expropriation and political terror that attempted to remove them from their land and livelihood. For both indigenous peoples and peasant colonists the alternatives have been to secure the state's meager presence and protection in the small towns or, willingly or not, to be subjugated to the authority of the main agents of the armed conflict, the guerrillas (the Colombian Revolutionary Armed Forces, FARC, in particular) and paramilitaries. In fact these have been the general dynamics for both populations in recent decades, as it was the articulation of the local economy with the global markets, both in the case of extractive oil development and in the case of coca cultivation and subsequent cocaine production.

Nevertheless at the beginning of the twenty-first century the absence of a labor market different from coca cultivation, together with the intensification of the armed conflict and the introduction of new methods for instilling terror in the local population, have forced a good portion of this indigenous and peasant population to leave rural settings in favor of urban centers. The new social conditions confronted by these displaced populations have led them to develop new cultural and political strategies so as to make their social reproduction viable.

Economically, however, the stressful and uncertain dealings related to the coca economy have brought both rural and urban Putumayan inhabitants to increasingly participate in "occult economies" of financial schemes such as pyramids, which share with the drug trafficking economy "the allure of accruing wealth from nothing."[4]

Along with displacement and within this political framework, the social dynamics of the region (and the nation), whether in the rural or urban context, have been marked by an intense process of redefinition of identity. Persistently individuals and collectives seek their inclusion into one or several official categories in order to benefit from state resources. *Desplazado/a* (refugee), *mujer cabeza de familia* (female head of household), *indígena* (Indian), and "below the poverty line" are only some of these categories. Such demographic categories of governmentality become the ground that defines both their identities and their claims (Chatterjee 2004). In this context the reconstruction of ethnic identity by peasant colonists and de-Indianized indigenous populations, who see in this crossroads a strategic opportunity to establish better terms for reevaluating their social condition vis-à-vis the dominant society, the state, and even indigenous peoples, has been prominent. In this way the peasant and indigenous populations have put into motion new cultural, political, and social processes that allow them to configure new social identities and to calibrate their position in the framework of the power relations that prevail in the region.

The Authentication of Indigenous Identity and the Politics of Indigenous Territorial Rights

For the purposes of this chapter it is crucial to highlight the role of the state in the dynamics of ethnic identity reconfiguration. Through its attempts to create mechanisms of administration and control in the region and through its policies of ethnic recognition and land allocation for indigenous populations, the state has managed to impact the logic of identity politics among indigenous peoples and peasant colonists. In 1999 and 2000 the General Administration of Indian Affairs of the

Ministry of the Interior issued four communiqués that enunciated the state's criteria for determining the validity of the increasing demands for recognition of indigenous ethnic identities. Among the outlined criteria that those groups petitioning such recognition must meet, "the existence of an indigenous *parcialidad* [community settlement] in which there will be a small *cabildo* created by them [its members] in keeping with their practices and customs" was constantly reiterated (Chaves 2003b:125). These three elements (a single territory, a specific form of government, and a distinct culture), supported by numerous laws and decrees, revealed a constraining concept of "indigenous community" on the part of the state. However, it did not weaken the efficacy of legal performativity on the part of re-ethnicized people. On the contrary, rituals of seamless blending and difference became everyday practices (for a detailed analysis of this process, see Chaves 2005), and although the requirements for determining who is an Indian were somewhat vague, the fixed nature of the criteria for recognition serves to fill in the absence of a "state's code of ethnicity." The result has been a reinforced construction of indigenous identities within the parameters of isolation and the display of cultural difference rooted in timeless "practices and customs."

In this context re-ethnicized indigenous peoples and peasant colonists find themselves navigating between the possibility of articulating some discursive coherence to their identity projects so as to link them to the creation of innovative political platforms and new subjectivities, or being co-opted in the reproduction of a government dynamics through their inscription in fixed identity categories to gain access to these benefits. In the first case, the state's anchoring of indigenous identity in a single territory and its nonacceptance of "a mere description of how people live" (Povinelli 2002) as an expression of their distinctive culture has encountered varied responses on the part of the indigenous *mestizo* populations and re-ethnicized peasants directly affected by it. Through the redefinition and negotiation of the cultural and political referents that mediate their interactions with the state, these re-ethnicized subjects have accomplished the destabilization of the power and influence not only of already recognized groups, but also of the state itself. This is particularly clear in regard to the exponential increase in those classified as indigenous following the state's delivery of ethnic criteria for recognition.

As I said before, instead of halting the multiplication of indigenous constituencies, the structuring of a code of indigenous ethnicity facilitated the labor of those who appealed to the exclusive juridical, political, social, and economic privileges granted to indigenous peoples in the constitution of 1991. In fact this normativity prompted re-ethnicized peasants to articulate identity discourses that subvert the original purpose of such normativity, that is, the administration and control of populations and territories. The paradoxical consequence of this very particularized legislation is that, even though it has made ethnic authentication more complicated, it has also produced seemingly complex and effective responses by those who seek ethnic recognition, thus challenging the state to envision new actions.

The dynamics of identity politics among indigenous and peasant colonist populations has not necessarily been accompanied by the development of a conscious and explicit questioning of the normative and ideological character of identity-making state policies. This holds true even in those cases in which indigenous or re-ethnicized peasant populations have been able to destabilize state intervention (Chaves 2003b). In this sense the modus operandi of these groups has been conditioned by the state's logic in its attempt to control the production of identity and indigenous territorial rights. To the extent that issues of territory constitute a component of the production of identities, the regional political geography is also state-produced. Following Porto-Gonçalves (2001), I mean by "geo-graphy" the inscription of the physical space, and in that sense the symbolic representation of the environment, and by "territory" I mean the physical space consciously appropriated by a social group, be it indigenous or governmental. The territory, physically and conceptually defined by the state, thus constitutes an institution of social control (Lefebvre 1991). The state converts the institution of territory as well as control over its cultural and political definitions, which imply the notion of its production, into an object to be manipulated. Therefore the territory becomes a space of confrontation among the different agents that seek to exercise power and affirm social, political, and economic dominion throughout a determined geographic area, in this case, Putumayo. But this confrontation does not imply that the tension between identity and territory is less central for the political and cultural dynamics of diverse social groups in Putumayo. In this sense the representations of identity that emanate from the state and from indigenous communities and peasant colonists, as well as the political constructions of territory articulated by all of them and challenged by armed actors, deserves serious and rigorous anthropological and sociological reflection that takes into account the political and economic nature of those moments (Dirlik and Prazniak 2001). This political framework allows us to understand debates related to the conceptualizations of space and ethnic claims by indigenous and peasant populations vis-à-vis state normativity crystallized in "ethnic codes," geo-graphic control, and institutions for territorial administration.

Territorial Anchorages, De-anchored Identities, Geopolitical Discourses

The anchoring of identity in territory poses diverse problems that need to be understood by looking at the different actors involved and their mapping of political space. I outline some of these problems in the following discussion about their theoretical and practical implications.

Territorial Anchorages

In Putumayo identity as a form of representation essentially linked to territory or a "lived space," as conceptualized by Lefebvre (1991), has a practical expression especially in the discursive agency related to identity politics among indigenous people that inhabit rural areas. The conflation of identity and territory has acquired particular relevance in indigenous politics because, to a great extent, indigenous construction of difference and ethnic singularity is rooted in the premise of their "aboriginality," that is, of their being original inhabitants of a territory or even a continent (Briones 1998). This discursive agency has been powerfully nourished by academic and political discourses generated nationally and globally, with which indigenous peoples maintain an ongoing dialogue. The case of colonists, indigenous or not, seems to be the inverse. Their identity politics reclaim a lived space from the discursive position of subjects who are not originally from the territory they inhabit today. The lack of coincidence between place of origin and place of residence constitutes a disadvantage when they advance their territorial claims to the state. This is clearly seen in cases when re-ethnicized indigenous peoples who are originally from Putumayo get to enter the political negotiation of ethnic rights recognized by the Constitution of 1991, for they have a relative advantage over re-ethnicized immigrants, even though both share similarities in terms of the process of reconstructing identity.

It is interesting that a contrast can be drawn between re-ethnicized indigenous communities in Bogotá and Putumayo with respect to place and legitimacy. In the nation's capital city outsider origin is more highly valued than insider. Re-ethnicized Muiscas, original inhabitants of Bogotá's high plateau, occupy a bottom rung in the ethnic hierarchy (cf. Zambrano 2006). The situation in Putumayo is exactly the opposite: autochthony ranks higher than the status of migrant. This difference has to do with dominant representations about the "proper" location for indigenous peoples. Bogotá figures as a developed urban center, where indigenous presence can be explained only as migration from the outside. Putumayo, due to its representation as an eminently rural and backward rainforest region, is instead imagined as prime indigenous territory within which migrants ought to be nonindigenous.

In this context state policy regarding the formation of indigenous *resguardos* in the area deserves analysis. The situation of *resguardos* in Putumayo differs radically from that in the Andean region. In the latter the *resguardo* is a form of collective land property, and the *cabildos* are a form of communal government; both date from the colonial period. Although both institutions were introduced by the Spanish, highland indigenous peoples appropriated them and they now serve as pillars of their social movements.[5] In the Amazon, however, both *resguardos* and *cabildos* came into being only recently. In the municipalities of Mocoa, Puerto Guzmán, and Puerto Asís, located in the piedmont (Map 1), *resguardos* formed during the 1970s.[6] In the rest of the region they appeared only during the mid-1980s, when the state undertook an aggressive policy to constitute areas of special protection, including indigenous *resguardos* and natural parks.[7] It is also important to note that most existing *resguardos* in Putumayo were created prior to recent environmentalist and multicultural legislation, under which enormous areas in the Amazon came under special protection. Therefore in the Amazonian context indigenous peoples in Putumayo have been the least favored in terms of the creation of new *resguardos*.[8] These *resguardos* are generally small and face serious obstacles to securing land access for their members: three of the four *resguardos* created in Putumayo in the 1990s do not exceed one hundred hectares.[9]

The exception is the recently created (June 2001) *resguardo* La Torre, located in the municipality of Puerto Guzmán, which illustrates the state's view of space with regard to indigenous territorial rights. This *resguardo* has 68,357 hectares, 15 percent of the municipal area of 4,565 square kilometers (see Map 1). While tracing the details of its creation I encountered contradictory practices and discourses accompanying a presumed generous territorial policy.[10] The official beneficiaries of the *resguardo* titles are Ingas from Villa Catalina, a small community located in the environs of the town of Puerto Guzmán. However, the studies carried out for its creation purported that this *resguardo* should

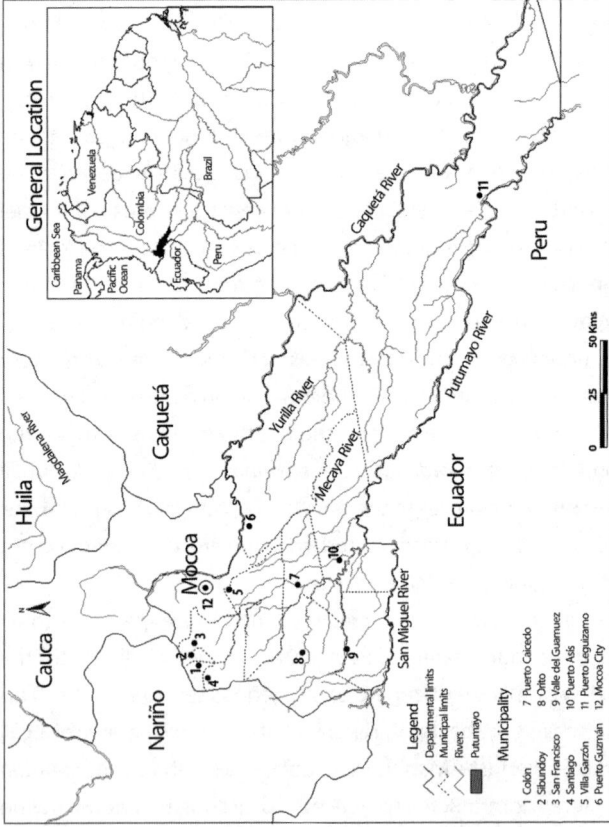

Map 1. Putumayo municipalities. Prepared by Manuel Pérez.

restore lands to Kofán, Inga, and Siona communities from the rural areas of Valle del Guamuez and Puerto Asís, located far from Puerto Guzmán (see map 1). These communities, which lost an important portion of their lands to peasant colonists who came to Putumayo in the bust of oil exploration in the 1960s, today benefit from national prestige due to the *yagé* healing rituals performed by their shamans, or *taitas* (Taussig 1987), which are regularly attended by the technical cadres of the state, especially those involved in environmental programs and sympathetic to the notion of the ecological native (Ulloa 2004). But contrary to the official discourse that supported the constitution of an indigenous territory distant from their settlements, the communities involved were far from willing to move to a territory located in an area under strict FARC military control and bordering areas of forest and oil reserves slated for future exploitation, where they might repeat previous loses. In addition this *resguardo*, like many others in the Amazonian region, had a series of overlapping normativities pertaining to environmental protection areas (forest reserve) and indigenous territorial rights (*resguardo* entitlement), which in this case had been mixed and went unquestioned by both community members and public administrators. Furthermore the official procedure and paperwork for *resguardo* creation, which is generally lengthy, was accomplished in less than a year thanks to the efforts of Zio-Ai, an organization of Kofán traditional healers whose actions articulated with global eco-governmentality (Ulloa 2004).[11] Paradoxically, up to the present the *resguardo* La Torre is entirely uninhabited except for the transit of guerrilla personnel through their territory.

I consider this case to be emblematic of current state visions of indigenous territoriality. In zones of colonization such as the Putumayo state policy for the constitution of *resguardos* has frequently been imbued with a normative vision that aims to secure indigenous territories through the definition of juridical parameters alone, colonizing in this way indigenous visions of the territory. To the extent that the *resguardo* is understood as a juridically bounded geographic space, the indigenous spatial perspective implicit in ordinary spatial experience is negated. The indigenous spatial experience does not reduce territory to the physical boundaries administered by the state but articulates multiple forms of spatial construction defined in accord with practical and cultural principles: domestic space, spaces for intra- and intercultural socialization, hunting territories, agricultural territories, trading territories, and so on (Lefebvre 1991). On the one hand, normalized representations, such as the representation of the *resguardo,* have a form of hegemonic power that obscures the intrinsic relationships between forms of production and the reproduction of social subjects and between the practical construction of the territory and the cultural and political production of geography as a social act. Moreover the normative vision of space proposed in the official structure of the *resguardo,* at least in this region, ignores the indigenous representation of territorial boundaries as a place of convergence instead of a place for dividing spaces and people. Patricia Vargas (1999) mentions something along these lines in her work on the Pacific region of Colombia, which concerns fluid territorial and social boundaries that are crisscrossed by relationships of cooperation and trade between neighboring Afro-Colombian, indigenous, and *mestizo* populations. The riverine Afro-Colombian communities of the Pacific Cauca region of Colombia studied by Oslender (2001) provide a similar case.

On the other hand, by tracing rigid boundaries among peoples that are not de facto spatially isolated the juridical act of *resguardo* creation can promote segregationist and essentializing attitudes toward indigenous populations. The following statements about the supposed separation between indigenous peoples and the rest of the regional population, voiced by a key government agent in charge of territorial indigenous affairs, helps clarify this point:

Following the delimitation and legal adjudication of indigenous territories [in the Amazon], the state has proceeded to acquire facilities and

establishments introduced in some of these territories by non-indigenous
people with the goal of returning these areas, free of non-indigenous
occupation, to their ancestral and legitimate owners. . . . The indigenous
communities that have received lawful adjudications have secured relative
tranquility in their internal lives, and a great number of these have been
able to reorganize their traditional forms of government and have even
made significant efforts towards the creation of new ones that stand in
harmony with the requirements posed by their contemporary condition
of relatedness with an external world. (Roldán 1993:67, my emphasis)

In a contradictory fashion, the protectionist goals that inspire the
creation of *resguardos* are surpassed and also negated by the very
artificiality of the proposed territorial boundaries. Indeed political and
economic processes such as oil exploitation, agrarian colonization,
and the armed conflict led this same government agent to recognize,
years later, the ephemerality of the *resguardo's* ability to control the
spatial expansion of these processes in Putumayo. In the short span of
fifteen years more than 50 percent of the territory initially assigned to
Inga and Kofán indigenous *resguardos* was lost (Roldán 1995:275).

De-anchored Identities

The anchoring of identity to territory has also led to the rejection,
by the state and some indigenous peoples themselves, of identity
claims by urban indigenous populations. Such claims are increasing
in Putumayo and other regions of Colombia. This denial finds support
in the forced association between the indigenous condition and rural
settings where *resguardos* are located. Among the urban indigenous
populations of Putumayo nowadays it is possible to identify (1) indigenous groups whose urban settlement predates steady processes
of urbanization; (2) re-ethnicized indigenous populations that for a
long time have settled in urban areas; (3) populations that belong to
diverse ethnic groups who have migrated voluntarily from their ancestral territories to urban centers with the goal of enjoying services

such as education and health; (4) individuals and families displaced because of the armed conflict; and (5) migrant indigenous populations who classify themselves into categories related to displacement. In all of these cases the quotidian space of identity re-creation is not isolated from that of other urban dwellers and is not circumscribed to their households, neighborhoods, or streets. On the contrary, these territories are constructed in the common spaces of symbolic production of identity, bounded in practices indigenous peoples deem autochthonous but that in reality are hybrid products not necessarily different from those of other urban populations.

Thus against the state's territorial hegemony re-ethnicized indigenous peoples redefine the terms of their territoriality and urban indigenous identities and take over the categories implied in public policy to include meanings that allow them to widen the regimes of democratic representation and pluralism proposed by the state. In the process the sizable population of indigenous and re-ethnicized people in Mocoa, Putumayo's capital city, as well as in the other municipal centers of the region has become evident to nonindigenous people. Their sites of congregation, their periodic celebrations and festivities, the modern building of their indigenous regional organization in Mocoa, the *yagé* houses or the *malocas* (longhouses) located in indigenous neighborhoods where indigenous shamans carry out healing sessions, their tenacious political response to the state, all suggest that urban indigenous territoriality is marked importantly by enunciating the place of indigenous ethnic identity in the process of urbanization of this area of colonization. In this way the normative discourse that fixes identity in territory confronts urban indigenous constructions of identity and territory.

The situation of three Murui (Uitoto) indigenous families from Puerto Leguizamo illustrates this well. They were related by kin ties and included *colonos*, and I found them in 2002 in a settlement of displaced people in the periphery of Mocoa, close to the new highway that connects this urban center with Bogotá. This setting, similar to a squatter settlement, allowed me to see the organizational impetus of the representatives of the displaced population, who grouped and instructed them in how to settle as a community in order to gain legal title over the space they were now occupying. House architecture, although using basic materials, did not take away from a comfortable layout, which included bedrooms, kitchen and entrance, stove, refrigerator, television, and dining-room, all indicating that although construction could be improved, the intention was to settle permanently. House areas, although small, were surrounded by open yards in which people planted manioc, plantain, pineapple, and ornamental plants, pointing to the rural background of their inhabitants. When I inquired into the reasons for displacement, which had occurred three years earlier, I learned that, in their case, it had been voluntary and motivated by the desire to access better basic services and the powerful appeal of urban centers. That this was included under the rubric of displacement was the result of state strategies that had offered people the opportunity to be brought to the state's attention under the category of "vulnerable population,"[12] which differentiates them from displaced people, who have been expelled by the armed conflict and fumigation programs. This is how Marina Nofuya, one of the three Uitoto siblings, explained it to me:

We came three years ago because the situation was too difficult there [in Puerto Leguizamo],[13] and we do not know if it is going to deteriorate. There are no jobs, the army is everywhere, and the children need a good education. It is better here and one is not locked indoors. Because one can only leave there by plane, which is way too expensive; instead here one can head to Bogotá or Pasto if one wants, and everywhere one can find the colonies of Leguizameños. Our elders stayed there on the farms, in the resguardo. Since we are here already, the family has a place to go in case of necessity.

Her analysis of why she decided to be a *desplazada* in Mocoa factors in the capacity of other actors, with greater influence, to intervene in territorial matters and the diverse interests of family members of different generations. Her reasoning displays a strategic vision about space and identity, one that privileges awareness of the historicity of subjects and therefore of a changing, flexible, and operationalized construction of identity responsive to context. The way she enunciates it, Murui identity is woven along diverse lines, in multiple webs, which connect her not only with those belonging to the "Murui people," as she said, but with people related to the place from which she traces her roots, Puerto Leguizamo. The reference to "the colony" is no more than a sign of the important role that urban setting has played in the socialization of Murui people, allowing her to alternate her ethnic identity with her locally rooted identity that highlights the importance of the interaction between indigenous and nonindigenous people and of neighboring social networks. Access to locally rooted identities also enables the combination of various sources of social recognition, creating a highly diversified pattern that is structured on the grounds of transcultural experience. This permits indigenous and nonindigenous people to resist processes of individualization and social atomization typical of urban settings. In this way they gain organizational capacity and can generate a sense of belonging in new territories. When conditions are favorable, they can even articulate new cultural identities.

Just as in the case of territorial anchorages, the *resguardo* promotes the subordination of social practices of territorial construction to juridical normativity, and among certain indigenous sectors the normative power of identity anchoring promotes the utilization of the link of indigenous identity with rural setting to claim territorial rights. A form of strategic essentialism is produced in this case, as defined by Spivak (1988), in that an essentializing and stereotyped discourse is momentarily embraced with the prospect of political gain (titling of land in rural areas). Despite being problematic, as this often gives way to territorial claims that contradict contemporary indigenous urban conditions, identity anchorages sometimes constitute the only way subaltern subjects can relate to a dominant society (Povinelli 2002), paradoxically contributing to the rural typification that negates the diversity of contemporary indigenous locations, neutralizing indigenous emancipation in urban settings.

Geopolitical Discourses

Geopolitical discourses promoted by the state, implicit in the revindication of identities anchored in *resguardo* territories, resonate with the struggles of indigenous organizations. This struggle is presented as a normative and legal discourse that assumes land acquisition and protection to be a function of legal boundaries, just as the aforementioned government agent suggests: "The conversion of wide territories into the patrimony of diverse indigenous populations of Colombia has come to constitute a juridical instrument, in the hands of those entitled, to secure the defense of these territories against the advance of colonization and against the incursions of those that loot natural resources. These adjudications also have the effect of allowing indigenous peoples to define a rational model of amplitude of physical spaces" (Roldán 1993:68).

The similarity between this assertion, the ecological rationale that underlies the creation of natural parks and reserves, and the global discourse on sustainable development and biodiversity is noteworthy.[14] In both instances it would seem that the legal creation of space as park, reserve, and *resguardo* suffices to consider them protected from whomever and for whatever. But the reality is different wherever political and economic agents (such as guerrillas and drug traffickers) with greater capacity for spatial intervention than indigenous peoples are present, permanently challenging the state's legitimacy. In these cases the normative legal and geopolitical vision implicit in the creation of *resguardos* and natural parks not only fails to translate into effective territorial defense, but also does not solve the problems of indigenous populations or peasant colonists affected by the geopolitics of armed violence and transnational capital.

As Van Vliet indicated two decades ago when criticizing policies dealing with national parks and *resguardos* as a strategy for the conservation of natural resources in the Colombian Amazon, "It is useful to put side by side the juridical and normative construction implicit in this policy to geopolitics, defined as a reflection about the relationship between space and power structures (power in its various forms: legal/formal, political domination, economic domination, as well as cultural, ideological and physical domination)" (1990:69). Perception of space differs depending on one's position, be it the perspective of state agency, indigenous agency, or settlers. Further, space perception varies within these groups of actors depending on the level on which one analyzes the situation: the perception of a national indigenous leader differs from that of a local leader. From this one can comprehend the apparently contradictory territorial strategies of re-ethnicized indigenous peoples and peasants, inscribed in forms of spatial and identity mobility to claim roots in a specific territory while constructing both rural and urban networks. These complementary strategies of territoriality have allowed them to produce political and cultural identities that are situated in multiple spaces.

Territories of Identity and Displacement

The ever new, ever different character of migrations and displacement of identities among rural and urban populations of Putumayo pose serious challenges for the affected population, as well as for scholars. This is because migrations question the territorial policy of both state and social subjects that place in this territory the construction of their representations of identity, and in the process question theoretical and methodological constructs of an anthropology itself anchored in territory. Without an interrogation of these perceptions, which constitute a key piece in the operationalization of dominant ideologies, it is not possible to understand the dynamics of urban spaces such as Bogotá or Mocoa, or of rural areas such as the Colombian Pacific or the Amazon.

One of these constructed sociospatial images of indigenous populations advanced in the modern discourse of social science and in state
policy is that of community. This abstract and idealized category, utilized to refer to a collectivity of individuals who have stable temporal
and spatial links, combines two central ideas (Rose 1997; Povinelli
2002). The first identifies a discrete population with a singular and
limited space, which can be the territory or any space susceptible to
geographic or juridical delimitation. This identity assumes that the
internal relationships that community members participate in are
more important than those conducted outside of the space of the
community. This in turn distinguishes among those who are part of the
spatialized community and those who are not, generating practices
of inclusion and exclusion based on the assumption that community
members are isomorphic and intimately related, which, as stated by
Young (1990, cited in Rose 1997), does not permit the creation of opposition politics. The notion of community also assumes that communal space or territory constitutes for its members the privileged
arena for decision making and action, and that therefore community
interaction is greater than interactions performed in wider arenas,
such as the region, or narrower ones, such as the family, where indi-
viduality prevails.

Second, community as an idealized category implies a certain coherence produced by a tidy assemblage of parts that form an integrated
functional whole, be it the result of a shared livelihood that creates
replication of social action or, better, of a set of reiterated social norms
that are consistent with values and beliefs. From this perspective the
complex heterogeneity of contemporary communities is explained
by reference to external interactions or to transitional stages in which
one form of social integration is being replaced by another form.
This interpretation obviously loses ground when social mobility is
considered. To the extent that mobility in the form of migration,
displacement, or cyclical movement shows that the social nature of
the space is constructed and reproduced through the capacity for

collective human agency, the boundaries imposed by dominant arrangements of spatial realities are susceptible to change (Massey 1994). In this sense displacement and migration, understood as a form of mobility among places, challenge spatial images such as that of the stable and functional community (Rose 1997). In other words, the realities associated with mobility in the form of migration or "voluntary" displacement should be used as a platform from which to critically review the images emanating from hegemonic representations of indigenous, Afro-Colombian, or *mestizo* communities as linked to fixed territories, as the latter negate the actual social dynamics of urban and rural populations that have historically reconstructed their identities and spatial referents.

Given the ubiquity of these forms of mobility and the depth of their influence, the raw material of this new cartography, as proposed by Appadurai (1991), must be exposed precisely in the quotidian experience of moving populations. In this sense the goal is to debunk the dominant idea that migration associated with colonization signifies a rupture with former social relations and an entrance into new relations. Changes, as much as continuities, must be identified, as well as the new networks and associations and the multiple anchorages and de-anchorages in unlike territories constructed by subjects in displacement.

With respect to populations involved in the quotidian processes of cultural dynamics of deterritorialization and our attempts to ethnographically describe them, Appadurai's words are useful here:

As groups migrate, regroup in new locations, reconstruct their histories, and reconfigure their ethnic "projects," the ethno in ethnography takes on a slippery, nonlocalized quality, to which the descriptive practices of anthropology will have to respond. The landscapes of group identity—the ethnoscapes—around the world are no longer familiar anthropological objects, insofar as groups are no longer tightly territorialized, spatially bounded, historically unselfconscious, or culturally homogeneous....

Put another way, the task of ethnography now becomes the unraveling of a conundrum: what is the nature of locality, as a lived experience, in a globalized, deterritorialized world? (1991:192, 196)

As far as the science of ethnographic production and its interpreters go, it is useful to remember the critical reflections of Gupta and Ferguson:

For now, it is sufficient to note a certain contradiction. On the one hand, anthropology appears determined to give up its old ideas of territoriality, fixed communities and stable, localized cultures, and to apprehend an interconnected world in which people, objects, and ideas are rapidly shifting and refuse to stay in place. At the same time, though, in a defensive response to challenges to its "turf" from other disciplines, anthropology has come to lean more heavily than ever on a methodological commitment to spend long periods in one localized setting. What are we to do with a discipline that loudly rejects received ideas of the "local," even while ever more firmly insisting on a method that takes it for granted? (1997:4)

The contradictory character of the local is, however, a matter of debate. Could it be that Gupta and Ferguson perceive a contradiction because they see the local merely as a closed space and not so much as a site of resistance (in Foucault's sense) to extralocal (global, national, regional) forces?

Notes

This text is a revised and expanded version of a paper I presented at the first meeting of researchers of the project "Identities and Mobilities: Regional Societies in New Political and Migratory Contexts. A Comparison between Colombia and Mexico" (IDYMOV), in Mexico City in November 2004 (published in www.idymov.com). I thank Ulrich Oslender, Anne Marie Locsonz, and other fellows of IDYMOV in Colombia whose comments were very useful at the time of converting my presentation into this chapter. Jean Jackson patiently read the version in Spanish and suggested revisions that helped to substantially improve the English version. I thank her very much. My research in Colombia was conducted thanks to the financial support of the Colombian Institute for the Development of Science and Technology. This text was translated from Spanish by Andrea M. Cuéllar and Patrick C. Wilson.

1. Because the English translation of *colono* as "colonist" has a strong connotation of a powerful colonizing actor, I use the expression "peasant colonists" to emphasize the peasant socioeconomic status generally attached to *colonos* as landless peasant migrants. Furthermore in Putumayo *colonos* currently utilize the term *colono* to identify themselves as coming from another region. Although the local elites do not use that term to refer to themselves, from an external point of view they might be considered *colonos* too.

2. As Oslender (1999) notes, the rediscovery of Lefebvre is not accidental. It is related to the necessity of interpreting struggles between spatial representation and spaces of representation that are central in many places today.

3. *Resguardo* was a colonial collective form of land tenure originally created to protect Indian labor and organize the payment of tribute in the Andean region. Law 89 of 1890 retained the legal figure of the *resguardo*, abolishing the payment of tribute. Its acknowledgment of official status for the *resguardos* and their autonomous government through the *cabildos* became a powerful legal instrument in the hands of indigenous peoples to defend their land rights.

4. Comaroff and Comaroff 2001:22; "¿Quién quiere ser millonario?" *Semana*, January 26, 2008, www.semana.com/wf_InfoArticulo.aspx?IdArt=109036.

5. Before the Constitution of 1991, and for over a century, indigenous territorial rights were ruled under Law 89 of 1890, which acknowledged communal property in *resguardos* as well as their *cabildos* as governmental bodies. These rights, according to Law 89, were applicable only to the extent that indigenous people had assimilated to "civilized living" and therefore did not apply for a long time to lowland groups in the Orinoco and Amazon, which were considered to be in a state of "savagery." The assimilation of the Amazon groups was left in the hands of Catholic missionaries (Arango and Sánchez [1998] 2004:35). The Constitution of 1991 maintained the fundamental principles of Law 89 as far as indigenous territorial rights, but it eliminated false evolutionary considerations and stated the importance of valorizing cultural diversity. Further, it expanded the autonomy given by the state to indigenous peoples, including autonomous jurisdiction and administration of their territories as well as of the resources transferred from the state for them to manage internal affairs (such as health and education). In short the 1890 and 1991 Constitutions differ in terms of how autonomy, communal property, and indigenous government are framed as a structure for the valorization of cultural difference.

6. The exception is the *resguardo* of Yunguillo, constituted in 1953 to give lands to the Inga populations of Mocoa and its surroundings.

7. The Colombian Amazon covers 399,183 square kilometers, which represents 35 percent of the national territory. The areas protected through the system of national parks, natural reserves, and indigenous *resguardos* is 24,217,703 hectares, about 60 percent of the Colombian Amazon, mostly in its eastern-

most portion. In 1988 national parks covered 3,810,000 hectares; natural reserves, 1,900,000 hectares; indigenous *resguardos*, 18,507,703 hectares (Comisión amazónica de desarrollo y medio ambiente 1988).

8. The department of Putumayo covers 24,885 square kilometers. According to the Plan de Desarrollo Departamental of 1996 Putumayo had a population of about 340,000 people, averaging thirteen people per square kilometer. The indigenous population corresponds to 9 percent of this total. In 1996 there were twenty-six *resguardos*, with an average area of 2,500 hectares each, 194,601 hectares in total. That same year there were 1,288 families and 7,272 people living in the twenty-six *resguardos*. About half of these *resguardos* were located in the easternmost, most isolated zone of Putumayo, close to the municipality of Puerto Leguizamo.

9. La Aguadita (1994) and El Descanso (1997) border the municipal center of Puerto Guzmán and cover 74 and 98 hectares, respectively. Huasipungo de Villagarzon (2000) has 90 hectares.

10. This information was obtained during an interview carried out in Bogotá (March 2000) with the representative for indigenous affairs of the National Program for Alternative Development. See www.desarrolloalternativo.gov.co.

11. According to the head of the Office of Participation in the Ministry of the Environment, in 2001 the budget of Zio-Ai was double that of the Office of Participation and was the reason why members of Zio-Ai offered to finance negotiations for the management of hydraulic resources in Putumayo.

12. "Vulnerable" is the category proposed by the United Nations in its policy on human security. It refers to populations that lack basic services such as water, food, health, and education.

13. Puerto Leguizamo is on the shore of the Putumayo River at a point where the Caquetá and Putumayo Rivers, two of the major tributaries of the Amazon, are very close to each other, separated by a distance of only twenty-five kilometers. This is a strategic position for controlling the transit through these two major navigable tributaries, motivating the Colombian Navy to build a military base in Puerto Leguizamo to guard the borders with Ecuador and Peru. Recently Puerto Leguizamo has become an important center of operations for the counterinsurgency army. Puerto Leguizamo has traditionally been the settlement of the Murui indigenous population. It is connected by river (ten hours from Puerto Asís) or plane to the rest of the country.

14. This is the case of the project Biopacífico, one of the Consolidación de la mazonía projects sponsored by the European Community in the Colombian Pacific and in the Amazon.

References

Asociación Latinoamericana para los Derechos Humanos. 2000. Embassy of Colombia, Plan Colombia: General description. www.aldhu.com/paginas/fs_info/plan.htm#plan.

Appadurai, Arjun. 1991. Global ethnospaces. In *Recapturing anthropology: Working in the present*, ed. Richard Fox, 191–210. Santa Fe NM: School of American Research Press.

Arango, Raúl, and Enrique Sánchez. [1998] 2004. *Los pueblos indígenas de Colombia en el umbral del nuevo milenio*. Bogotá: Departamento Nacional de Planeación.

Briones, Claudia. 1998. *(Meta)cultura del estado-nación y estado de la (meta)cultura: Repensando las identidades indígenas y antropológicas en tiempos de postestatalidad*. Serie Antropología 244. Brasilia: Universidad de Brasilia.

Chatterjee, Partha. 2004. *The politics of the governed: Reflections on popular politics in most of the world*. New York: Columbia University Press.

Chaves, Margarita. 2002. Economía propia. In *Palabras para desarmar: Una aproximación crítica al vocabulario del reconocimiento en Colombia*, ed. M. Serje, C. Suaza, and R. Pineda, 145–57. Bogotá: Mincultura and ICANH.

———. 2003a. Cabildos multiétnicos e identidades depuradas. In *Fronteras, territorios y metáforas*, ed. Clara Inés García, 121–35. Medellín: Hombre Nuevo Editores and INER.

———. 2003b. Jerarquías de color y mestizaje en la amazonia occidental colombiana. *Revista Colombiana de Antropología* 38:189–216.

———. 2005. "¿Qué va a pasar con los indios cuando todos seamos indios?" Ethnic rights and reindianization in southwestern Colombian Amazonia. PhD diss., University of Illinois at Urbana-Champaign.

Comaroff, Jean, and John Comaroff. 2001. Millennial capitalism: First thoughts on a second coming. In *Millennial capitalism and the culture of neoliberalism*, ed. Jean Comaroff and John Comaroff, 1–56. Durham NC: Duke University Press.

Comisión amazónica de desarrollo y medio ambiente, con la colaboración de Gabriel García Márquez. 1988. Amazonia sin mitos. Bogotá: Departamento Nacional de Planeación–Programa de las Naciones Unidas para el Desarrollo.

Dirlik, Arif, and Roxann Prazniak. 2001. Introduction: Cultural identity and the politics of place. In *Places and politics in the age of globalization*, ed. Roxann Prazniak and Arif Dirlik, 1–13. Boston: Rowman & Littlefield.

Gupta, Akhil, and James Ferguson. 1997. Discipline and practice: "The field" as site, method and location in anthropology. In *Anthropological locations: Boundaries and grounds of a field science*, ed. Akhil Gupta and James Ferguson, 1–46. Berkeley: University of California Press.

Jansson, Oscar. 2006. Triadas Putumayenses: Relaciones patrón-cliente en la economía de la cocaína. *Revista Colombiana de Antropología* 42:223–47.

Lefebvre, Henri. 1991. *The production of space*. Oxford: Blackwell.

Massey, Doreen. 1994. *Space, place, and gender*. Minneapolis: University of Minnesota Press.

Oslender, Ulrich. 1999. Espacializando resistencia: Perspectivas de "espacio" y "lugar" en las investigaciones de movimientos sociales. In *Antropologías transeúntes*, ed. E. Restrepo and M. V. Uribe, 191–221. Bogotá: ICAN.

———. 2001. La lógica del río: Estructuras espaciales del proceso organizativo de los movimientos sociales de comunidades negras en el Pacífico colombiano. In *Acción colectiva, estado y etnicidad en el Pacífico colombiano*, ed. M. Pardo, 123–48. Bogotá: ICANH.

Porto-Gonçalves, Carlos Walter. 2001. *Geo-grafías: Movimientos sociales, nuevas territorialidades y sustentabilidad*. Mexico City: Siglo XXI.

Povinelli, Elizabeth. 2002. *The cunning of recognition: Indigenous alterities and the making of Australian multiculturalism*. Durham NC: Duke University Press.

Roldán, Roque. 1993. Reconocimiento legal de tierras a indígenas en Colombia. In *Reconocimiento y demarcación de territorios indígenas en Amazonia*, 56–88. Bogotá: Fundación GAIA and CEREC.

———. 1995. Aproximación histórica a la explotación de petróleo en territorios indígenas. In *Tierra profanada: Grandes proyectos en territorios indígenas de Colombia*, 241–304. Bogotá: Proyecto ONIC-CECOIN-GhK.

Rose, Guillian. 1997. Performing inoperative community: The space and the resistance of some community art projects. In *Geographies of resistance*, ed. S. Pile and M. Keith, 184–202. London: Routledge.

Spivak, Gayatri. 1988. Can the subaltern speak? In *Marxism and the interpretation of culture*, ed. Cary Nelson and Lawrence Grossberg, 271–313. Urbana: University of Illinois Press.

Taussig, Michael. 1987. *Shamanism, colonialism and the wildman: A study in terror and healing*. Chicago: University of Chicago Press.

Ulloa, Astrid. 2004. El nativo ecológico: Movimientos indígenas y medio ambiente en Colombia. In *Movimientos sociales estado y democracia en Colombia*, ed. M. Archila and M. Pardo, 286–320. Bogotá: CES Universidad Nacional ICANH.

Van Vliet, Geert. 1990. Reflexiones sobre geopolítica en la Amazonia colombiana. In *Amazonia: Identidad y desarrollo*, ed. Geert Van Vliet et al., 63–76. Bogotá: FEN and Fundación Manoa.

Vargas, Patricia. 1999. Propuesta metodológica para la investigación participativa de la percepción territorial en el Pacífico. In *De montes, ríos y ciudades: Territorios e identidades de la gente negra en Colombia*, ed. J. Camacho and E. Restrepo. Bogotá: Ecofondo, ICAN, and Fundación Natura.

Watts, Michael John. 1999. Collective wish images: Geographical imaginaries and the crisis of development. In *Human geography today*, ed. John Allen, Doreen Massey, and Philip Sarre, 85–107. Cambridge: Polity Press.

Zambrano, Marta. 2006. El gobierno de la diferencia: Volatilidad identitaria, escenarios urbanos y conflictos sociales en el giro multicultural colombiano. Presentada en la tercera reunión del proyecto IDYMOV (Identidades y movilidades), Xalapa, México, Enero de 2006. www.idymov.com.

8. Indigenous Leadership and the Shifting Politics of Development in Ecuador's Amazon

Patrick C. Wilson

In early 1998 I walked into the usually tranquil offices of the Federation of Indigenous Organizations of Napo, now renamed the Federation of Kichwa Nationalities de Napo (FONAKIN), as I did almost every morning, only this time to find a bustle of activity. The president of the Federation, Mariano Huatatoca, enthusiastically greeted me. It wasn't that he normally was cold to me, but during the three months since I had begun my fieldwork, Mr. Huatatoca and the rest of the Federation leaders had received my proposal to do research with their organization with some hesitation. On this day, in contrast, he wanted to talk. He ushered me into his office and explained that the Federation would be holding a congress the following week, and that it would please him greatly if I were to attend. I was thrilled by his invitation and by what I perceived to be a change in attitude toward my presence at the Federation office, and I eagerly set out for the congress on the morning of its inaugural day. After a short twenty-minute bus ride I walked an additional half-hour with several other attendees to the community hosting the congress and quickly got the sense that this was no ordinary assembly. In fact the purpose of the congress was to evaluate the performance of the leadership at midterm and consider the possibility of a regime change. Public opinion ran that Huatatoca and other elected leaders were ineffective in their management of projects sponsored by nongovernmental organizations, were unable to attract new projects for the Federation, and were engaged in questionable negotiations with multinational oil companies working in the region. When the congress eventually got under way inside the community center, a large rectangular cement structure dimly lit by several lightbulbs hanging in bare sockets from the rafters and with a tin roof that thundered from the incessant rain that fell during the two-day gathering, approximately two hundred attendees huddled close together on wooden benches to protect themselves from the cold. Each leader in turn presented a report on his or her achievements during the past two years.[1] When Mariano Huatatoca spoke he focused his attention on development projects during his tenure, particularly on the attempt by his administration to secure access to new projects and funding from NGOs. It was at this moment that his motivation for inviting me to the congress became clear: he requested that I stand, explaining to the assembly that I had recently arrived at the Federation and, much to my surprise, that I would be bringing new projects to the organization over the next two years.

Huatatoca and several other leaders were removed from office at this congress amid concerns about the economic hardships facing a Federation that suddenly found itself almost broke, with limited financial and technical support from the NGO community, and with concerns stemming from the onset of oil exploration in its territories. The inability of these leaders to control development is a central theme that I explore in this chapter, and one that I suggest has become critical for understanding Amazonian leadership and the changing legitimacy of indigenous federation leaders in the present.

I wish to explore the contemporary situation of indigenous politics in Amazonian Ecuador by examining the intermingling of divergent understandings of development from the perspectives of sustainable development NGOs and the members and leaders of an indigenous organization. In particular I analyze how leaders' legitimacy and prestige may be impacted by the nature of the relationship those leaders have with development projects and the national and international NGOs that administer them, suggesting that the small-scale projects that proliferate in Ecuador's Amazon carry distinctive values for the different participants in the development encounter. From the vantage point of NGOs working on sustainable development and poverty alleviation, development projects are understood primarily from an economic perspective, where these projects are thought to hold the potential to ameliorate the economic hardships of marginalized communities in the Amazon. Even with those projects designed to have a cultural dimension, such as the numerous ethnotourism and folkloric handicraft projects in indigenous communities throughout the Amazon and Andes regions, and labeled in development circles as "culturally appropriate sustainable development" or "development with identity," the ultimate goals of the projects are still tied to poverty alleviation. Forging cultural linkages in these contexts is seen as the pathway through which the NGOs administering the projects can attract and sustain local interest and participation in them.

Yet I suggest that indigenous federation leaders and their constituents understand development projects from a distinctive framework of value. It is not that they are uninterested in or unconcerned with poverty alleviation; quite the contrary, as working to alleviate economic hardship in indigenous communities has been a central goal of these organizations since their founding in the late 1960s. Rather, it is that development projects represent much more than just economic opportunity and carry a symbolic weight that is central to comprehending the relationships between indigenous leaders and members. As Beth Conklin suggests in her chapter in this volume, social relationships are forged and strengthened through material exchanges, and incidents of so-called indigenous materialism may be better understood as a different framework of value rooted in the strengthening of social ties through such exchange. In the current case federation leaders, as I will explain, are frequently evaluated by federation members in reference to their ability to attract and control the circulation of NGO-sponsored development projects. The logic guiding this relates to the widely held belief that a leader's authority, prestige, and legitimacy are tied to his (most of these leaders are men) generosity, where generosity is understood as a moral obligation of leaders to their subjects. In federation politics the circulation of development projects by indigenous leaders is evidence of their moral qualification to lead, making the mere distribution of these projects as important as, if not more important than, the tangible outcomes of the projects themselves. This is clearly in contrast to the perspective of NGO staff, who tend to be greatly concerned about project accountability and, in the context of my fieldwork, seemed unaware of the broader ritual and symbolic significance the projects themselves may hold for local people.

There is a second, and related, level of disjuncture in the conceptualization of development from the vantage points of NGOs and indigenous peoples. Particularly in the past ten years the concept of social capital has become central to how national and international development organizations evaluate the potential success of development projects in selected communities or with indigenous organizations (see Ramírez in this volume for a comparative case of how the notion of social capital is employed in the context of community development in Putumayo, Colombia). They seek social settings in which strong grassroots organizations exist, where they attract a broad base of support from the organizations' membership, and, in the case of development with identity approaches, where local people possess a keen awareness and appreciation of their cultural distinctiveness. From the NGO perspective these social settings offer the greatest promise for successful development initiatives. From the vantage point of indigenous peoples, in contrast, strong grassroots organizations are *outcomes* of receiving and effectively circulating development projects rather than a precondition for receiving them.

I explore these themes through an analysis of the political organization of the Napo Runa of Ecuador's Upper Amazon, focusing my attention on FONAKIN and one of its second-tier member organizations, the Unión Huacamayos. First I briefly sketch the organizational structure and history of indigenous organizing in Ecuador's Amazon since agrarian reform in the 1960s, paying particular attention to the interaction between FONAKIN and development organizations since the 1980s. I then provide an overview of the literature on Amazonian leadership, highlighting its relevance for explaining the current case of indigenous federation leaders. Anthropologists have long suggested that good leadership is personified in those individuals who are adept at consensus building, oratory skills, and mobilizing and circulating resources in conspicuous displays of generosity. This treatment of Amazonian leadership is useful for understanding contemporary indigenous federation leaders, in spite of the changing context. I am not, however, suggesting an ahistorical and static treatment of Amazonian politics; rather, I argue that the social and economic context in which these leadership traits are performed has been shaped in recent decades by the interaction between indigenous peoples and NGOs (among other actors). In the final section I suggest that these development agents have contributed, likely unknowingly, to the creation of expectations of federation leaders while, in recent years and probably inadvertently, making it increasingly difficult for these leaders to access the resources (in the form of development projects) required to effectively perform to the expectations of their constituents. The divergent understandings and meanings attached to development projects and their goals have contributed to conflicts over the appropriate organization and management of the projects, ultimately resulting in a shift away from NGOs directly involving indigenous organizations in the development process. This new politics of development has factored into the declining legitimacy of indigenous leaders and the current crisis within FONAKIN, where in the past eight years two former presidents of the Federation served time in prison on corruption charges, two Federation presidents were removed from office before completing their terms, and others have relinquished their posts disenchanted with indigenous federation politics.

Indigenous Organizations and
Development in Ecuador's Amazon

Indigenous social movements in different parts of Latin America emerged as prominent social and political forces in the late 1980s and early 1990s (Warren and Jackson 2002). Based on a degree of romantic wonderment, encouraging empirical evidence that spoke to the capacity of some of these movements to influence state-society relations and speak for the most marginal members of society, and the hope that these movements may represent an important bridge between environmentalism and human rights in parts of the Amazon and elsewhere, the movements were embraced by academics and international advocacy groups as compelling examples of progressive new social movements. As these movements and their leaders captured the attention of the international media, social scientists, and activists, they were buoyed by a massive influx of international support. The timing was also crucial: their rise to prominence in places like Ecuador and Brazil was facilitated by the social space opened by the return to democracy in those two countries, and with the strategic, economic, and technical support garnered through relationships with NGOs, which were rapidly growing during this period in terms of both raw numbers and the scope of their labors. These NGOs followed in the tracks left by the gradual (and not so gradual) withdrawal of state services through neoliberal reforms and became prominent actors promoting social justice and poverty alleviation for marginal sectors of society, including indigenous communities. Hence indigenous federations in Ecuador, many of which already had years of organizational experience, took advantage of a changing political and social climate to strengthen their organizations both locally and nationally.

Indigenous federations in Ecuador's Amazon are structured into nested organizations, hierarchical in terms of size and scope. The Federation of Kichwa Nationalities de Napo is a provincial-level federation; its office is located in Tena, the capital of Napo Province and a city of roughly twenty-five thousand inhabitants. Formed in 1969 FONAKIN had as many as 150 member communities at its peak in the early 1990s. The current number of member communities is roughly one hundred, although the number of active members (those that are regularly represented at congresses, assemblies, or other meetings and mobilizations) is often substantially fewer. The changing number of active member communities tends to grow or diminish based on perceptions of the Federation's effectiveness at different moments.

At the local level the community forms the elemental unit of the Federation's structure. At a level above the community is the association or the cooperative. Several of these are members of FONAKIN, such as the Unión Huacamayos, and each has multiple member communities, although not all communities that are members of FONAKIN are also members of a second-tier association or cooperative. The Unión Huacamayos formed in 1995 at the behest of Ecuadorian NGOs, and at its peak comprised eleven communities located to the west of the cities of Tena and Archidona. It is also a member organization of FONAKIN. The Federation itself is a third-tier organization, representing indigenous communities and organizations throughout Napo Province. At the uppermost levels FONAKIN is a member organization of CONFENIAE, the Amazonian regional confederation in Ecuador, and CONAIE, the national indigenous confederation.

Each of these organizations, from the community level up, elects leaders, and the particular structure of the Federation's executive committee may hark back to attempts by missionaries and the Ecuadorian state to consolidate Amazonian peoples into delineated, sedentary communities and to secure access to reliable sources of Indian labor. Members of the community of Santa Rita, located about a forty-five-minute walk west of the city of Archidona, date the history of electing community representatives to at least the early 1960s, when the Josefina mission delegated individuals as community representatives. Blanca Muratorio (1991) traces this practice back much earlier, to the mid-nineteenth century, when a system of Indian hierarchy known as *varayuj* was instituted by colonial administrators. In the 1960s the community representatives were called *capitanes*; these individuals served as the public face of the community in discussions with the mission and later with the Ecuadorian agrarian reform and colonization institute (IERAC) and other state officials. While these first *capitanes*, at least in Santa Rita, were likely delegated by the mission, the community began nominating their own shortly thereafter, electing first, second, and third *capitanes*. Over time the titles of elected offices changed, and it is now more common to elect a president, a vice president, a treasurer, and a secretary, as well as a possibly longer list of *vocales*, where representatives attend to specific areas of community interest, such as education and health care.

Each community sends representatives to participate as voting members in congresses and assemblies of FONAKIN, and the Federation's leadership structure is similarly made up of elected officials occupying different posts. (There were eight such offices in the late 1990s: president, vice president, treasurer, secretary, and representatives of agriculture, health, education, social promotion, and land.)

The early years of FONAKIN coincided with the acceleration of colonization of Ecuador's Amazon by peasants from the highlands, who were encouraged to migrate to the Amazon by the 1964 agrarian reform and colonization legislation promoting frontier expansion in the region. Colonization was also facilitated by the onset of commercial oil production in the region in 1967 and the construction of limited infrastructure, particularly in the form of roads, which eased access to the region. As a result of the influx of colonists and the

accompanying land disputes, FONAKIN served as an intermediary between its member communities and IERAC, helped settle disputes
over territory, and aided in the formalization of communities with
legalized boundaries. During this time the Federation had a handful
of member communities, primarily nucleated near the urban centers
of Tena and Archidona.

The Federation underwent a process of growth and consolidation
of authority in the mid to late 1980s. During this period the organization grew to well over one hundred member communities spread
throughout the western half of Napo Province. A new set of opportunities confronted indigenous leaders during this period, spurred
by the return to democracy coupled with a dramatic increase in the
presence of international development NGOs in Ecuador. Federation
archives detail the arrival of a sizable number of NGOs to work in the
region and speak to the regularity and frequency of dialogue and col-
laborative work between them and the Federation. By the mid-1980s
international NGOs, including Oxfam, the Inter-American Foundation,
Cultural Survival, and Pan Para el Mundo, provided funding directly
administered by the Federation for a range of community and leadership projects: agroforestry, leadership training seminars, accounting
and administration of projects, resources for constructing an office
building, and agricultural commercialization projects, among others. By the early to mid-1990s the Federation boasted a computer
lab, mapping facilities, a technical team, medical extension workers,
legal counsel, a radio station, and two automobiles.

Several scholars have documented the importance of the links
between international NGOs and local and regional indigenous organizations for the political consolidation of the latter in the 1980s and
early 1990s (Brysk 1996; Perreault 2003a). Thomas Perreault (2003a,
2003b), for example, examining networks of scale, suggests that the
ability of local and regional federations (including FONAKIN and its
member communities, also the focus of his research) to forge relationships with a range of international actors has been crucial for the

strengthening of these organizations and their ability to contribute to concrete processes of socioeconomic empowerment at the local level. These ties also contributed to training a generation of indigenous leaders in project administration through a range of training seminars, the creation of an active youth organization within the Federation, and scholarships to provide promising young leaders with access to university education. As such, interaction between NGOs and these leaders became a common element of leadership activity. In fact many of the most prominent and enduring FONAKIN leaders, those who have gone on to serve as public officials in local or national government and even to hold ministry posts, were trained in the leadership seminars and education programs of the 1980s.

Less attention has been paid to how interaction between indigenous federations and the development community may shape the internal institutional identity and goals of the federations. As interaction with these NGOs increased, there was a gradual shift in the objectives of the Federation. By the late 1980s the organization moved its focus away from issues of land titling and community consolidation (the themes that drove indigenous organizing in the 1960s and 1970s) to community development projects, writing project proposals and submitting them to international NGOs for financing. By the early 1990s and due to its success in attracting NGO resources, FONAKIN managed a budget thought to have surpassed that of the municipality of Tena.

In academic circles attention focused on the organization of these federations, their primary goals, and a resurgence of interest in the nature of Amazonian leadership. Anthropologists were attempting to make sense out of these new leaders, who were typically young and possessed a command of Spanish or Portuguese, with the prevailing literature on Amazonian leadership that suggested that authority was rooted in being a member of an older generation, possessing superior oratory skills, lacking coercive authority over their subjects, and cementing prestige and legitimacy through conspicuous displays of generosity. Most FONAKIN leaders fit the recent mold of the younger, more cosmopolitan indigenous leader. In their dress and accessories they provide visible evidence of the central role they play as mediators between their communities and the state, multinationals, and NGOs; the typical Federation leader wears a dress shirt, slacks, and dress shoes and carries a day-planner and cell phone. These are more than practical necessities, as they also make a statement about the capacity of these leaders to represent their constituents in NGO offices, multinational boardrooms, and state agencies. At the same time, as Michael Brown (1993) has argued, these new leaders retain elements of traditional authority, such as a persuasive oratory style, often conspicuous generosity, and leadership by example. This has contributed to the common conceptualization of the new Amazonian leader as a leader who can "walk in both worlds," as comfortable in a government office in Quito as in the local member communities (Vickers 1989). As Matthew Lauer (2006) illustrates for the case of the Ye'kwana in Venezuela and which also resonates with the experiences of the Napo Runa, these new leaders have gradually usurped authority from more "traditional" leaders because of changing social, political, and economic dynamics that require them to be able to effectively negotiate with agents of the state, multinational corporations, and NGOs, among others.

Amazonian Political Authority

The literature on Amazonian leadership and authority owes much to Lévi-Strauss's (1967) influential work on Nambikuara chiefs. This treatment of leadership, common throughout the literature on political hierarchy in the Amazon, coalesces around a general agreement about the fragile and consensus-oriented nature of Amazonian political authority, whereby the legitimacy of leaders rests on certain acquired traits, such as oratorical abilities, critical for a leadership based on persuasion rather than on coercion. The success of leaders in this context is thought to be rooted in their capacity to mobilize willing cooperation, and this is often cemented not only through oratory practices but through displays of generosity, such as by providing supporters with gifts of food and *chicha* (manioc beer; Lorrain 2000; Kracke 1979), and leaders proving themselves to be effective providers for their supporters in a more general sense (Erikson and Santos Granero 1988; Lorrain 2000; Rosengren 2003). As Gertrude Orte (1966) illustrated for the case of the Kuikuru, leaders often recruit labor or support by sponsoring a party and engaging in ritual activity. Such cooperative activities in turn are often closely associated with kin ties, as individuals with large kin sets often have more ample bases of support from which to draw as well as greater domestic labor to call on to respond to the economic demands of leadership in these public displays of generosity (Basso 1973; Smole 1976; Wagley and Galvao 1969).

The norms of leadership behavior are ultimately moral mandates, and leaders gain prestige and maintain or enhance authority by exhibiting proper moral behavior, rooted in generosity and the ability to circulate valued, exogamous goods (Lauer 2006). Conspicuous acts of generosity, as Ellen Basso (1973) observed in her work with the Kalapalo, are critical if leaders are to acquire prestige, and also serve to cement social ties and increase the number of individuals that the leader can call on for support. In this way acts of giving and receiving structure social relationships. Michael Uzendoski (2005) has suggested for the Napo Runa that turning commodities into gifts and the act of giving itself create social value and ultimately produce identities and relationships between individuals. One learns who one is and how one relates to others through these exchange and gift-giving relationships. Hierarchical relationships are the outcome of giving; put another way, where hierarchy exists it is the moral obligation of the more powerful member of the relationship to give. Therefore relationships of giving establish and maintain hierarchical relationships, while the act of giving also soothes the social tensions that may emerge from the inequality itself. The inequality emerging from these social relationships of giving is not solely, or perhaps even primarily economic in nature, even though the outcome of the circulation of resources may have

PATRICK C. WILSON

economic dimensions. Although the objects being exchanged are important, they are important not as commodities in terms of their exchange value, but in terms of what they communicate about the nature of social relationships between people and the intertwined nature of politics and economics.

Social inequality is comprehended therefore through rituals of production and exchange. Further, as Uzendoski (2005:113) has noted, if the moral obligation to give carries with it a social value resulting in the establishment of relationships, then it is preferable to satisfy someone else's desire than to address one's own, as satisfying the desires of others is to live convivially. This preference is articulated in a commonly noted dichotomy of individual types in the region, between those who *siempre colaboran* (who always contribute or collaborate) and those who work for *intereses personales* (personal interests). This dichotomy is used in daily situations, but I also heard it frequently used as a measure for evaluating the legitimacy and prestige of indigenous federation leaders, where those who were perceived to collaborate with member communities were spoken of and remembered fondly and contrasted starkly with unpopular leaders who were accused of seeking individual advancement.

As I suggested earlier, it is the moral obligation of leaders to provide for their followers, and their ability to do so is often considered a validation of their ritual prowess and critical for cementing legitimacy. Powerful shamans among the Pianoa of Venezuela, for example, are thought to possess what Santos Granero (1986) refers to as the "mystical means of production." This entails mystical knowledge and ritual skills to ensure the well-being and reproduction of both the social group and the natural world on which people depend for survival. The shaman's power is affirmed by the abundance of highly prized game and the fertility of gardens, and through ritual activity he guarantees bounty in both hunting and horticultural activities. The ability to "attract" game and to be especially skilled at hunting can enhance a leader's prestige, in turn attracting more followers (Maybury-Lewis 1967). In a similar vein a decrease in available game or a shortage in food for sponsoring feasts or merely for subsistence can lead to a decline in a leader's prestige. The ebbs and flows of leadership prestige and authority may thus be tied, at least in part, to the ability of leaders to satisfy the desires of followers through rituals of production and generous gift-giving and redistributive acts.

Pierre Clastres (1987 [1974]) concludes that the exchange value of leaders is decidedly negative, in the sense that the leader does not acquire a coercive capacity or the ability to demand labor at his behest. In fact the fragility of authority is a common characteristic of Amazonian leadership. Maybury-Lewis (1967), in his discussion of the Akwẽ-Shavante, noted the lack of a formal institution of authority in that society and the frequency with which those who are recognized as chiefs are ignored or overruled by the members of their communities. Commonly these chiefs would survey public opinion before announcing their "commands," which often serve as no more than a recapitulation of the dominant sentiment of the community (see also Wagley and Galvao 1969). In this context leaders help to build community cohesiveness more than they exert power over others.[2]

Blanca Muratorio (1991) similarly suggests that leadership positions among the Napo Runa have been fragile. Addressing the historical case of Napo Runa leaders designated by missionaries and colonial authorities, she shows how those delegated as *varas* lacked coercive power over those they represented. Instead newly appointed leaders needed to achieve legitimacy in order for their requests to be heard by demonstrating, from the outset, their generosity. At events marking the inauguration of new *varas*, for example, the recognition of their authority was not complete until the newly appointed leaders sponsored drinking parties. These elaborate parties provided them with the legitimacy to extract resources and labor from community members at the behest of colonial authorities.

Serving as community president or a leader of the indigenous federation today entails substantial expectations in terms of comportment, and FONAKIN and the Unión Huacamayos leaders are evaluated by a similar concern for generosity and a consensus-based approach to leadership. As I examine in the next section, the centrality of development projects to current conceptualizations of effective leadership makes a leader's ability to secure and circulate development resources a central component of his or her perceived legitimacy. As such, while expectations of Federation leaders have retained central elements from previous forms of Amazonian political authority, the material signs of generosity (or stinginess) have been transformed by the influence of the developmentalist state, sustainable development, and conservation NGOS working in the region.

Indigenous Leaders and NGOS

Matthew Lauer has argued that the "reworkings of political authority are related to transformations in how the lowland Ye'kwana communities conceptualize community well-being" (2006:62), suggesting that the specific exogamous goods and commodities that are central in these conceptualizations may change in concert with the specificities of the historical moment. In the case of lowland Ecuador, NGO projects have become one such desired exogamous good in the current moment, and the ability of leaders to mobilize NGO resources in the form of development projects has become central to the effective exercise of leadership. As Frank Hutchins (this volume) describes for the case of indigenous ecotourism, the locally inscribed goals and meanings attached to ecotourism contribute to a process of indigenizing modernity, whereby the actions and their significance are mediated by Napo Runa priorities and notions of value. Similarly Federation leaders and members likewise interpreted the significance of the development encounter from the framework of local systems of value, with implications for the organization of Federation-community relationships and the construction of leadership legitimacy and morality. As Federation leaders increasingly turned their attention to administering projects and seeking funding for new Federation initiatives since the 1980s, member communities began to view the Federation as an organization tied to community development. Every year the leaders would survey the member communities, and community presidents would provide the Federation with a list of necessities that the organization would then seek to address through external financing from NGOs, among others. It would be overly simplistic to suggest that the Federation replaced the state in terms of providing community development, as community leaders would seek resources from a variety of different sources, including the Catholic mission, multinational corporations, and the state, but it did come to be viewed as one such provider of resources for community development and as a conduit for development projects sponsored by international NGOs.

Theorists of NGOs and development have understood their involvement with indigenous federations and ultimately the motivations and goals behind "doing development" differently from their indigenous counterparts. First, supporting these grassroots social movements fits with the political leanings of many of these organizations, and many development theorists have considered those NGOs working with indigenous organizations to be "grassroots support organizations," capable of aiding in the process of the maturation of these organizations while also providing the practical expertise necessary for the success of development projects (Carroll 1992). Second, it is often argued that indigenous and other grassroots organizations possess the social capital necessary to ensure extensive local participation and support for NGO-funded projects (Bebbington and Perreault 1999). More recently this has become a central theme of global development work and is endorsed by organizations such as the World Bank (DeFilippis 2002). The current influence of notions of social capital in development circles is based on the assumption that economic growth is contingent on sociocultural factors, seen as the existence of "stocks" of social capital, that form the foundation of successful development activity (Mayer and Rankin 2002). The goal of development work, then, becomes identifying social contexts in which strong grassroots organizations exist, which thereby are assumed to possess the social conditions necessary for development to occur; the NGO-sponsored development work should, as a consequence, achieve its goals (Mayer and Rankin 2002). In the 1980s and early 1990s indigenous federations were seen as illustrative of the organizational capacity and social cohesion necessary for successful development, and they attracted support from NGOs (and others) for their projects.

Yet the circulation of NGO resources was not without difficulty for Federation leaders, and financial management of project resources became a central source of contestation between indigenous leaders and NGOs. These resources were earmarked for specific purposes, and FONAKIN leaders were required to keep strict accounts of how resources were being used. The parameters of NGO project demands presented obstacles to the ability of Federation leaders to respond to requests by community members. Elected leaders did not always receive salaries for their work, nor did they manage budgets with built-in flexibility that could be mobilized to respond to diverse community requests. These pressures may have led some leaders to reallocate NGO project money for other purposes, actions interpreted by NGOs as misusing project funds. In fact by the late 1980s and early 1990s the constant dialogue between Federation leaders and NGOs was not simply related to project proposals or providing updates on project status; NGOs were writing the Federation with increasing frequency to analyze and attempt to resolve problems that the NGOs saw in the use of funds, and Federation leaders likewise attempted to establish formal mechanisms to ensure that funds were used in the ways outlined by project proposals. Yet from the perspective of Federation members, responding to community wishes and needs (even when this involved the "misuse" of NGO funds) was interpreted as leaders' generosity and willingness to collaborate with community members in satisfying members' needs and desires.

Partly as a result of a shift in development theory and partly as a critique of the perception of Federation mismanagement of resources, international development NGOs and funding organizations began to work with intermediary Ecuadorian NGOs on the implementation of development projects. Rather than work directly with indigenous organizations Ecuadorian NGOs would design and implement projects with funding from the international sector. The role of FONAKIN in this new arrangement was often simply to bless the projects and perhaps to suggest possible recipient communities. This effectively left Federation leaders outside of the development loop, with limited input into the nature of the projects being introduced in the region, some (although generally minimal) control over the destinations of these projects, and no access to or control over project finances. These projects, as one Federation leader put it, no longer came to member communities in the name of the Federation and as a Federation project, but instead came in the names of the NGOs that implemented them.

Such was the experience of the Unión Huacamayos with development projects funded by the Canadian Fund for Ecuadorian Development (FECD) in the late 1990s. These projects (ecotourism, tourist-oriented ceramic production, and an ethnographic museum) were designed by the Quito-based NGO Sinchi Sacha. With some consultation from the Unión Huacamayos, Sinchi Sacha determined where to implement the projects, and project implementation was overseen by the NGO itself, involving local people primarily as laborers in the construction of the buildings associated with the projects. Over time, and for a variety of reasons that I develop elsewhere (see Wilson 2003a, 2003b), relationships between Sinchi Sacha and the Unión deteriorated. One element of the conflict between them centered on the frustration felt by Unión Huacamayos leaders due to their inability to effectively harness and control the development process. This feeling was only reinforced during a meeting between the two organizations and the funding organization FECD, called to seek reconciliation between the feuding parties. At this meeting the Unión requested financial and administrative control of the projects, a request that FECD denied, suggesting that it was the policy of the organization to always work through intermediary NGOs—as a FECD representative later told me, for the purposes of fiscal responsibility. While Unión Huacamayos leaders were excluded from decision making regarding the location of development projects and the distribution of project funds in its member communities, Sinchi Sacha effectively used project money to reward community support for and loyalty to the NGO, ultimately contributing to political instability within the Unión. The inability of indigenous leaders to control the circulation of project resources left them vulnerable to accusations of greed and corruption.

In fact the way that indigenous leaders are evaluated by their constituents in terms of honesty and fiscal responsibility is not necessarily directly related to adhering to NGO budgets or spending plans. Rather, as long as resources circulated effectively and community members felt that leaders were responsive to their requests, leaders were not accused of corruption from the membership. In contrast, when the Federation could no longer access and control the circulation of NGO resources, which was the case by the mid-1990s, FONAKIN and Unión Huacamayos members increasingly accused their leaders of corruption and of working for personal interest instead of the betterment of the communities.

With projects becoming more directly associated with the activities of NGOs,[3] current Federation leaders are now confronting decreased access to development projects, and the inability of leaders to attract and control the circulation of NGO resources has contributed to a dip in leader and Federation legitimacy. The experiences of two former leaders, one who served as a leader of FONAKIN for a number of years from the mid-1980s to the early 1990s, and the other who was president of the Unión Huacamayos in the late 1990s, illustrate the impacts of their different relationships with development NGOs on the way members of their organizations perceived their authority and legitimacy as leaders.

In early 1999 I attended a FONAKIN assembly that was to address the arrest of a former Federation leader. This leader, whom I will call

Efraín Calapucha, was a leader of the Federation for several years from the mid-1980s to the early 1990s, during which time he also served as the Federation's administrator of a large NGO-sponsored project. He became a leader during the Federation boom years and was one of the young leaders who benefited personally from the series of leadership training courses organized by NGOs during this period. In the mid-1990s he was appointed to a ministry post by Abdalá Bucaram, the flamboyant (and corrupt) populist politician elected president of the Republic in 1996. The rampant corruption and ineptness of the regime led to Bucaram's removal from office by civil coup the following year. Bucaram promptly received political asylum in Panama, but lower ranking government officials such as Calapucha paid the price for the regime's corruption by serving time in jail. In 1999 FONAKIN members examined his case and explored possible legal alternatives to gain his release. Interestingly, although his arrest was for a charge of corruption, that charge was summarily rejected by the vast majority of people who spoke at the assembly. Recalling his history as a leader, speakers emphasized his generosity when visiting member communities, both as a Federation leader and later as a government representative. In concrete form Calapucha was praised for visiting the different communities (something that became harder for leaders to do regularly in the late 1990s due to the lack of travel funds), and the evidence that he was not guilty of corruption was his common practice of distributing televisions and VCRs to the communities on his visits. Following his release from prison he was again elected to the Federation's leadership. Much of this may be nostalgia for a prior time of Federation prosperity, but it also speaks to a construction of effective leadership rooted in collaboration and the circulation of resources, one that does not necessarily see the "correct" use of resources as tied to the intentions of NGO personnel and notions of fiscal responsibility.

Calapucha's experiences contrast sharply with those of an indigenous leader of the late 1990s, Artemio Patucue, who was president of the Unión Huacamayos. The Unión's relationship with the NGO Sinchi Sacha is reflective of the broader shifts in development theory and practice in the late 1990s. As measured by NGO standards, Patucue was a fiscally responsible leader. Though having access to very limited resources, he was careful to ensure that those resources were used for their intended purpose, primarily for small-scale productive projects such as fish farming and raising chickens by local women's groups. But in this changing context, meeting leadership expectations became increasingly difficult. Patucue, and the Unión Huacamayos more generally, did not manage resources that could be mobilized to meet a range of requests by local people, unlike Federation practices in the late 1980s and early 1990s. This placed Patucue in a difficult position. He was observed interacting regularly with NGO representatives who arrived from Quito in SUVs, and this raised expectations about his ability to provide the Unión's communities with resources from these NGOs. Yet he claimed that he did not have the resources thought to result from those interactions to circulate in demonstrations of generosity, even though such acts were critical for his legitimacy as a leader. Patucue was also an elementary school teacher, and the pressures of leadership in the Unión led him to spend a substantial part of his salary to attempt to address at least some of the requests brought to him by the organization's members. In contrast to the case of Calapucha, who remained a popular leader in spite of being convicted of corruption in Ecuadorian courts, Patucue was accused of corruption by a faction within the Unión Huacamayos. While the circumstances that contributed to those accusations are complex, they were conceivable from the viewpoint of some Unión Huacamayos members because of the structural constraints that limited his capacity to regulate the flow of NGO projects and resources in the member communities.

Returning to the example that opened this chapter, Mariano Huatatoca's removal from office in 1998 was also related to accusations of corruption stemming from his inability to attract and regulate the flow of development resources. If leadership authority is related to the circulation of certain goods, and if the expectation of federation leaders is that they regulate the flow of development projects and NGO resources, this has become increasingly difficult for indigenous leaders in Napo since the late 1990s. Erikson and Santos Granero (1988), examining contexts in which leaders are ritually responsible for ensuring success in hunting, argue that scarcity of resources is blamed on the failure of leaders to attract those resources. In a similar way the inability of federation leaders to attract and regulate NGO resources in the late 1990s was also interpreted by members as a failure of leadership, in this context through conceptions of corruption and collaboration. From the perspective of federation members, corruption was illustrated by the inability of their leaders to attract, or their unwillingness to be generous with, NGO resources. Because Patucue and other leaders were still regularly seen with NGO representatives and would make frequent trips to Quito for meetings with them, the assumption that leaders had access to development resources persisted in spite of the change in the relationship between the federations and the NGOs. This shift is ultimately what made leaders incapable of collaborating with community members according to expected patterns, and has contributed to the crisis of leadership and a fragmentation of indigenous federations in recent years.

Conclusions

There has been a tendency to overemphasize the consensus-based and egalitarian nature of Amazonian indigenous leadership in the approaches employed by many NGOs working in the region. On the one hand, this may stem from romanticizing the notion of indigenous leaders as "first among equals" and the seeming tendency to arrive at decisions through consensus building. On the other hand, it may relate to a practice of "sanitizing politics" of subaltern actors based on the perception that exposing the internal complexities of indigenous politics (Ortner 1995), and thereby deconstructing the authenticity of models of consensual politics, may be harmful for indigenous peoples and their social movements (Friedman 1996). Yet I suggest that the failure to recognize the fragility of indigenous leadership and the complex and sometimes conflictual nature of indigenous politics may present obstacles to the effective exercise of leadership in these contexts, particularly when the sanitation of indigenous politics informs the agendas of sustainable development and human rights NGOS, anthropologists, and others who may wish to contribute to dismantling the socioeconomic inequalities confronting indigenous peoples in the Amazon and elsewhere. The outcome of such representations and the actions guided by these representations may be to weaken rather than strengthen indigenous social movements in the long run.

The changing nature of NGO development practice in indigenous communities of Amazonian Ecuador has had consequences for the nature of leadership in the region. I argue that the legitimacy of indigenous federation leaders is influenced by a broad social context that, in the case of FONAKIN in Napo, is closely related to changes in development policy and practice. The resources of NGOS, both in terms of direct funding and in terms of particular projects, came to be seen as material symbols of leaders' generosity and morality and as a guidepost for measuring their ability to effectively regulate the flow of resources according to culturally expected patterns. Furthermore the changing identity of the Federation toward an organization that increasingly emphasized its role in accessing and distributing development projects and resources reinforced these expectations in the minds of local community members. From this perspective good leaders are those who collaborate with Federation members by circulating resources generously to the base communities; bad leaders, in contrast, are those who are working for personal interest and who fail to distribute NGO resources generously.

The expectation of generosity has been misinterpreted as serving as an economic leveling mechanism designed to prohibit the accumulation of resources by particular individuals. The executive director of Sinchi Sacha, for example, blamed the failure of development projects the NGO designed and administered in the Unión Huacamayos' communities on the social prohibitions on capital accumulation,[4] a necessary component (from his perspective) of the effective commercialization of the projects. Instead, the problem does not seem to be due to the accumulation of wealth, but rather due to circulation of resources. Janet Chernela (2006) argues that if Amazonian leaders possess wealth, it becomes problematic only in the absence of the circulation of resources. She suggests that there are not leveling mechanisms that prohibit indigenous leaders from accumulating wealth, but social expectations that indigenous leaders will be generous and effective in the circulation of cherished exogamous goods, thereby satisfying the collective desires of community members. In this context hoarding is a moral offense (Chernela 2006:102), but, when accompanied by consistent acts of generosity the accumulation of wealth is not. As a consequence it is overly simplistic to interpret lavish displays of generosity as social and economic leveling mechanisms in this context. Instead, conspicuous acts of generosity may reflect recognition of inequality and the moral obligation of individuals in positions of power to give. This observation is useful for comprehending the different receptions that Huatatoca, Patucue, and Calapucha received from their constituents. Calapucha, in spite of being guilty of corruption in Ecuadorian courts, was not guilty in the eyes of his followers of the moral offense of working for personal interest because he constantly circulated desired exogamous goods. On the other hand, Huatatoca and Patucue could not command resources for circulation (nor for personal profit, for that matter), and they were both accused of corruption and working for personal interest.

Some research on indigenous organizations and development has suggested that the capacity of indigenous federations to build international networks of financial, administrative, and ideological support has been central to their vitality (Brysk 1996; Perreault 2003a). Although this has certainly been true in some cases and in particular contexts, the specific contexts become very important for understanding the impacts of development activities on indigenous social movements. In fact we should not treat the social capital of grassroots organizations as an a priori condition that they possess; rather, if the concept of social capital is at all useful for thinking of the potential for development in different social contexts, it needs to be understood as constructed or dismantled in particular historical moments and social contexts, the changing development context being one of them. What I am suggesting is that the changing fortunes of indigenous federations may relate to the capacity of indigenous leaders to effectively fulfill the expectations placed on them as leaders, and their capacity to do so may change along with the fads of development policy and practice or other structural conditions. Therefore the activities of NGOs may just as easily debilitate as strengthen grassroots indigenous organizations if those activities do not facilitate the exercise of indigenous leadership according to locally expected cultural patterns. These scalar networks therefore are not necessarily productive and empowering (Bebbington and Perreault 1999), as NGO practices can instead divide and weaken indigenous organizations, as was the case with the Unión Huacamayos and FONAKIN in the past few years.

The crisis of leadership within these indigenous organizations in Napo has had repercussions for other facets of FONAKIN and the Unión Huacamayos as social movements. In recent years FONAKIN has encountered difficulty mobilizing coordinated resistance to the arrival of oil companies and the deepening of racist, neoliberal practices of the Ecuadorian state in the region (Wilson 2002, 2008). This has also led to fragmentation within the movement, as there are a growing number of local and kin-based cooperatives emerging that refuse affiliation with FONAKIN and the Unión Huacamayos. The Unión in fact has essentially ceased to operate; it is no longer calling meetings and a number of former members have withdrawn from it. The atomization of the movement in recent years toward smaller, kin-based organizations that (like the Federation) seek access to external resources for local development projects may in the end have detrimental consequences for the capacity of the Federation to serve as a nucleus of social movement organization and activity.

Notes

1. There was only one female leader, the vice president at the time. Federation politics have typically been male-dominated, with female leadership restricted to offices such as the *vocal de mujeres* (the women's representative), the *vocal de salud* (health representative), and the *vocal de educación* (education representative). Suggestive of the skewed representation in favor of men, the most common arena of women's direct involvement in the Federation is through the Women's Group, and even this had male oversight at the time of its founding.

2. Some scholars have challenged the implications of depictions of Amazonian leadership made by Pierre Clastres (1987 [1974]) and others, on the grounds that they overstate the egalitarian nature of politics (see Santos Granero 1986, for example). Others have challenged these depictions because of their failure to recognize gendered or class hierarchies (Lorrain 2000) or because of the occasionally coercive nature of Amazonian politics (Brown 1993; Santos Granero 1986). Even so there remains general agreement on the tenuous nature of authority in these social contexts. Further, the line dividing willing support for a leader and coercive authority is often difficult to read clearly, particularly in contexts in which a leader's base of support is close kin.

3. Multinational oil companies also adopt the guise of community development NGOs in their negotiations with local communities by creating "NGOs" financed by the company that offer local communities small-scale development projects in exchange for consent by the community for the oil company to proceed with its work.

4. See Wilson 2003a, 2003b for further discussion of these projects.

References

Basso, Ellen B. 1973. *The Kalapalo Indians of central Brazil.* New York: Holt, Rinehart and Winston.

Bebbington, Anthony, and Thomas Perreault. 1999. Social capital, development, and access to resources in highland Ecuador. *Economic Geography* 75 (4): 395–418.

Brown, Michael F. 1993. Facing the state, facing the world: Amazonia's native leaders and the new politics of identity. *L'Homme* 126:307–26.

Brysk, Alison. 1996. Turning weakness into strength: The internationalization of Indian rights. *Latin American Perspectives* 23 (2): 38–57.

Carroll, Thomas F. 1992. *Intermediary NGOs: The supporting link in grassroots development.* West Hartford CT: Kumarian Press.

Chernela, Janet M. 2006. Lex talionis: Recent advances and retreats in indigenous rights in Brazil. *Journal of Latin American Anthropology* 11 (1): 138–53.

Clastres, Pierre. 1987 [1974]. *Society against the state: Essays in political anthropology.* New York: Zone Books.

DeFilippis, James. 2002. Symposium on social capital: An introduction. *Antipode* 34 (4): 790–95.

Erlksun, Philippe, and Fernando Santos Granero. 1988. Politics in Amazonia. *Man: Journal of the Royal Anthropological Institute* 23 (1): 164–67.

Friedman, Jonathan. 1996. The politics of de-authentication: Escaping from identity. A response to "Beyond authenticity" by Mark Rogers. *Identities* 3 (1–2): 127–36.

Kracke, Waud H. 1979. *Force and persuasion: Leadership in an Amazonian society.* Chicago: University of Chicago Press.

Lauer, Matthew. 2006. State-led democratic politics and emerging forms of indigenous leadership among the Ye'kwana of the Upper Orinoco. *Journal of Latin American Anthropology* 11 (1): 51–86.

Lévi-Strauss, Claude. 1967. The social and psychological aspects of chieftainship in a primitive tribe: The Nambikuara of northwestern Mato Grosso. In *Comparative political systems: Studies in the politics of pre-industrial societies,* ed. Ronald Cohen and John Middleton, 45–62. Garden City NY: Natural History Press.

Lorrain, Claire. 2000. Cosmic reproduction, economics and politics among the Kulina of southwest Amazonia. *Journal of the Royal Anthropological Institute* 6:293–310.

Maybury-Lewis, David. 1967. *Akwe-Shavante society.* Oxford: Clarendon Press.

Mayer, Margit, and Ketherine N. Rankin. 2002. Social capital and (community) development: North / South perspective. *Antipode* 34 (4): 804–8.

Muratorio, Blanca. 1991. *The life and times of Grandfather Alonso: Culture and history in the Upper Amazon.* New Brunswick NJ: Rutgers University Press.

Orte, Gertrude. 1966. Anarchy without chaos: Alternatives to political authority among the Kuikuru. In *Political anthropology,* ed. Marc J. Swartz, Victor Turner, and Arthur Tuden, 73–87. Chicago: Aldine.

Ortner, Sherry B. 1995. Resistance and the problem of ethnographic refusal. *Comparative Study of Society and History* 37 (1): 173–93.

Perreault, Thomas. 2003a. Making space: Community organization, agrarian change, and the politics of scale in the Ecuadorian Amazon. *Latin American Perspectives* 30 (1): 96–121.

———. 2003b. Social capital, development, and indigenous politics in Ecuadorian Amazonia. *Geographical Review* 93 (3): 328–49.

Rosengren, Dan. 2003. The collective self and the ethnopolitical movement: "Rhizomes" and "taproots" in the Amazon. *Identities: Global Studies in Culture and Power* 10:221–40.

Santos Granero, Fernando. 1986. Power, ideology and the ritual of production in lowland South America. *Man: Journal of the Royal Anthropological Institute* 21 (4): 657–79.

Smole, William J. 1976. *The Yanomamo Indians: A cultural geography.* Austin: University of Texas Press.

Uzendoski, Michael A. 2005. *The Napo Runa of Amazonian Ecuador.* Urbana: University of Illinois Press.

Vickers, William T. 1989. Traditional concepts of power among the Siona-Secoya and the advent of the nation-state. *Latin American Anthropology Review* 1 (2): 55–60.

Wagley, Charles, and Eduardo Galvao. 1969. *The Tenetehara Indians of Brazil: A culture in transition.* New York: AMS Press.

Warren, Kay B., and Jean E. Jackson, eds. 2002. *Indigenous movements, self-representation, and the state in Latin America.* Austin: University of Texas Press.

Wilson, Patrick C. 2002. Indigenous federations, NGOs, and the state: Development and the politics of culture in Ecuador's Amazon. PhD diss., University of Pittsburgh.

———. 2003a. Ethnographic museums and cultural commodification: Indigenous organizations, NGOs, and culture as a resource in Amazonian Ecuador. *Latin American Perspectives* 30 (1): 162–80.

———. 2003b. Market articulation and poverty eradication? Critical reflection on tourist-oriented craft production in Amazonian Ecuador. In *Here to help: NGOs combating poverty in Latin America,* ed. Robin Eversole, 83–104. Armonk NY: M. E. Sharpe.

———. 2008. Neoliberalism, indigeneity, and social engineering in Ecuador's Amazon. *Critique of Anthropology* 28 (2): 127–44.

9. Worlds at Cross-Purposes

Alcida Rita Ramos

What do chapters 5 through 8 have in common? Beyond the obvious context of interethnic relations in four South American countries, they raise issues that clearly speak to each other. Despite the diversity of local situations, one can easily detect the pervasive concern with goods, territories, and ethnic identity. With these three elements in hand I shall analyze what may be regarded as the most salient features of contemporary indigenism.

Commodities versus Gifts

Wari', Kichwa, Yanomami, Kayapó, and virtually all indigenous people with whom the ethnographer works display a seemingly universal fascination for trade goods, in some cases, such as the Brazilian Kayapó Xikrin, with hyperbolic gusto (Gordon 2006). We experience their craving for or even addiction to trade goods as a sort of exacerbated consumerism out of proportion to the value we impute to those objects; in other words, their taste for goods does not fulfill quite the same material needs as ours. We would never admit that emotions can be measured in handfuls of beads, and although we put up with the proverbial diamonds and flowers as compensation for an unfaithful husband's guilt feelings, we take such action as the epitome of deception and insincerity.

Like Conklin (this volume), I was taken aback when, around 1974, a Sanumá woman, having mimicked the shedding of tears for having missed me during my prolonged absence, put out her hand and asked for beads. Beads for tears! It took all my anthropological training and sixteen years of retrospection to overcome the shock and see that act in a relativistic light. For my own peace of mind I chose to interpret her gesture as follows: "In stark contrast to our ethos that nourishes 'uninterested' feelings, the Sanumá woman employed her most cherished symbol of value to convince me that she really was glad to see me again" (Ramos 1995:9).

Unconvincing as it may be, the argument had the merit of shifting my attention from sheer emotional discomfort to intellectual curiosity. What matters here is to show the glaring contrast between the way the Sanumá, among others, objectify their emotions and the peremptory refusal of the dominant society's educated sector to mingle affect with material gain. A court case in the 1990s is an apt illustration of this aversion to monetize sentiments. Having been removed by the state Indian agency (Fundação Nacional do Índio, Funai) from their invaded lands to the Xingu National Park, the Brazilian sanctuary of cultural diversity, the seventy-nine (out of an estimated three hundred to six hundred) Panará Indians of Central Brazil who survived the trauma of first contact were forced to live as self-conscious and involuntary intruders in the lands of either former enemies or remote strangers. For a quarter of a century the Panará moved seven times within the Xingu Park in search of a piece of land that might resemble their lost territory (Arnt et al. 1998) With the aid of a nongovernmental organization they filed a lawsuit against the Indian agency and the Brazilian state for the losses they had suffered, including the death of more than 170 of their companions during the "pacification" process and removal to the Xingu in the 1970s. The federal judge in charge of the case ordered the state to pay a large sum to the Panará as compensation for their losses but was very careful to exclude the dead with the following argument: "One cannot pay for the pain suffered, as pain cannot be the object of compensation, that is, it is not susceptible to economic calculation, for it would be immoral to measure such sentiment in terms of money" (quoted in Ramos 2008:100). The same logic justified the British Empire's interference in the numerous cases of blood compensation in its African colonies, thus creating some anthological examples of worlds at cross-purposes (John Comaroff and Comaroff 2004).

Three of the chapters in this section describe situations that evidence the omnipresent conundrum resulting from a given common experience that turns into the object of deep-rooted misunderstandings, or, in the words of the Portuguese anthropologist João de Pina Cabral, "equivocal compatibilities" that frequently come across "situations of prolonged intercultural contact" (2002:108). In contexts where apparently the same assumptions conceal enormously different interpretations, the parties involved are left to act in often irreconcilable ways. The consequences can be particularly damaging to the weaker side (Ramos 1996).

Underlying the chapters by Conklin, Ramírez, and Wilson is the theme of meeting grounds and opposed expectations. We find frustrated anthropologists who expect to be treated as real people instead of conveyors of goods and services, investors who come to "develop" indigenous communities and find general lack of interest, and humanitarian types who bring "green" ideas to the Indians and capitulate in frustration at their ecologically incorrect choices. But in all three cases the virtues of anthropological scrutiny lead each of the authors through the detective work of trying to identify the place where the indigenous reasons actually sit. I shall use my colleagues' ethnographic expertise to refine my understanding of what is at the core of these equivocal compatibilities.

There is a Portuguese saying: *Amigos, amigos, negócios à parte* (Friends and business must be kept apart). This formula reminds us of the chasm that must exist between lucre and sentiment and of the judge's argument in the Panará case, according to which it is immoral to pay for pain. Most of us, however, do not follow the long trajectory of the West to arrive at such a rigid compartmentalization. The saying *Amigos, amigos, negócios à parte* is the perfect antithesis of most indigenous peoples' understanding of how persons and goods should relate to each other, for nothing could be more at odds with the logic of the gift according to which objects for trade are the quintessential lubricant for the smooth running of social relations.

We find the central contradiction between indigenous and nonindigenous principles in the most unanticipated contexts. In the Colombian case, foreign aid donors expected the local peasants to accommodate to the demands of capital, that is, abandon illegal activities, congregate in peasant organizations, curb violence, and in general eliminate all the signs of the stereotyped coca-growing *campesino*. But could this European illusion become reality when "coca is seen by small growers as a means to improve their standard of living" (Ramírez, this volume)? Among the Kichwa of Amazonian Ecuador good leaders are not the impartial administrators, regarded as "working for *intereses personales*," who seek to benefit the whole collectivity rather than some of its parts, but, ironically for us, those "who *siempre colaboraron*" by dispensing their generosity among relatives and friends (Wilson, this volume). It is not difficult to envision the outcome of such a mismatch of expectations in the context of government or private funding put into the hands of those leaders.[1]

What passes for us as nepotism and outright corruption on the part of indigenous project managers is regarded by their companions as the unquestionable virtues of the correct person who dutifully distributes benefits among kith and kin. A great many of the complaints by funding agencies about indigenous mismanagement of funds is, again, the result of a tremendous unequivocal incompatibility (my excuses to Pina Cabral for taking this liberty with his concept). At the indigenous end these moneys are taken to be like any other material object whose value is precisely its capacity to nurture very concrete social relations. In the so-called gift economy, you are what you give, and conversely, you give what you are, a trope that is plainly untranslatable into the idiom of its counterpart, the so-called commodity economy. By means of a metonymic operation the given stands for the giver, and vice versa, in countless versions of the Maori *hau* of Mauss's (1954) famous analysis. In other words, human beings and objects are fused and become a virtually inseparable ontological entity. In contrast, at the Western end money is regarded as an impersonal commodity with a logic of its own, which should not be contaminated by personal affairs. Moral acts are thus gauged by the distance one is capable of maintaining between being and thing: the farther apart, the better.

But like Weberian ideal types, these two economic modes are not as pure as they seem. As we find market-inclined Indians capable of betraying their companions' confidence (as in Ramírez's examples in this volume), so we find some interesting escape routes to "irrationality" among emotionally abstemious capitalist practices. We might ponder, for instance, about a telling irony that comes out of the U.S. banking system. From time to time we are treated to news that someone, often an old lady who trusted the security of her bank, finds that her money has been confiscated by the state due to abandonment. A long-dormant bank account, like a child, needs constant nourishment and care; otherwise its owner, like a neglectful parent, loses the right to exercise parenthood or ownership over it. Thus hypostatized, money takes on a fragile human quality that is curiously at odds with the overall detached monetary system. So much for aloof impersonality.[2]

Rather than be aghast at the apparent callousness of the Indians toward the providers of Western goods, perhaps we should retrace the steps that Louis Dumont (1977) so laboriously took to open up the Pandora's box of Western history and reveal *Homo aequalis*, the epitome of that chasm between market and sentiment, the champion of the autonomous economic sphere, disruptor as he is of the totality of things social. Ingrained in the socialization process of Euro-Americans is the axiom that mercantilism is incompatible with sociability, and, as with so many other axioms, they cannot believe that this incompatibility is not shared by the rest of humanity.

Having come across Westerners well after they instituted their "modern" compartmentalized world (*pace* Bruno Latour 1991, who, in a fit of wishful thinking, attempts to deconstruct modernity), the Indians had no reason to suspect that such a thing as compartmentalization existed. To the contrary, they had all the reasons in the world to think that, for non-Indians as well, feelings and objects are like communicating vessels. Let us take as evidence the Brazilian phenomenon of "attraction," formerly known as "pacification," the elaborate set of procedures to bring wayward Indians into intercourse with state agents. At first contact what these agents display to the Indians are not the deep structures of mercantilism but the most obvious and pedestrian of its products: knives, machetes, mirrors, and matches hanging from ropes between trees in forest clearings. After what can be a months- or even years-long wait, at last the Indians are lured into that silent trade to which they contribute bows and arrows, basketry, and feathers. The climax of this "attraction" is the indigenists' long-desired hug between attractor and attracted, an embrace that is bound to bring unending troubles to the latter (Ramos 1998: chapter 5). As a ploy to entice the Indians into the hands of the state, goods and hugs are profusely dispensed (remember the proverbial diamonds and flowers). Not surprisingly the Indians equate goods with hugs as part and parcel of the same deal. What are we anthropologists doing when we distribute gifts to our "informants" if not buying their precious goodwill, usually for a short-term sojourn? Do we feel guilty of bribing? And when we stop visiting our indigenous hosts after our thirst for data has been completely and definitively quenched, do we ask ourselves what they think of our disappearing act? Deeply ingrained in our Western selves, the mercantilist logic is presented to the Indians, and to many of us, in its most innocent attire (what, after all, is a bunch of glass beads?) until they feel the bite of conquest when their consciences as well as their pockets are thoroughly colonized (Jean Comaroff and Comaroff 1991:26).

After such clear demonstrations on our part that objects and emotions go together, to then expect of the Indians a spontaneous display of decorum and frugality à la the Protestant ethic would be laughable if it weren't potentially tragic. The GAIA Foundation representatives were shocked at the long list of Xavante demands and blamed the Indians for not seeing the light they had brought along with their promises. But to the ethnologist's trained eye, those do-gooders seemed to be less interested in helping the Indians on their own terms than in helping them do "what outsiders think they should do" (Conklin, this volume). By all accounts the hyperreal Indian will die of very old age, if at all.

Territories and Identities

In a different key, Chaves presents us with another set of issues that have been around the field of indigenism, albeit with less visibility than they deserve. In a nutshell these issues hinge on the following question: Is ethnic identity a mere corollary of territoriality? The Putumayo case she describes is multiply interesting because it deals with indigenous and *campesino* people claiming old and new ethnicities, occupying rural and urban settings, and suffering various sorts of compulsions all the way from armed assaults to economic deprivation. In the face of the resulting social unrest and subsequent exodus to towns and cities, Chaves appropriately challenges the assumption that one needs a territory of one's own lest one's ethnic identity is irremediably lost.

Other things being equal, ethnicity and territoriality go together. But other things are not and have never been equal. Fixed territories are a product of colonialism as it impinged upon most peoples in the Americas a sense of dominion that was utterly foreign to them. Considering that before conquest land occupation took place with no call for rigid boundaries, drawing the limits of a given indigenous territory is nowadays a fictitious act to satisfy the need of state control. To this day we find indigenous peoples, at least in Brazil, who are at a loss when it comes to land demarcation. What limits are the white men talking about? Those fuzzy borders of five hundred years ago? Those itinerant and not always consensual fringes resulting from multiple moves along the generations? Or the more recent constraints imposed by state operations, agribusiness, and smallholders alike? It is not fortuitously that the state delegates to non-Indians the task of identifying, delimiting, and demarcating indigenous lands in the country. For it is the non-Indian who has full command of the political grammar of land demarcation as a crucial element in the ideal order of things: one territory, one culture, one polity.

Take for instance the Guarani of southeastern Brazil. True to their historic quest for the Land without Evil, the legendary Terra sem Males (Clastres 1978), whenever possible they pursue that quest by periodically moving their villages to a new place. What matters most to them is to maintain their esprit de corps rather than a fixed territory. Regardless of where they are, their ethnic identity accompanies them and is preserved as long as they continue to be a cohesive social group. Central to being Guarani is to hold together as a group, independently of the locale where they happen to live. "We might say that . . . a Guarani defines himself in terms of tribe, for any area where there are Guarani is equally suitable for living" (Pires 1980:205). Hence the locus of ethnicity is for them (as it has been for the Gypsies and still is for many Jews) the human component of their social life. In stark contrast to their Kaingang neighbors in the state of Paraná (Pires 1980) or the Tupiniquim in Espírito Santo (Guimarães 2004), the eastern Guarani show no special interest in fighting for the demarcation of the land they occupy at a given moment, for the idea of confinement in an enclosed territory, large or small, is not compatible with the spirit of their traditional marches in search of the Land without Evil.

A dramatic counterexample is the western Kaiowá Guarani in the state of Mato Grosso do Sul, who have been driven to an extremely reduced piece of land that has been suffocating them for decades. Their confined life and the inexorable "impossibility of withdrawal" with nowhere to run have been deemed mostly responsible for the many suicides of their young people (Morgado 1991). But their case is one more exception that proves the rule: with no way out of a virtual incarceration, plagued by chronic infant mortality and famine, their only escape routes have been suicidal acts in epidemic proportions and very severe confrontations with encroaching landowners.

If we think in terms of the historic long run, the Guarani are not an exception. What they seem to aspire to today fits well into the pattern of the preconquest American continent. We read, for instance, about the Arawak diaspora that occupied most of the Amazon (Heckenberger 2004:43; Santos-Granero 2002); we are told by archaeologists that the location of a given indigenous group today is not the same as in the past; and we hear from the people we study about the spatial movements of successive generations. In other words, when we consider *longue durée* trends, "such as ancient diasporas, as large as any on the planet" (Heckenberger 2004:xiv), the equation of ethnic identity with a specific territory is a relatively recent phenomenon that mimics the imagined homogeneous nation-state. If this is the case, why is there now so much emphasis on this anchoring (Chaves's *anclajes*) of ethnicity on territory to the point that a divergent position needs to be elaborately justified, as Chaves does in her chapter? Why does it still feel awkward, like going against the grain, to ensure that uprootedness does not destroy ethnic identity? Could it be that the idea of indivisibility of identity and territory has filled certain political spaces as an incontestable truth? If so, perhaps a diachronic view of interethnic relations can help us understand it.

The notion of a fixed territory associated with a given people came to the Americas as part of the colonial design, along with the concept of privacy and of private property with market value. For those European powers that imposed their rule in the New World, nothing was more natural than to associate a bounded territory with a particular polity, following the Greek tradition of what a *polis* or civil society should be. The flexible boundaries of indigenous territories were an irresistible temptation to the colonizers, who were quick to lure the Indians into transferring to them most of the continent. It took a few centuries for most indigenous peoples to realize that the occupation of territories was no longer the result of a sort of gentlemen's agreement between neighbors, and the only way to guarantee their subsistence base was to accept the terms of the conquerors, namely, seclusion in drastically reduced and enclosed lands. To then tie indigenous identity to territory, after the model of the European nation-state, was an easy step and a convenient ploy for exercising control.

Indigenous people who, for a variety of reasons, were uprooted and displaced became the target of a stigma that, adding insult to injury, punished them for being victims. The image of the landless ex-Indian has been the result of yet another misunderstanding constructed on the premise that Indians without land are no longer Indians. A particularly blatant example comes from Argentina, where the very word "Indian" was carefully avoided in parliamentary debates in the early twentieth century (Lenton 2001) after the colossal indigenous defeat in the infamous "Conquest of the Desert" that covered them with a thick layer of invisibility. This tremendously equivocal incompatibility has been deeply lodged in the minds of those with power to decide what an Indian should be, anthropologists not excluded. The result of this extremely disruptive process was that many ethnic identities went underground to reemerge in the late twentieth century as, in Chaves's words, *campesinos reetnizados*. In some cases — perhaps much more numerous than we suspect — remnants of old ethnic groups reunited as a new composite entity, such as the Piro in Peru (Gow 1991), the indigenous people of the Brazilian Amazon region of Tefé (Faulhaber 1983), the Krahó in central Brazil (Ávila 2004), and a number of groups in the Brazilian Northeast (Oliveira 1999). For those peoples emerging from ethnic oblivion the most obvious and meaningful thing to do to regain recognition is to adopt the idiom of the state and claim their right to an indigenous territory. The past few decades in Brazil have witnessed myriad such demands from various parts of the country. On the basis of the simple criterion of self-identification, the Indian agency Funai, usually following anthropological expert reports, proceeds to certify or deny the legitimacy of such claims. If a group's rights are confirmed, the process of land demarcation takes place. In these cases it is an officially recognized territory that operates as a guarantor of ethnic authenticity and not the other way around: they possess an indigenous territory, hence they are Indians, rather than they are Indians, hence they possess an indigenous territory.

Chaves's chapter raises yet another question, regarding the role of migrations in the making of multisite indigenism. The mere fact of settling in towns and cities does not suppress indigeneity. The pioneer work of the Brazilian anthropologist Roberto Cardoso de Oliveira (1968) among the Terena Indians of western Brazil revealed back in the 1960s that the bonds between town and village not only are tightly maintained, but actually contribute to enlarge the social horizon of both migrants and their rural relatives. Since then numerous examples have been added to the list of situations in which "urban" natives prove themselves capable of straddling two very different worlds. In fact this theme has become a recognizable subset of interethnic studies. Michael Kearney identifies five different spaces crisscrossed by Mixtec Indians of Mexico: the traditional peasant communities, the agribusiness sites in northern Mexico, the shantytowns of Mexico City, the informal forms of work on the border zone between Mexico and California, and a variety of occupations in towns and cities. He characterizes these mobile peoples as an example of what he dubs "transnational multiethnic groups" (1996:174–82). Marshall Sahlins, impressed with the "indianization of modernity" (1997:114), reports the success of Samoan immigrants in the United States both as professionals in an industrialized world and as vigorous members of their distant homeland as an example of what he calls "transcultural societies" (109–10). Anthropological neologisms for this phenomenon abound.

In none of these cases is there a question about indigenous migrants having lost their ethnic identity. Very often these migrants manage to transpose to their new urban setting a number of significant features that demarcate their ethnic allegiances. The Putumayo migrants from rural to urban Colombia, the Pankararu Indians from the Brazilian Northeast to the São Paulo megalopolis, and a still unknown and fast-growing number of deterritorialized Indians and peasants belong to this category, recently discerned by anthropology and assigned to a new slot, no longer "savage" (Trouillot 1991) but "multisited." How successful or doomed their efforts are in the long run to maintain their identity and ties to their homeland is an empirical question that only intensive and long-term research may be able to answer.

Notes

My thanks to Wilson Trajano for his useful reminders.

1. For a superb contrast between two experiences with cooperative manage ment among the Ashaninka in Brazil, see Pimenta 2006.
2. This affect toward wealth reminds me of the European colonizers when they blamed the Indians for the sin of disdaining the value of gold, which gave the intruders ample reason to deplete America of its precious mineral and to persecute the Indians for their negligent indifference to it.

References

Arnt, Ricardo, Lúcio Flávio Pinto, Raimundo Pinto, and Pedro Martinelli. 1998. *Panará: A volta dos Índios gigantes.* São Paulo: Instituto Socioambiental.

Ávila, Thiago. 2004. "Não é do jeito que eles quer, é do jeito que nós quer": Os Krahô e a biodiversidade. Master's thesis, Departamento de Antropologia, Universidade de Brasília.

Cardoso de Oliveira, Roberto. 1968. *Urbanização e tribalismo.* Rio de Janeiro: Zahar.

Clastres, Hélène. 1978. *Terra sem mal: O profetismo tupi guarani.* São Paulo: Brasiliense.

Comaroff, Jean, and John Comaroff. 1991. *Of revelation and revolution: Christianity, colonialism, and consciousness in South Africa.* Vol. 1. Chicago: University of Chicago Press.

Comaroff, John, and Jean Comaroff. 2004. Criminal justice, cultural justice: The limits of liberalism and the pragmatics of difference in the new South Africa. *American Ethnologist* 31 (2): 188–204.

Dumont, Louis. 1977. *From Mandeville to Marx: The genesis and triumph of economic ideology.* Chicago: University of Chicago Press.

Faulhaber, Priscila. 1983. Índios civilizados: Etnia e alianças em Tefé. Master's thesis, Departamento de Antropologia, Universidade de Brasília.

Gordon, Cesar. 2006. *Economia selvagem: Ritual e mercadoria entre os índios Xikrin-Mebêngôkre.* São Paulo: Editora UNESP.

Gow, Peter. 1991. *Of mixed blood: Kinship and history in Peruvian Amazon.* Oxford: Clarendon Press.

Guimarães, Silvia. 2004. A marcha ceremonial guarani-mbyá. *Anuário Antropológico* 2002/2003: 151–92.

Heckenberger, Michael. 2004. *The ecology of power: Culture, place, and personhood in the Southern Amazon, AD 1000–2000.* New York: Routledge.

Kearney, Michael. 1996. *Reconceptualizing the peasantry: Anthropology in global perspective.* Boulder CO: Westview Press.

Latour, Bruno. 1991. *Nous n'avons jamais été modernes.* Paris: La Découverte.

Lenton, Diana I. 2001. Debates parlamentarios y aboriginalidad: Cuando la oligarquía perdió una batalla (pero no la guerra). *Papeles de Trabajo* 9:7–36. Centro Interdisciplinario de Ciencias Etnolingüísticas y Antropológico-Sociales, Rosario, Argentina.

Mauss, Marcel. 1954. *The gift: Forms and functions of exchange in archaic societies.* London: Cohen & West.

Morgado, Anastasio F. 1991. Epidemia de suicidio entre os Guarani-Kaiwá: Indagando suas causas e avançando a hipótese do recuo impossível. *Cadernos de Saúde Pública* 7 (4): 585–98.

Oliveira, João Pacheco de, ed. 1999. *A viagem da volta: Etnicidade, política e reelaboração cultural no Nordeste indígena.* Rio de Janeiro: Contra Capa.

Pimenta, José. 2006. *Reciprocidade, mercado e desigualdade social entre os Ashaninka do Rio Amônia.* Série Antropologia 392. Departamento de Antropologia, Universidade de Brasília. Available at www.unb.br/ics/dan.

Pina Cabral, João de. 2002. *Between China and Europe: Person, culture and emotion in Macao.* London: Continuum.

Pires, Maria Ligia Moura. 1980. Bugre ou índio: Guarani e Kaingang no Paraná. In *Hierarquia e simbiose: Relações intertribais no Brasil,* ed. Alcida Rita Ramos, 183–240. São Paulo: Hucitec.

Ramos, Alcida Rita. 1995. *Sanumá memories: Yanomami ethnography in times of crisis.* Madison: University of Wisconsin Press.

———. 1996. A profecia de um boato: Matando por ouro na área Yanomami. *Anuário Antropológico/95*: 121–50.

———. 1998. *Indigenism: Ethnic politics in Brazil.* Madison: University of Wisconsin Press.

———. 2008. Uma crítica da (des)razão indigenista. *Anuário Antropológico/2006*: 95–115.

Sahlins, Marshall. 1997. O "pessimismo sentimental" e a experiência etnográfica. *Mana* 3 (2): 103–50.

Santos-Granero, Fernando. 2002. The Arawakan matrix: Ethos, language, and history in Native South America. In *Comparative Arawakan histories: Rethinking language family and culture area in Amazonia*, ed. Jonathan Hill and Fernando Santos-Granero, 25–50. Urbana: University of Illinois Press.

Trouillot, Michel-Rolph. 1991. Anthropology and the savage slot: The poetics and politics of otherness. In *Recapturing anthropology: Working in the present*, ed. Richard G. Fox, 17–44. Santa Fe NM: School of American Research Press.

Contributors

Margarita Chaves is a researcher and coordinator of the Social Anthropology Group at the Instituto Colombiano de Antropología e Historia (ICANH). She studied anthropology at the Universidad Nacional de Colombia and received her doctorate at the University of Illinois in Urbana-Champaign. She has been editor of the *Revista Colombiana de Antropología* and a visiting professor at various anthropology and cultural studies programs in Colombia. Her research focuses on indigenous and peasant social and political dynamics in colonization zones of the Colombian Amazon. Her work has appeared in various edited volumes and academic journals; her most recent publication is *La multiculturalidad estatalizada: Indígenas, afrodescendientes y formaciones regionales de estado en Colombia y Latinoamérica* (State-Sponsored Multiculturalism: Indigenous Peoples, Afro-descendants, and Regional State Formations in Colombia and Latin America, ICANH, 2009). She is currently engaged in research on consumerism, markets, and cultural heritage in the context of expanding cultural industries in Colombia.

Beth A. Conklin earned her doctorate in 1989 from the University of California at San Francisco and Berkeley. She is a cultural and medical anthropologist at Vanderbilt University specializing in the ethnography of indigenous peoples of lowland South America (Amazonia). Her research focuses on the anthropology of the body, religion and ritual, health and healing, death and mourning, the politics of indigenous rights, and ecology, environmentalism, and cultural and religious responses to climate change. Her publications include *Consuming Grief: Compassionate Cannibalism in an Amazonian Society* (University of Texas Press, 2001), "Body Paint, Feathers, and VCRs: Aesthetics and Authenticity in Amazonian Activism," "The Shifting Middle Ground: Brazilian Indians and Eco-Politics" (with Laura Graham), "Ski Masks, Nose Rings, Veils and Feathers: Body Arts on the Front Lines of Identity Politics," "Shamans versus Pirates in the Amazonian Treasure Box," and "Environmentalism, Global Community, and the New Indigenism."

Frank Hutchins is an associate professor of anthropology at Bellarmine University. His dissertation research at the University of Wisconsin–Madison focused on cultural change in the Upper Amazon of Ecuador, particularly on issues of ecotourism and development. He is the director of the University of Wisconsin–Madison Summer Field School for the Study of Language, Culture and Community Health in Ecuador. His recent research looks at ritual fighting associated with the Inti Raymi festival in the northern Andes.

Jean E. Jackson is a professor of anthropology at the Massachusetts Institute of Technology. She received her master's and doctoral degrees from Stanford University. Her 1983 book, *The Fish People: Linguistic Exogamy and Social Identity in Northwest Amazonia* (Cambridge University Press, 1983), examined the Tukanoan cultural complex of the Vaupés region. She has published numerous articles on the Vaupés peoples and on Colombia's indigenous movement. She and Kay Warren coedited *Indigenous Movements, Self-Representation, and the State in Latin America* (University of Texas Press, 2002). Jackson also conducted ethnographic research in a rehabilitation hospital, which resulted in several published essays and a book, *"Camp Pain": Talking with Chronic Pain Patients* (University of Pennsylvania Press, 2002).

María Clemencia Ramírez is a research associate and the former director of the Colombian Institute of Anthropology and History. She attended the Universidad de los Andes and the National University in Colombia, earning a bachelor's degree in anthropology and a master's degree in history. She holds a doctorate in social anthropology from Harvard University and was the 2004–2005 Santo Domingo Visiting Scholar at Harvard's David Rockefeller Center for Latin American Studies. She has taught in Colombia at the Universidad de los Andes and the National University. Her work explores the intersections of violence and identity through the lens of public policy and state-citizen relations, focusing on the Amazon region of Colombia, specifically the department of Putumayo, where the implementation of Plan Colombia began in 2000. The impact of Plan Colombia on the small coca growers of Putumayo has become a main focus of her research. She is the author of *Between the Guerrillas and the State: The Cocalero Movement, Citizenship and Identity in the Colombian Amazon* (forthcoming from Duke University Press), a revised and updated English-language version of *Entre el Estado y la Guerrilla: Identidad y ciudadanía en el movimiento de los campesinos cocaleros del Putumayo* (2001). She is also the author of *Frontera Fluida entre Andes, Piedemonte y Selva: El caso del Valle de Sibundoy, Siglos XVI–XVIII* (1996) and coauthor of *Atlas Cultural de la Amazonia Colombiana: La construcción del territorio en el siglo XIX* (1998) and she has recently written several book chapters and journal articles on the politics of global security and the war on drugs in Colombia.

Alcida Rita Ramos is a professor of anthropology at the University of Brasília and a senior researcher at the National Council of Scientific and Technological Development (CNPq) in Brazil. Having done extensive fieldwork among the Yanomami in Brazil, she is currently working on a comparative perspective of indigenism and nation, focusing on Brazil and other South American countries. Along with several dozen articles published mostly in Portuguese, English, and Spanish, she is the author of *Sanumá Memories: Yanomami Ethnography in Times of Crisis* (University of Wisconsin Press, 1995) and *Indigenism: Ethnic Politics in Brazil* (University of Wisconsin Press, 1998). For decades she has dedicated a good portion of her professional time to advocacy work in defense of indigenous peoples in Brazil, particularly the Yanomami.

Michael A. Uzendoski holds a doctorate in anthropology and is an associate professor of modern languages and linguistics at Florida State University. He is the author of *The Napo Runa of Amazonian Ecuador* (University of Illinois Press, 2005) and has published several journal articles dealing with Amazonian Quichua ethnohistory, culture, and language. Uzendoski has won grants from Fulbright and the National Science Foundation. He is currently working on a book about Napo Runa mythology and storytelling.

Neil L. Whitehead is a professor of anthropology, Latin American and religious studies at the University of Wisconsin–Madison. He is the author of numerous works on the native peoples of South America and their colonial conquest, as well as on the topics of sorcery, violence, sexuality, and warfare. His most recent works include a new edition of Hans Staden's sixteenth-century account of captivity and cannibalism among the natives of Brazil (Duke University Press, 2008) and essays on terrorism, torture, and cybersex. He is currently studying the cultural aesthetics of sex and violence and the emergence of posthuman and digital subjectivities.

Patrick C. Wilson is an associate professor of anthropology at the University of Lethbridge (Canada). He has conducted research in Amazonian Ecuador since 1995 on indigenous social movements, development, NGOs, and the state. He is currently conducting research on transnational artisan fair trade and indigeneity.

Index

Brazil, 136, 253, 255–56; and the
Bororo people, 42–43; indigenous
social movements in, 135, 223, 256;
media in, 71; and "pacification"
("attraction"), 251–52; and the
Panará Indians, 247–48
Bucaram, Abdalá, 237
buen vivir, 10
Buitrago, Francy, 91, 94
Bush, George W., 157, 163–64

cabildos (councils), 74, 80, 85, 90, 197,
201, 214n3, 214n5
Caja de Compensación Familiar. *See*
Fund for Family Compensation
Campo en Acción, 182–83. *See also*
Plan Colombia
Canadian Fund for Ecuadorian
Development (FECD), 235–36
Cañari Indians, 16–17
Canelos Kichwa. *See* Kichwa
cannibalism, 106–7, 111, 120–21
Capirona, Ecuador, 3, 4, 20, 34
capitalism: and globalization, 8, 28,
115–17, 130–31; history of, 28–29,
41, 65n3; indigenous responses to,
xxiv–xxv, xxviii, 4–5, 6–7, 30, 39, 64,
115, 130–32, 133
Cardoso de Oliveira, Roberto, 256
Carib people, 110–15, 119–20, 122n1
Carvajal, Gaspar de, xii, xiv
ceremonial dress. *See* clothing, indigenous
Chakrabarty, Dipesh, 6–7, 27–29,
65n3
Chemonics International Inc., 170–72,
174–76, 178, 186n1; mission of, 152;
and social capital, 161, 164–65, 169,
171, 179, 180–84; and USAID funds,
160
Clastres, Pierre, 42, 231, 243n2
Clinton, Bill, 157–58, 163–64
clothing, indigenous, 83, 95, 96, 133
coca: cultivation of, 152–55, 158–59,
165–69, 187n12, 194–95, 249; eradication of, xxvi, 152, 157, 158, 159–61,

163–64, 167, 174–76, 180, 186nn8–10,
193, 194; media representations of,
88. *See also* drug trade
Cocama people, 46–47
Colombia: and alternative development agribusiness projects, 151–52,
164, 165–66, 174–83, 184, 194; armed
conflict in, xxi–xxii, 76, 78–81,
89–90, 98, 154, 155, 167, 194–96;
coca cultivation in, 152–55, 158–60,
163–64, 165–67, 187n12, 194–95;
colonization of Amazon territory
in, 154–55; constitutional reform
in, 74, 75–76, 214n5; departments
(politico-administrative units) of,
72, 152, 186n4, 201; displacement in,
xxi–xxii, 76, 89, 155, 192–93, 195–96,
206–9, 210; ethnic recognition in,
xx, 191–92, 193, 196–201, 203–9;
land ownership in, 75, 154–55;
media in, xxii, 70–73, 76–91, 93–99,
118, 154; narcotrafficking in, 79, 153,
154–58, 162–64, 166–67, 181, 186n8;
and nation-building, 74, 84; NGOs
in, 169–72, 175–85, 186n1; population of, 73–74, 185; and *resguardo*
system, xxi–xxii, 75, 195, 201, 203–5,
208–10, 214n3, 214nn5–7, 215n8;
and state corruption, 74, 86, 98–99,
100n5, 166–67, 170, 171; storytelling
in, 39, 43–46; *veredas* in, 172–74,
175–79, 184
Colombia Alternative Development
Program (CAD), 175, 179–80, 183–84
Colombian Antinarcotics Police
(DIRAN), 154
colonialism, xxiv, 107, 119–22, 257n2;
and acculturation through commodities, xiv, 131–32; and territorial
boundaries, 252–53, 254–55; and
tourism, 109, 110–12, 113–14, 115
colonos, 55, 85, 153–55, 166, 214n1
Columbus, Christopher, 110, 111, 119
commercial goods, 131–33, 134, 143–
44, 147–48, 246–52

commodification: of culture, xxvii,
3–4, 5, 6, 7, 11–16, 20, 26, 29, 30,
112–15; as "negotiated" process, 30
commodities. See commercial goods
commodity transactions. See mate-
rial exchanges
Communal Action Committees. See
Juntas de Acción Comunal (JACS)
community: definitions of, 25, 196–
99, 211–13; and resguardo system,
xxi–xxii, 195, 201, 203–5, 208, 209–
10, 214n3, 214nn5–7, 215n8; veredas
in, 172–74, 175–79, 184
Condamine, Charles-Marie La. See La
Condamine, Charles-Marie
Confederación de Nacionalidades
Indígenas de la Amazonia
Ecuatoriana, 22
Confederación de Nacionalidades
Indígenas del Ecuador. See
Confederation of Indigenous
Nationalities of Ecuador
Confederation of Indigenous
Nationalities of Ecuador, 16–17, 22
conflicts, armed: and coca produc-
tion, 154–55, 167, 194–96; and
displacement, xxi–xxii, 76, 155, 193,
195–96; media representations of,
76, 78–81, 89–90, 98
Conrad, Joseph, xiv
Consultancy on Human Rights and
Displacement, 155
consumerism, xxiii, 89, 132, 134–36
Coordinadora de las Organizaciones
Indígenas de la Cuenca
Amazonica, 22–23
Corporación Ecuatoriana de Turismo
(CETUR), 11, 23
cosmic bodies, 53, 54, 55–56, 57–58,
63–64; and circulatory relationships, 45–46, 51–52; and music, 63;
and predatory flows, 48–49
Cuentos Amazónicos (Galeano), 58
cultural flow frameworks, 7, 11–13, 15,
18, 25, 26–27, 30, 117

de-anchored identities, 205–9
"despondency theory," 16
displacement, 89, 192, 206–9, 210,
255; and armed conflicts, xxi–xxii,
76, 155, 192–93, 195–96
Dominica, 110–15, 122n1
Driver, Felix, xiv–xv
drug trade, xxvi; and narcotrafficking, 79, 153, 154–58, 162–64, 166–67,
181, 186n8, 194–96; and perverse
social capital, 161–66; and war on
drugs, 153–54, 155–61, 163–64, 181,
186n10, 193, 194

ecotourism, xxvii, 6, 27, 28, 122n2;
community-based, 6–7, 18–23, 24,
34, 179; and cultural commodification, 7, 11, 18–20, 29; on Dominica,
112–13; in Ecuador, 3–12, 14–17,
18–24, 27, 30–34, 116, 179; and envidia over resource sharing, 30–34.
See also tourism
Ecuador: and buen vivir, 10; colonization of Amazon territory in, 225–26;
Constitution of, 9, 10; ecotourism
in, 3–12, 14–17, 18–24, 27, 30–34, 116,
179; folktales of, 39, 42, 50–52, 55;
and government activities, 9–10,
11–12, 13–15, 18, 23; indigenous
social movements in, 16–24, 25,
26–27, 222–28, 231–42; and Kichwa
culture, xxviii, 3–6, 7–8, 20–21,
30–33, 34–35, 39, 40, 42; land ownership laws in, xix; legal system in,
xix, 13–14, 23; media in, 13; NGOs in,
219–23, 226–28, 232–42
envidia, 30–34
environmentalism, xxi, xxvi–xxvii,
76–77, 86–88, 146–47
Escobar, Carlos Ossa, 75
ethnic identity: and "community,"
211–13; and geopolitical discourses,
209–10; and land ownership,
133–34, 191–92, 193, 196–97; in
Putumayo, Colombia, 191–93,
196–201, 203–9; and race, 111, 114;